T0247430

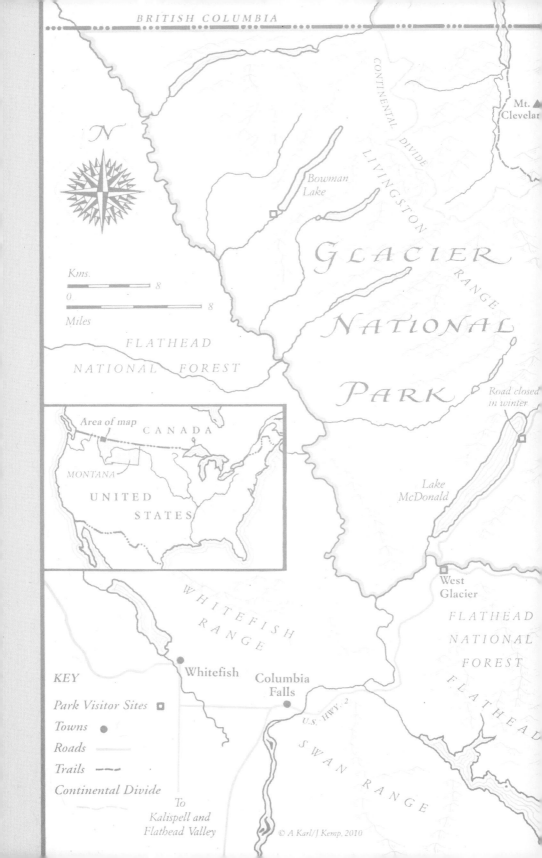

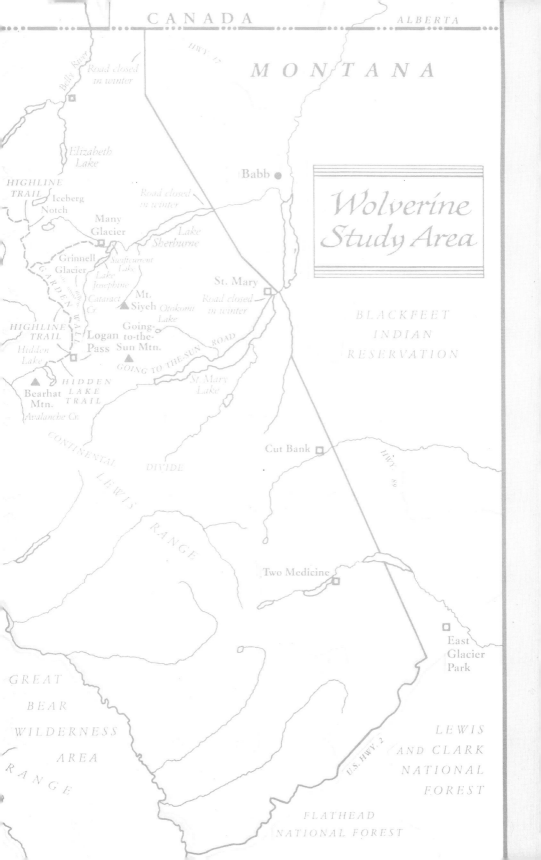

The Wolverine Way

By Douglas H. Chadwick

patagonia

THE WOLVERINE WAY

Softcover edition
Printed in Canada

Patagonia publishes a select number of titles on wilderness, wildlife, and outdoor sports that inspire and restore a connection to the natural world.

Project Management - Jennifer Sullivan
Editor - John Dutton
Photo Editor - Jane Sievert
Book Designer - Annette Scheid
Production - Melissa Beckwith, Rafael Dunn

ENVIRONMENTAL BENEFITS STATEMENT

Patagonia Inc saved the following resources by printing the pages of this book on chlorine free paper made with 100% post-consumer waste.

TREES	WATER	ENERGY	SOLID WASTE	GREENHOUSE GASES
51 FULLY GROWN	23,907 GALLONS	23 MILLION BTUs	1,600 POUNDS	4,408 POUNDS

Environmental impact estimates were made using the Environmental Paper Network Paper Calculator 32. For more information visit www.papercalculator.org.

End maps: Anita Karl & Jim Kemp

ISBN 978-0-9801227-4-9

TABLE OF CONTENTS

Foreword

Most people, even if they don't know any of the details about the natural history of wolverines, know that they are fierce. Maybe it's the name – *wolverine* – with that core root *wolve* that leaves a sense of distilled, implacable fierceness. Or maybe it's a memory of a tale of some hapless victim – human or otherwise – who had the misfortune of crossing paths with a wolverine.

But take the time to look into their natural history, and you come across facts such as the observation that wolverines sometimes force grizzlies off a kill. When you weigh 30 pounds that, as Doug Chadwick tells us, is pretty badass. You also discover that while wolverines turn out to have a surprisingly sociable side to them, they remain mostly solitary for much of the year and claim huge amounts of territory that they fiercely protect. You also find out they travel widely, covering hundreds of miles a year, and if they are to survive into the future they need space to move around in. They need the freedom to roam.

At the clothing company Patagonia we are committed to using our company "to implement solutions to the environmental crisis." A few years ago we decided to focus resources on the protection of wildlife corridors, so that animals had the ability to move within and between territories, ensuring genetic diversity. Borrowing the name from a book by the celebrated wildlife photographer Florian Shultz for which Doug Chadwick wrote the introductory chapter, we called the initiative Freedom to Roam. We soon spun it off as an independent nonprofit coalition representing an array of constituencies, including large corporations, government agencies and environmental nonprofits.

One of the goals of Freedom to Roam is to increase awareness of what wildlife corridors are. Another is to highlight why - in the face of the dual pressures from habitat fragmentation, due to human development, and habitat shift, due to global warming - corridors are the best bet for wildlife's survival into the next century. At Patagonia we knew the way to increase awareness of wildlife corridors was to tell stories about this concept of landscape connectivity. In the case of Freedom to Roam, that meant telling good animal stories.

So we approached one of the eminent animal storytellers of our time, Doug Chadwick, and soon he delivered an essay about wolverines to be printed in one of our catalogs. "When I say these might be the toughest animals in the world," Chadwick wrote, "I'm . . . including the way wolverines relentlessly roam vast territories . . . taking on cliffs, icefalls, and summits through some of the nastiest weather modern winters can throw at a mammal. Climbers and extreme skiers come back from such expeditions and tell riveting tales of survival. Wolverines just growl and keep going 24/7."

Chadwick's' essay resonated with our customers, and we suspected we might have identified the four-legged mascot we were searching for that could catch people's attention long enough that they would listen to the bigger message of large-scale habitat conservation. In the initial stages of building the coalition, we received an invitation from Governor Freudenthal of Wyoming to give a presentation on Freedom to Roam at the annual meeting of the Western Governors Association. As host of the meeting Freudenthal was tasked with setting the agenda, and he wanted to propose to the other governors that they consider the importance of protecting wildlife corridors in their states.

The meeting was in Jackson Hole; there were 600 people in the audience, including the 14 governors and their staffs, four premieres from Canada's border provinces, dozens of corporate CEOs and government officials of all stripes. I narrated the presentation, showing slides and maps and animations as I told them about Freedom to Roam.

The highlight though was the story of M3, the biggest, snarliest and most badass wolverine any of the biologists had ever encountered. I told how wildlife biologists finally managed to trap M3 and put a radio collar on his neck programmed to uplink his position every five minutes. I told how the biologists were then astounded to learn how far a male wolverine roams, as they observed M3 leaving Montana, heading north into Waterton, cruising over to British Columbia and working his way back to Montana.

"The most astounding thing they observed, however, was when M3 left Montana in February, the height of winter. To get to Waterton," I told the crowd, "M3 approached the base of Mount Cleveland and then started up the south face - 9,000 feet, 9,500 feet, 10,000 feet." On the screen I had an artist's rendition of Mt. Cleveland, with a progression of dots showing M3's position as he climbed the steep south face, gained the ridge and kept going toward the summit. "Finally M3 topped out on the highest peak in Glacier National Park," I said. "Why? You guessed it: Because it was there."

M3 got a thunderous applause, and when I finished my presentation Governor Freudenthal gave me a bear hug, Governor Schweitzer from Montana high-fived me, Governor Napolitano from Arizona said she was a Freedom to Roam convert, and we heard months later that while on a fact-finding trip on global warming in the high Arctic, Governor Ritter from Colorado regaled his ship-mates with a retelling of the story of the most badass wolverine of them all.

What you have in front of you is that story of M3 and the story of what we have discovered about wolverines. All told by Doug Chadwick from the research of committed field biologists like Jeff Copeland and Rick Yates. It's an adventure story, a surprising story . . . a badass story.

– *Rick Ridgeway*

The author, age 6 or 7, and his mining geologist father, Russell Chadwick, at a prospecting camp in the western Rockies. CHADWICK COLLECTION

Prologue

The Way is limitless,
So nature is limitless,
So the world is limitless,
And so I am limitless.

LAO-TZU
from the *Tao Te Ching*, translation by Peter Merel

WHEN I WAS 17, I SPENT THE SUMMER WITH MY GEOLOGIST FATHER prospecting a rolling sweep of Alaskan tundra northeast of Nome. We traveled miles downstream one day to visit the nearest neighbor, though he was anything but a neighborly man. He was a hermit who sought out people only when he desperately needed supplies. A rusty generator ran near his camp and powered a high-pressure hose. He used the stream from its nozzle to bust loose the gravels of an old riverbed and sift them for gold. Yet unlike any placer-mining operation I'd ever seen, his took place underground. This man had sluiced his way inside the hills, carving tunnels and caverns through the permafrost.

The floor of the mine, where the water drained, was a half-congealed sludge that grabbed at our boots. The walls and ceilings were rimed with icicles and frost patterns sparkling like subterranean galaxies when we played a flashlight across them. Our strange, reluctant host used no posts to shore up the roof of this burrow. Portions had fallen onto the floor in heaps. It seemed only a matter of time before one of the rooms he kept enlarging collapsed to entomb him in crystals and muck – and perhaps a few flakes of gold.

I studied the hermit's face below the cone of light from his headlamp, taking care to keep my own light pointed somewhere else so he wouldn't catch me staring. His skin was striated with welts. The sections in between didn't fit together right. Some patches looked like dried-out hamburger. The movements of light beams and shadows made the overall effect even more grotesque, as if his features were writhing. I could understand why he preferred solitude. I had no way of knowing whether or not his appearance was what drove him to accept this level of risk while mining. Though young, I'd seen ordinary-looking men do amazingly heedless things to follow a streak of gold in the ground. Still, the questions kept revolving in my mind: What was going on with this hermit? What in the world would leave a man with this wreck of a visage?

"Wolverine."

When we were alone, my father explained that he had heard the man used to run a trapline in winter. One time he caught a wolverine in a set of steel jaws and caved in its skull with a club. The man didn't want to skin his prize right away; the fur was valuable and he wanted to do a careful job back at camp. Yet he was looking at a long snowshoe trip to get there. While wolverines aren't nearly as large as their reputation for malice and mayhem, they can reach 45 pounds in northern climes like that of Alaska. The easiest way to pack the carcass, he decided, was to tie the front legs together and loop them around his neck like a harness so the body rested against his back.

A wolverine's paws, which serve as its snowshoes, are as broad as a 120-pound wolf's. Each paw has five toes with a stout, slightly curved claw up to two inches long. Suppose you put the forepaws in place around your neck, and you haven't smashed the owner's skull as lethally as you thought, and the wolverine somehow fights its way back to consciousness while you're walking with its body still warm against your back. You, too, might end up hiding your face from the day in a faraway mine dark as the grave.

I wasn't 100 percent convinced that something else hadn't rearranged that guy's physiognomy – a really nasty bar brawl with broken bottles or a god-awful mistake with machinery – but the trapping accident story just sounded better. All the same, I promised myself to steer clear of wolverines and never let one up close. That seemed an easy enough vow to keep. Who runs into wolverines?

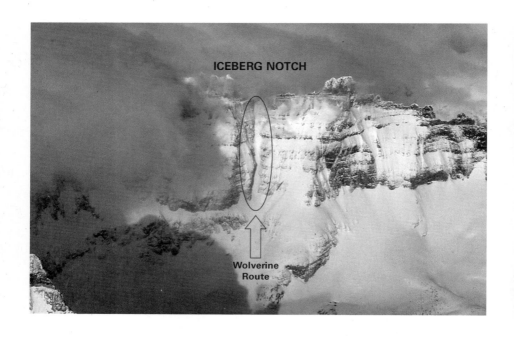

ICEBERG NOTCH

Wolverine
Route

M1's vertical route (regularly used both winter and summer) over the Continental Divide. RICK YATES

CHAPTER ONE

Many Glacier, March 2006, Part I
A Personality of
Unmeasured Force

"The wolverine is a tremendous character . . . a personality of
unmeasured force, courage, and achievement so enveloped in a mist
of legend, superstition, idolatry, fear, and hatred, that one scarcely
knows how to begin or what to accept as fact. Picture a weasel –
and most of us can do that, for we have met the little demon of
destruction, that small atom of insensate courage, that symbol of
slaughter, sleeplessness, and tireless, incredible activity – picture
that scrap of demoniac fury, multiply that mite by some fifty
times, and you have the likeness of a wolverine."

ERNEST THOMPSON SETON
from *Lives of Game Animals: Vol. II, 1925–1927*

FINE SNOW STREAKED THE AIR, RIDING SIDEWAYS ON A GALE, in early March
2006. Biologist Rick Yates led the way, breaking trail on skis through the powder. Great cliffs striped with avalanche tracks rose on all sides. Somewhere
higher up among the clouds stretched the icefields that gave this valley – Many
Glacier – its name. We crossed two frozen lakes and finally passed into an old-
growth spruce forest that took the edge off the storm. Beneath the branches,
half-buried in snow, stood a large box made of logs six to eight inches thick.
It looked a little like a scaled-down cabin. But it was a trap, and there was a
wolverine inside.

The animal had entered during the night. We knew from its radio frequency
that this was M1: M for male, Number 1 because he had been the first wolverine caught and radio-tagged during a groundbreaking study of the species

underway here in Glacier National Park, Montana. Sometimes the researchers called him Piegan instead, after a 9,220-foot mountain at the head of the valley. To me, he was Big Daddy, constantly patrolling a huge territory that straddled the Continental Divide near the heart of the park. His domain overlapped those of several females, and he had bred with at least three of them over the years while successfully keeping rivals at bay.

We paused a short distance from the trap to listen. M1 was silent. Predictably, he began to give off warning growls as we drew nearer. They rumbled deep and long with a force that made you think a much larger predator lay waiting inside, something more on the order of a Siberian tiger – or possibly a velociraptor. I lifted the box's heavy lid an inch or two to peer in. The inside of the front wall underneath was freshly gouged and splintered, its logs growing thin under Big Daddy's assault. Raising the lid another notch, I could finally make him out as a dense shadow toward the rear of the trap. Wolverines have dark brownish eyes, but in the light from my flashlight those orbs reflected an eerie blue-green color that glowed like plutonium, surrounded by the rising steam from his breath. The next things I saw were white claws and teeth and stringers of spit all flying at me with a roar before I dropped the lid shut and sprang back.

Inside the trap, the roaring and growling continued – wolverine for "Hope you won't be needing your face for anything, Tame Boy, because I'm going to take it off next time!" – followed by the sound of more wood being ripped apart. Given a few more hours, M1 would have an escape hole torn through the mini-log cabin. From time to time, the tips of his claws poked out just above the uppermost log of the front wall while he rammed his head against the lid. He was trying to shove the thing upward, though the ice-encrusted logs that formed the top of the box must have weighed 100 pounds.

I looked round at the trees and the snow swirls beyond and shook my head, thinking of my long-ago vow to steer clear of these creatures. Having joined the Glacier Wolverine Project in 2004, I was going into my third straight year of breaking that vow in just about every way it could possibly be broken. No regrets. These animals' off-the-charts strength and survival skills had become a source of inspiration for me by now. Even so, I was never going to get used to dealing with the intensity of a wolverine when it's up close and cornered. Nobody did.

M1's radio was a VHF (very high frequency) transmitter, standard in wildlife telemetry studies. But a wolverine's neck is short and as wide as its head, and there isn't much of a furrow between them to hold a radio collar. The animal can use its powerful rear legs to shove it off in short order. Subjects in the Glacier Wolverine Project carried their transmitter and battery in a capsule implanted beneath the skin of the belly. We then tracked their general whereabouts with a handheld antenna – when we were lucky enough to catch up to one of these nonstop mountaineers and keep within a few miles.

Volunteer Alex Hasson at the Avalanche trap, 2005. ALEX HASSON COLLECTION

Newly fitted with a bulky early version of a GPS radio collar, Big Daddy, M1, looks over his captors.
ALEX HASSON

As part of a new phase of the study, M1 was also wearing a lightweight GPS (global positioning system) collar. Using satellite signals, the device would record his location much more precisely than we could with an antenna, and it could do so at regular intervals whether we were awake or asleep, nearby or lagging behind and dropping out of radio range. Of course, M1 was still likely to work this technological wonder loose and leave it lying on some high slope or crag. That was fine with us as long as he didn't do it in the first 8 to 10 days. After that, the computer's memory chip should be out of data storage space anyway because the researchers had programmed it to take a reading every five minutes. When we retrieved the collar and downloaded the full chip, we stood to gain a bonanza of brand new, very detailed information about the movements and activity patterns of one of the least understood animals on the continent.

Since Yates had just put the satellite radio on M1 the day before, our only task this morning was to check his condition along with that of the collar and then, as project members liked to say, just kiss the wolverine on the lips and let it go.

"Ready?" asked Yates. "I'll open the trap. You kiss him good-bye."

"Oh darn. You know what? I forgot to brush my teeth this morning. He might get offended. How 'bout I open the trap and you kiss him on the lips?"

Using an overhead pole attached to the front of the box trap, I levered the lid open wide. Like most captive wolverines, M1 waited a while, evaluating the sudden change before jumping out. And as usual for him, he didn't run very far before he stopped cold and looked over his shoulder as if he'd suddenly remembered the beaver carcass left in the trap and was wondering why the hell he shouldn't go back and take it along with him. He then started circling us at a distance of 40 to 50 feet, pausing to rub his belly and urinate on some alder brush nearly buried in snow, scent-marking the branches. After all, this was his territory. He had a claim to that beaver carcass we'd used for bait.

Marci Johnson, a former assistant on the project who continued to volunteer on breaks from her graduate studies in wildlife, had told me that when she raised the lid on a trap that held M1 one time, he didn't leap out at all. He jumped atop the front of the box and perched there, regarding her, as if challenging Johnson to make the next move. Her take on M1 was, "He's exactly what I think a wolverine is supposed to be: fearless."

Once released from a trap, no wolverine we'd handled had ever attacked us or attempted to bluff us into leaving by making threatening rushes. Still, wolverines have been reported fighting over food with larger carnivores, up to and including grizzly bears. That wolverines were willing to even try driving off a full-grown grizz was astounding. The fact that they sometimes succeeded tended to stick in your mind when one was circling, especially when the circler was a big gnarly guy with anger management issues like M1. In his worldview, we likely appeared to be tall, gangly, weirdly behaving competitors who were messing with him because we wanted the half-eaten beaver for ourselves.

I doubt M1was seriously weighing his chances of shredding the two-leggeds between him and that meat. But he might have been. It was a lean and hungry time of year. At the very least, he would probably stick around the trap and return for the bait after we moved out. He had already gone in after it two nights in a row. We wanted him and the fancy GPS collar out roaming his vast realm, gathering data on behalf of his kind. So Yates and I left the trap lid propped open with a log so that he could dive in once more, quickly finish what little remained of the bait if he wanted to, and then resume his normal rounds.

We blew M1 his kiss good-bye and skied back to the lake through the dark spruce sighing and groaning under the storm's relentless fury. Once out in the open, we stood straight and spread our arms to the gusts at our backs and sailed home over the ice. In the final half-mile, we passed through a dense fir grove in the shelter of a hill, and I was startled by a new sound: the whisking of my skis through the snow. I could finally hear it above the wind.

As for Big Daddy, we all but forgot about him during a burst of other wolverine activity that day. When he did depart Many Glacier for another area, he often chose a route that led several miles straight toward a headwall marking the east edge of the Great Divide. There, he would scale a nearly vertical, 1,500-foot chute in about 20 minutes and cross through Iceberg Notch to the Pacific side of North America in a plume of stirred-up snow. The ridgeline would block his radio signal. And just like that, the sharp-clawed, sharp-toothed, tireless climber was gone, off to patrol the rest of his turf, which encompassed almost 200 square miles along the crest of the Rockies.

◇◇◇

This unprecedented study of the most important population of wolverines left in the lower 48 states had been underway since mid-2002. Jeff Copeland, the principal investigator, split his time between the field and an office at the U.S. Forest Service Rocky Mountain Research Station in Missoula, Montana, a couple hundred miles south. Yates directed the day-to-day fieldwork, carried out with logistical support from the park (special permits, the use of equipment and cabins) and an assistant when money was available. He and Copeland also relied heavily on the help of a band of unpaid volunteers.

In January of 2003, Copeland arranged for a veterinarian he had previously worked with on a separate study in Idaho to come to Glacier and perform the project's first radio implant surgery. Everything went smoothly, and M1 was released with a transmitter to begin his long and successful career of broadcasting from the wild. However, it was plain that as other animals were captured over the months to come, the Glacier study was going to need a local animal doctor – someone who not only would be available on short notice but who could also be counted on to reach remote traps under all kinds of winter conditions.

Colleagues suggested Dan Savage, who had a practice in the Flathead Valley 30 miles southwest of the park. An avid mountain explorer, he was also the kind of telemark skier who climbed cliffs to carve turns down the chutes in between. Copeland got in touch immediately. Within days of volunteering, Savage found himself en route to a Many Glacier trap to operate on the second wolverine captured.

"I'd just met Dan," Copeland recalled, "so I had no idea how this was going to work out. I'll admit I was a little worried. I mean, my new vet has a Prince Valiant haircut. The guy's so handsome he's pretty, and he eats tofu. But we weren't very far down the trail before I knew I would never be able to keep up with him skiing. He was the real deal in the backcountry. When we got to the trap and sedated the wolverine, I unpacked a folding table for Dan to operate on. I'm down on my hands and knees trying to make sure the table's legs are level on the snow. And by the time I get up to tell Dan we're ready to start, he's already got the transmitter implanted and is closing up F2 with sutures. OK, I'm exaggerating, but I couldn't believe anybody could operate that quickly with that level of skill under field conditions. Talk about a find! From then on, Dan was the key to our success."

The year before Copeland came calling, Savage and his wife, Sally Hash-Savage, had hiked to Avalanche Lake in the park. When they reached the high-elevation basin filled with zinging-cold meltwater, Hash-Savage stayed to explore the lake's outlet. Savage went exploring upstream and spied dark objects moving on one of the snowfields above. "They weren't bears, which is what I originally thought," he said. "They were three wolverines" – the first he'd ever seen in a lifetime of venturing through Montana's backcountry.

"I couldn't have told you a thing about their natural history," he continued. "For all I knew, wolverines always traveled in groups like that. But from their reputation, I certainly didn't expect to find them playing. That's what these three were doing, though – taking turns hiding under a melting snowbank, running out to climb up onto a rock, then jumping off to go sliding down the snow a ways. They kept at it for quite a while. All the mystery around wolverines, and now: play! I think watching play is one of the things that bonds us to animals. It allows us to see the qualities that we have in common more easily. More, there's this sense of a shared spirit. When I was asked to help with the project, all I had to hear was the word *wolverine*. I didn't even think about it. Hey, I'm in."

I was a volunteer as well for Copeland, not the park. Being a National Park volunteer involves a more formal arrangement. While I didn't instantly jump aboard the way Savage had, it wasn't long before all my outdoor clothing and gear began to smell like dead beavers and live wolverines. To this day, I can't quite explain what drove me to get involved in the first place. Curiosity, naturally; my life has largely been ruled by a fascination with wild creatures. The fact that I was a wildlife biologist who'd become a journalist and sorely missed doing hands-on research also played a role.

Glacier Wolverine Project field coordinator Rick Yates keeping a sedated wolverine warm during a capture.
MARCI JOHNSON

Then there was the lure of the setting itself. Glacier National Park is the centerpiece in the section of the Rockies many call the Crown of the Continent. When I'm away from this tall, never-tamed country, I ache to be back within its folds the way other folks miss home. I chose to live close by the 1,500-square-mile reserve, and it's never taken much of an excuse to get me out hiking and skiing its contours on a moment's notice. It makes sense to me to wander around in Glacier purely to air out the soul.

But there was an especially pressing reason to go wandering after wolverines. To use a phrase that sounds shopworn because the words apply to so many life forms these days: The animals are in serious trouble.

Still fairly widespread in the far North, *Gulo gulo* was also common across northern states from Washington to Montana during the 19th century and occasionally reported from the Great Lakes to New England. Its range continued south along the Pacific Coast range and Sierras far into California and all the way down the Rockies into Colorado and New Mexico. Today, the wolverines of the Lower 48 are confined to a few remote parts of Montana, Idaho, and northern Wyoming, with perhaps a dozen more in Washington's North Cascades. They total no more than 500 and more likely number just 300 or fewer. To make a point about their present status, you could cram all of them into one person's mountainside trophy home. It would be a snarlfest, but they'd fit.

Part of the predicament for this hunter-scavenger is that it has proved so hard to find and follow that much of its existence remains a blank. The public scarcely knows what a wolverine actually is apart from cartoon versions and trappers' yarns about the beast. Unfortunately, natural resource managers don't have much more to go on when deciding how best to promote the species' survival.

For example, female wolverines den deep in the snowpack from February into May. This is a central feature of their lives and absolutely critical to the population as a whole. The insulated shelters are where the females give birth and rear their young – the litter size varies from one to four, with an average of two – until they are strong enough to keep up with her. Wolverines don't hibernate. Far from it; each mother actively hunts a large area around the den site and carries food back to the babies once they begin to eat solid food. A mother may dig several dens in succession through the late winter and spring, transferring the infants from the natal, or birth, den to different maternal, or young-rearing, dens as they grow older. She is especially likely to move her babies if she detects some sort of alarming or unfamiliar activity in the area. But what sort of places do mothers pick for a den? High slopes or low ones? Steep or gentle? Open habitats or sheltered spots? What would managers need to do to protect dens from disturbance? As with most questions about wolverine life, the answers were either vague or nonexistent.

When Copeland first looked into studying wolverines at the start of the 1990s, several dens in Alaska were the only ones ever reported in North America. Only a few dozen more have been located since then. Just 20 or so are known from the lower 48 states, and more than half of those were found during the Glacier Wolverine Project. We were hunter-scavengers of new information. Somebody had to get busy scouring big swaths of corrugated terrain the wolverine way, scrabbling across cliff faces, squirming under overhanging ledges, and probing fresh sign to see where it might lead.

The future of this long-mysterious, often-reviled species in the contiguous states depends upon people quickly uncovering enough about its behavior and ecology to assemble the first true-to-life portrait of what this animal does and what it requires to survive.

Adding to the urgency is the current rate of climate change. What little was known about the range of wolverines made it plain that they are tied to environments with fairly heavy snowfall and cool year-round temperatures. In southern Canada and the Lower 48, that translates into a number of small, widely separated subpopulations in the alpine and subalpine zones of high mountain ranges, rather than a single continuous population. As long as they maintain some degree of contact with one another in order to avoid the negative effects of isolation such as inbreeding and occasional dips to dangerously low numbers, the scattered groups can function as what ecologists term a *metapopulation*.

To endure over time, though, the animals are going to need wildland corridors that guarantee individuals the freedom to roam from one chain of peaks to the next. As wolverines struggle to adapt to changing weather and shifting habitats in the warmer years to come, linkage zones running in a north-south direction may prove especially vital. Yet before ecologists can identify the best routes – the wildways that hold the most promise for keeping groups connected – many more gaps in our knowledge of the species' natural history have to be filled in.

◇◇◇◇◇◇◇◇◇◇◇◇◇◇◇◇◇◇◇◇◇◇◇◇◇◇◇◇◇◇◇◇◇◇◇

Four big log box traps had been set up at different sites in Many Glacier. Several more traps were positioned in other parts of the reserve. To avoid attracting grizzlies to the bait, we didn't start trapping until at least late November, after the last big bears had gone into dens for the winter, and we quit around the end of March or early in April, when they started to wake up.

Wolverines captured for the first time were anaesthetized, weighed, measured, and checked over for injuries or illness before being given a radio implant. As the study progressed, recaptured animals whose radio batteries were coming to the end of their approximately two-year life had their implants replaced, and a few of the study animals were fitted with the GPS satellite collars. Nothing was done to a captive that didn't appear fit enough to take the stress of handling. Like subjects already carrying the desired telemetry equipment, a wolverine found in rough shape would simply be freed with our best wishes and the usual cheap talk about a good-bye kiss.

Most of our efforts were devoted to tracking implanted animals, using the handheld antennas. Or trying, anyway. Wolverines keep on the move both day and night, covering territories of up to several hundred square miles. Without radios, it would be virtually impossible to chart their travels. With radios, it's still an overwhelming task in mountain terrain. Even when you're following a fairly close, strong radio signal, the straight-line VHF transmission is blocked the moment your subject drops over a rim, lopes into a side canyon, or ducks under rocks in a boulderfield. We usually had a dozen or more Glacier wolverines on the air at any given moment. Yet days went by when nobody managed to pick up a single electronic cheep anywhere. Some individuals disappeared for weeks or even months at a time.

Merely detecting a signal, thereby establishing that a known animal was in the general vicinity, always felt like an accomplishment. This was one more scrap of information about wolverines than had been available before. The next step was to start pinning down the subject's whereabouts by rotating the antenna back and forth to figure out where the strongest transmission was coming from. Once you had the direction, you took a compass bearing toward it and noted down your own location from a handheld GPS unit. This simple sequence could take a frustratingly long time to complete when signals were bouncing off cliff faces, giving you false directions, or echoing around a cirque basin shaped like a colossal amphitheater.

We tried to get readings from three successive points, each a quarter of a mile from the next. Only after drawing the three bearings on a map to see where they converged could we finally say that we had a fix on the wolverine's location. Taking into account the distances involved and the jumbled topography, plus the likelihood that the wolverine was moving the whole time, to say we had a fix might be overstating things. What we'd garnered was a rough idea of where the target was. This still counted as a coup, and you never knew what patterns it might illuminate when combined with other locations.

As for actually seeing a wolverine, that only happened about once every few hundred hours on the trail. While getting a sighting – "a visual" – gave you long-lasting bragging rights, it wasn't a priority in the study. Better to spend your time locating as many different radioed wolverines as you could in a day than to keep trying all day to get close to one. You'd likely just end up out of breath on a steep series of ledges, wondering where the creature had gone.

A GPS satellite radio collar with the round-the-clock ability to establish locations accurate to within a few feet represented a most welcome advance. The device and its batteries were bulky though. Researchers had been putting such packages on large species for years. But Copeland and Yates were reluctant to add such a burden to a modest-size carnivore that stays almost constantly on the move to make its living and frequently sticks it head and neck into narrow crannies and holes. The wolverines would have looked as though they were carrying a lunch box under their chins.

Fortunately, advances in technology were bringing smaller, lighter GPS satellite collars onto the market. The team had purchased several of them at a cost of around $3,000 each. This winter of 2006 marked the biggest push yet to get some on our Glacier *gulos*. It added up to a costly experiment, for we had little assurance that the new units would stay on long enough to gather meaningful sets of data. When the team tried out different brands of GPS satellite collars in earlier years, the wolverines sometimes got them off within hours. Most of those units didn't work worth a darn anyway. The circuitry fried itself, failed in supercold conditions, or drained the battery practically overnight.

◇◇◇◇◇◇◇◇◇◇◇◇◇◇◇◇◇◇◇◇◇◇◇◇◇◇◇◇◇◇◇◇◇◇

No study of wild animals gets by without its share of glitches and frustrations. If there were going to be days when about the only things still working for us were hope and stubborn determination, that was all right. They were enough. Sooner or later, some of the GPS collars would stay on and function half-decently, and when they did, there was every chance that whole new dimensions of wolverine life would start to unfold before our eyes. In the meantime, we would manage to keep putting several more members of the population on the airwaves with VHF implants each year, and at any given hour on any day, a set of ordinary radio signals could suddenly reveal a side to the animals almost nobody had ever suspected.

Out tracking with my handheld antenna one winter afternoon, I picked up the signals of two different wolverines near the base of some cliffs. The first was M1. The other was one of his yearling male offspring. From the way the signal strength varied from moment to moment, I could tell the animals were moving. Both seemed to be headed in the same direction. I guessed that they might be fairly close to one another, but I was still stunned when I skied that direction after a while and came upon their tracks.

The two sets of paw prints wove back and forth in a braided pattern with the first set crossing the second, then the second set crossing the first. This wasn't one animal following another independently. The two were trotting side by side. Partway across a clearing, the tracks joined in an aimless, looping pattern that almost seemed to say that the father and son were playing with each other – goofing around. Even if they weren't frolicking, I was looking at evidence of something that according to traditional lore simply didn't happen.

Except for mating, male wolverines were said to be strictly solitary – too volatile and vicious to tolerate company of any kind, least of all male company. Females were held to be equally short-tempered and unsociable apart from the six months during which they reared their kits. After that, the young were supposedly on their own. Yet from tracking radio signals on other days, I'd already gathered evidence of older juveniles spending time with their mother now and then. I'd also found M1 traveling with one of his mates outside the breeding season – more than once, suggesting that the pair maintained a long-term bond with each other.

Now I was documenting the case of a year-old youngster, already adult size, that had left its mother and gone on to hang out with Dad for a while – a sort of wolverine version of joint custody. What kind of mammal does that? None that I knew of other than *Homo sapiens*. Copeland had mentioned seeing juvenile wolverines of both sexes traveling with their father after leaving their mother's side during a separate study that he'd carried out years earlier in Idaho. However, his observations of such behavior mainly involved one particular adult male, raising the question of whether or not this was an anomaly – unusual behavior by a single individual. Studying the intertwined tracks as I skied along in the wake of M1 and his son, I thought, No, what Copeland reported wasn't a case of an odd wolverine. What seemed odd was that in the 21st century we understood so remarkably little about one of the most intriguing creatures to ever walk the wild.

The gated-off road into Many Glacier during a typical windstorm when drifts pile ten feet deep in places and the asphalt is scoured bare in others. RICK YATES

CHAPTER TWO

Many Glacier, March, 2006, Part II
Yates the Indefatigable

Even when wind caves the ribs of a fawn
The mountain, braced by blueness, is not stunned.

RICHARD HUGO
from *Triangle for Green Men*

FROM BROWNING, THE MAIN TOWN ON THE BLACKFEET INDIAN RESERVATION –
and the only town with stoplights and paved streets anywhere near Glacier's
eastern edge – it's an hour's drive to the little outpost of Babb. The park begins
five miles west of there. A gate marks the boundary, by the base of Lake Sherburne. It is locked over winter. To reach the ranger station in the heart of Many
Glacier, officially shuttered for the season, you've got another seven miles of
road to cover under your own power.

The prevailing airflow is from the Pacific. It washes up against the park's
western slopes and cools as it gains altitude, often condensing into clouds that
unload their moisture as rain or snow among the peaks. Still moving eastward,
the chilled air now wants to sink, and suddenly, there is all kinds of space to do
that just across the Divide, where the mountains fall off onto the Great Plains.
Like invisible floodwaters breaching a dam, heavy air spills over the heights, cascades through the passes, and comes pouring down the steep east-side ramparts
known as the Rocky Mountain Front.

My favorite mountainscape lies here on the million-acre park's eastern slope
where a major valley is fed by four branches, each of which leads up to the crest
of the Divide: Many Glacier with its necklace of icefields. It's no place for human
settlement. But the slopes suit plenty of mountain goats and bighorn sheep,
along with grizzlies and black bears, wolves and coyotes, lions and lynx, an elk

herd, scattered mule deer, and moose. Better yet, as I came to view things, the area seems to be just right for wolverines.

On the way to Babb, you may see Many Glacier reared up jagged and bright on the western horizon. Or you might find a curtain of snow-filled clouds hanging across the entrance to the main valley and hiding everything beyond. Held in check by a continental air mass over the Plains, the shroud doesn't advance or retreat. It just looms and roils at the mountain–prairie border. It waits. The skies can be clear in Babb, sunny almost to the park gate, but you know that as soon as you step behind that curtain, you're going to get tested to see if you're wolverine-worthy.

In early March of 2006, I parked my car in the lee of the hill leading up to Lake Sherburne and made a final check of gear and supplies. Some went into my backpack, the rest onto a long plastic sled. Since I planned to stay for a month, the load was heavy with fresh groceries. It made an ungainly stack on the sled. I secured it with lashings, clipped the sled's lead rope to the rear of my pack, and set off skiing. The temperature didn't seem too bad – probably somewhere in the high teens (F) – but I could hear the hiss and roar of a gale on the hilltop ahead. Wind chill was going to drop the effective temperature below zero fast. With snowflakes starting to spin into my face, I put on goggles, pulled my hat down more tightly, buttoned the parka's collar over my lower face, and headed in.

The worst spot would be where the air funneled off the end of the frozen lake. Five minutes later, I was in the thick of it, following a slot the wind had scoured through a drift that rose above my head. The curves and twists of the sides made this tunnel a turbine filled with whirlwinds of snow. There were no shadows, no distinct shapes to focus on for direction. The bottom slanted one way, then another. I could hardly tell up from down. It became nearly impossible to stand against the strongest blasts, much less make progress into them. Straining for all I was worth to get over a hump, I realized that it wasn't only the wind holding me back. The sled had tipped over, and I was dragging it on its side.

After this happened several times, I stopped to rearrange the weight. My goggles were fogging up. I cleared them yet could still barely see to the end of the sled in the whiteout. Slipping off my gloves to undo the sled's lashings was a mistake. My hands started to grow numb at once. As fast as I brushed snow off a knot with my increasingly useless fingers, new snow plastered everything over. The exposed skin on my face felt sandblasted and equally numb. My pants were pressed like a second skin onto the windward side of my legs, while the looser sections were snapping so hard that they stung. I'd forgotten to tie the draw cords on my parka hood together, and they were whipping my cheeks raw.

Well, shit! I thought: Welcome to Many Glacier. Here I am – what? – less than half a mile from my car going hypothermic and getting beaten to death by my britches and some string. I started talking back to the storm while I finished shifting the sled's weight. The situation was wretched but not truly dangerous.

Not yet. I'd be fine as long as conditions eased past this end of the lake. They did, somewhat.

Although the blizzard continued, nearly as much snow was being whisked up off the ground as was falling from the sky, and that was a good sign in a way. The flakes weren't piling up so quickly that I'd have to break a deep trail on the way in. I found patches of easy gliding between straightaways where gusts gathered strength until they threatened to topple me. My guess was that some were hitting 70 miles an hour.

Rather than fight a surge of headwind, I would plant my ski poles, lean forward onto them, and wait for the worst to pass before pushing ahead, knowing I might need all the energy I could conserve before the day was finished. I could always hang most of my burden from a conspicuous tree, hurry on with only light essentials, and ski back for the cache on a better day. I had no intention of doing that. But reminding yourself of good options is a useful distraction when you're marching along feeling like a penguin pulling a plow.

A couple of miles later, Rick Yates appeared out of a squall, having come from the ranger station. With his help and the distraction of his company, the rest of the trip seemed almost routine. No setbacks, no drama. A little more silent penguin plodding toward the end, and we were there. By the time we'd finished dinner at the cabin and sunk into chairs by the wood stove, listening to the wind's tantrums outside, being miserable seemed like something that happened to other people.

I'd been wolverining in Many Glacier for a good part of November and December during 2005 and for a few days in January of 2006. This was a homecoming to a familiar world, one more real in many ways than the one outside. Uncompromisingly harsh but less troubled, physically riskier yet somehow more reassuring and far more free, this was a world that wouldn't lie to you.

Yates had been on his own here in the valley for a while, operating the traps and carrying out surveys with his radio receiver. In particular, he had been tracking M1, who had carried an implanted radio since late January of 2003. From charting its signals, we knew that Big Daddy claimed more than half of Many Glacier as his territory as well as portions of several drainages across the Divide. He often traveled the same Many Glacier trails that we skied and hiked. His course took him past three of our four traps. Sometimes he ignored them. Often, he investigated the log boxes from the outside but left it at that. Then, after weeks of skipping by, he would suddenly climb in to get at the bait, as if he'd gone too many long winter miles without finding food and hunger had quenched his caution. Once in a while, we could hardly keep him out of the traps.

He'd been given a GPS collar earlier in the winter of 2006, but quickly got the annoying thing off. Where, was anybody's guess. For all we knew, it rested up on the shoulder of some towering summit. The pricey package included a small VHF transmitter so we could find it with a standard radio receiver. No one

A capture at the Two Medicine trap by Rick Yates (left) and seasonal ranger Al Hoffs. MARCI JOHNSON

had picked up its signal though, not even during an airplane flight. With luck, the transmitter had not died but only become buried by snow that muffled the signal, and someone could home in on it after the spring melt.

A detailed portrait of M1's movements here in the core of the park in relation to those of the other wolverines was important to understanding how the animals distributed themselves over the landscape and how that in turn influenced the dynamics of the population – breeding success, survival rates, dispersal to new habitats, and so forth. If M1 was caught again, Copeland wanted Yates to try fitting him with another GPS collar, a tad more tightly.

◇◇◇◇◇◇◇◇◇◇◇◇◇◇◇◇◇◇◇◇◇◇◇◇◇◇◇◇◇

From the beginning, the project's success hinged on sophisticated scientific analyses and electronic technology. Impressive. But they weren't getting anywhere without old-fashioned bushcraft. The different approaches converged at the trap sites. Picture an axe-hewn log box about six feet long by four feet wide and three to four feet high, half-buried by snow. Halfway along its length, a log arch straddles the box. A long pole rests lengthwise on the arch like a teeter-totter on a fulcrum. The front of this overhanging pole is connected by a length of cable to the front of the box's heavy log lid. A second cable runs from the rear of the pole down to the teeth of a set of locking pliers attached to the rear of the box. The locking pliers' release handle is attached to a wire that leads through a bottom log to the bait – typically a big chunk of road-killed deer or a skinned beaver carcass bought from fur trappers outside the park.

Now picture a wolverine climbing into the box and yanking on the prize. This pulls open the handle of the locking pliers, which opens their teeth, which releases the cable holding down the rear of the pole, which flies upward, allowing the front end of the pole and the heavy lid it has been keeping open to drop. Fast! Give a wolverine extra milliseconds, and it would be out in a blur. Two other devices, each with its own jury-rigged arrangement of wires and wood, come into play as the lid whams shut. The first is a small pole that falls into place beneath the log arch, locking down the lid. Second is a transmitter positioned so that the closing of the lid switches its signal from a slow pulse rate to a rapid one, alerting whoever is in the area listening to a receiver.

Except it's getting dark. Or it's after dark, which is when most of the wolverines we'd caught had gone in. You've been reading by the stove back at the cabin, warming your toes, and having trouble keeping your eyes open after a day of tracking. You know the temperature outside is sinking. Now, roused by the trap signal, you step out onto the porch to see how low the mercury has gone. If the clouds have cleared off and the starlight is glittering and the cold aches on your skin, you can tell before you even read the thermometer that the temperature might plunge below minus 10 F (minus 23 C) before dawn. You have no choice but to gear up and hit the trail. And when you get to the trap, all you're going to do is "kiss the wolverine on the lips and let it go," as Copeland first put it. The box is roomy enough to move around in, but keeping the animal confined through a bitter subzero night would still be unacceptable.

If it looks like a more typical night destined to stay above minus 10 or so, a wooden cave isn't such a forbidding place for a wolverine to be stuck. Wolverines are used to being in dens and to crawling or digging into tight spaces after food. The trap is sturdy as a vault. You could use logs that stout to build a full-size cabin, and in fact I have. Why not leave handling the animal for the morning when you can see what you're doing? The answer is, It's a wolverine. Your box contains a beast that, whether a tough male like M1 or a smaller female, is more than capable of clawing and chewing its way out before dawn. If the night is nearly half over, you can take a chance and wait for daylight. If not, you're obliged to strap on a headlamp and skis, hitch a sled full of gear to your pack, and go out to work with the captive, come rain, sleet, or snow.

The closest trap is less than a half-hour's ski from the ranger station, the farthest a bit more than an hour away if the ice cover of the two lakes en route is thick enough to travel on. If it isn't, you'll have to break trail for yourself and your loaded sled through the woods at the base of Mount Allen. That trip can take twice as long. You reach the site and crack open the trap's lid a couple of inches to shine a light in . . . and discover from the eyes shining back that it's not a wolverine in there after all. Lynx and martens were always gnawing on our baits, and every so often a red fox conducted a raid. They often got a meal without consequences, since we tried to adjust the trigger mechanism so a real wolverine-strength tug on the bait was required to trip it. Just the same, team members had found all those other species waiting inside at one time or another, especially lynx.

<hr>

We named one trap site the Boneyard, Boney for short. The other three – Fishercap, Swiftcurrent, and Josephine – were named for the lakes nearest to them. They became Fishy, Swifty, and Josey, respectively. Three days before I arrived, Yates picked up M1's radio frequency in the area. The signal showed Big Daddy going to Fishy, staying quite a while, moving straight to Swifty, and hanging around there as well. Nothing came of it in the way of an alert that a box lid had closed. Following the paw prints later, Yates saw that M1 had been in both boxes and eaten a good deal of their bait. Uncharacteristically, he had done this gently enough to avoid setting off either trap. However, the night before I reached Many Glacier, the signal from Josey, the most distant trap, went into rapid-pulse mode. Yates skied the two-and-a-half-miles there to check the box and found M1 inside.

For safety as well as efficiency, Project members worked in pairs whenever possible. Yates faced trying to put another collar on M1 by himself in the dark and a drizzling rain. This would mean kneeling or lying on his side in the deep snow, pushing open the heavy lid just a crack, and holding it there with one leg while using his hands to manipulate a jab stick – a fiberglass pole with a syringe at the tip – to sedate the animal.

Like most wolverines, M1 would interpret any opening of the lid as an opportunity to rush at the invader – to rage and roar and drip saliva and snap his formidable teeth, sending the message: I will rip you open if I can, and if I can't, I will die before I yield. Then almost without fail, he would wedge his head and claws into the crack and try pushing the lid upward to escape. When Yates first reached the trap, he noticed that M1 had already butted his head against the closed lid hard enough to jiggle loose the pole brace that was supposed to lock the top in place.

During a wolverine study in a different area, a guy lifted the trap lid a crack and shined a metal flashlight inside for a better look. The captive bit it out of his hand. Crunch. Gulp. The flashlight was never seen again. Whatever was left of it went off with the wolverine when it was turned loose. After hearing the story, I liked to imagine the animal roaming at night, often the most active time for these hunters. I pictured the creature covering mile after mile in that inexhaustible wolverine lope, making sharp detours, scent-marking tree roots and trunks, weaving in and out of cubbyholes, and generally driving its nose through the terrain until it caught a fresh scent. Then it would suddenly stop and open its mouth wide, and rays of light would come out to sweep across the forest floor until they fixed on a victim. Any animal lucky enough to escape would spend the rest of its life retelling the tale of how it was once half-blinded by unholy beams that shot from a wolverine's bone-mincing jaws.

Reacting to both the open lid and a probing pole, M1 was going to be a tornado of a target. Yates couldn't afford a partial hit or broken-off needle. He had to jab M1 exactly right to be sure he was delivering the correct dose of two drugs mixed together – a muscle immobilizer and a tranquilizer. Even then, a wolverine might react unexpectedly to the drugs, depending on its condition. The dosage required to act on certain males, especially pissed-off ones, was sometimes way higher than the charts prescribed for their weight. An overdose could be corrected with a drug that reversed its effects – unless the animal failed to respond. That hadn't happened yet but was always a worry. On the other hand, an underdose might leave Yates midway through the collaring process with an increasingly lively wolverine in his hands.

<hr/>

Rick Yates is a strapping man who stands six feet two inches with hulking shoulders and long arms that form a wingspan more than a match for his height. You'd want him at your back in a surly barroom. You'd want him with you whenever the high country turns testy because he is as strong as he looks with a will that is stronger yet, quick-witted, and brave – one of the most capable outdoorsmen I've ever met. More to the point, he is exactly who you'd want handling whatever situation developed at a trap site in Glacier's backcountry.

He had worked for years on trail crews in the park, gone back to college for a master's degree in wildlife biology while studying bald eagles in Glacier, and then signed on with the park again as a seasonal biologist. Among his other responsibilities, he handled problem grizzlies and trained rangers in bear capture techniques. Outside his seasonal park job, he trapped and surveyed grizzlies and black bears elsewhere in Montana and banded falcons and ravens in Greenland. Back in Glacier, he went on to conduct surveys of carnivores by skiing the backcountry for eight winters to locate their tracks in the snow. For recreation, he did more skiing in the park and climbed its summits during the warmer months.

I could easily see Yates as a mountain man from a century or two earlier. Scotch-Irish by background, he hails from the hills of Virginia and wears his dark hair long and his beard bushy. Though he is a handsome fellow and honest to a fault, one eye takes on a slant and focuses a bit off kilter when he grows tired, giving him a slightly feral expression at times. Adding to this aura is the fact that Yates has a horror of throwing anything away, and that includes the shirts he continues to wear in tatters and favorite pants resewn so many times you can't tell where the original fabric is.

One morning when I drove into the Many Glacier campground with a brand new volunteer, I saw Yates walking toward us on the road at his normal pace, which has some of the qualities of a fanatic on a special hurry-up mission from God, his upper body tilting forward to balance a ground-eating stride, long arms swinging from a shredded shirt, and hair flying in the wind.

"Oh boy," I whispered to my companion as I rolled up the car windows and locked my door, "It's that homeless guy that shows up around here. Don't let him catch your eye or he'll be hitting us up for something." My companion gave Yates a final, quick glance, surreptitiously locked the door on his side, and then stared fixedly the opposite direction until Yates came up to the window and said, "You look pretty pleased with yourself, Chadwick. Did you pick up some wolverine signals on your way in?"

◇◇◇◇◇◇◇◇◇◇◇◇◇◇◇◇◇◇◇◇◇◇◇◇◇◇◇◇◇◇◇◇◇◇◇◇

Back at Josey, Yates paced and beat his hands together for warmth – the gloves he liked had gradually been reduced to fragments of leather encased in duct tape – and weighed the circumstances. Handling M1 alone in the dark was inviting bad luck. The weather was getting sloppy wet, and the hour was late. M1 wouldn't suffer if left for the rest of the night. However, the trap surely would. This guy was a log demolisher. Usually, wolverines in a box trap stopped chewing when they heard noises outside. As long as we stayed nearby speaking loudly from time to time, the logs stayed in one piece; that was the rule. But M1

34

was an exception. Yates remembered a time he caught this wolverine and was talking at him through the slightly opened lid, trying to get him to quit biting away at the box's corner. M1 gouged out a fresh chunk of wood, spit it to one side, and sank his teeth in for another bite, glaring straight at the man all the while. He might as well have flipped Yates off with a middle toe.

Captured another night at Fishercap, M1 had chewed free by morning. But he didn't leave until he'd enlarged his escape hole so he could haul out the carcass and take it with him. Judging from his tracks, he then shot straight from Fishy to Josey, where the trap lid was down. F2, one of the females M1 mated with, was caught inside. He began chewing his way in toward her. While he might have wanted the bait, the story we told ourselves was that he was working to free his girlfriend, which may well have been a motive. He and F2 appeared to have a close and enduring bond.

Not surprisingly, we had to rebuild the boxes every so often. It was a chore, but the shredded logs actually testified to the wisdom of Copeland's choice to use this funky mini-log cabin of a trap. Besides being a cold conductor, a metal barrel or cage would have edges or seams that a wolverine might break teeth and claws on. Two other metal devices used in carnivore studies, a cable snare or a steel trap with padded jaws, would cause the same problems. Worse, a wolverine could tear joints and ligaments fighting those legholds. When nothing else worked to free it, the animal might pull off trapped toes or chew away its whole foot. What a wolverine would not do is cease struggling. In Copeland's capture system, only the wood got hurt.

Yates came to a decision. He propped the small pole back in place to hold the trap lid down and heaped snow on top to make it heavier – harder for M1 to jiggle. After packing more snow between the lid and the rest of the box so it might freeze in place, he left for the ranger station. Yet Yates was by no means finished for the night. At the cabin, he grabbed the battery-powered AM/FM radio we played for music and news, and then he skied back to Josephine. There, he tuned the radio to an all-night station, wrapped it in a plastic bag to keep out the drizzle, and set it under a tree near the trap to serve as a surrogate human voice. He and Copeland had heard about this technique from Scandinavian wolverine researchers during a visit to Norway. The distraction might slow down M1's breakout efforts. Even if it didn't, the night was now far enough advanced that the male would have to work nonstop to chew out by morning. Yates skied home to the ranger station to catch a bit of sleep. At daybreak, he was back on the trail to Josey.

M1 was still there. In the end, Yates managed to sedate him without much trouble. Needing room and light to fit the new GPS collar carefully in place around the male's neck, Yates lifted him out of the box and laid him on a heat-reflecting space blanket with a foam pad atop it. He draped his coat over the wolverine because the immobilizing drug lowers body temperature and wouldn't fully wear off for a while. The rain was changing to sleet with a strong wind behind it as the weather started to swing toward blizzard conditions. Yates stood by shivering until M1 began to stir. At that stage, he placed the wolverine back in the trap. Two hours would pass before Yates thought it safe to release him, sure that the male was fully alert and active, able to handle whatever came his way on the slopes. At last, Yates made the ski trip home to the cabin. Then he headed down the valley to meet me.

◇◇◇◇◇◇◇◇◇◇◇◇◇◇◇◇◇◇◇◇◇◇◇◇◇◇◇◇◇◇◇◇◇

The following morning, Yates the Indefatigable came hurrying down from the cabin's second floor, where we had an omnidirectional antenna positioned to pick up signals from all four traps. He woke me with the words, "Josephine's going off." We grabbed gear and a breakfast bar and hit the trail. In an ordinary winter setting, we would have been able to glide along the track Yates had broken during his recent commutes. In Many Glacier, a ski track rarely lasted long before fresh snow and winds obliterated it.

From the start of our trip, it was snowing and blowing heavily even in the forest. Our early progress where the trail wound through the lodgepole pines and bare white trunks of aspen was uninspiring. I readjusted the daypack's weight on my shoulders and fantasized about a steaming cup of coffee. We picked up speed crossing Swiftcurrent, the first frozen lake on the way. That the wind picked up too was a lousy sign because we were still somewhat sheltered in the lee of the massif called Grinnell Point. After three-quarters of a mile, the route from the lake's upper end climbed a hill. At the top, we could receive a straight-line radio signal from any wolverine at the trap site. Adjusting the receiver, Yates nodded to himself and said, "It's M1."

We dropped down to Josephine, the second lake, and started the exposed journey toward its head. Instantly, the trip turned Antarctic. We were now in a colossal bowl cupped at one end by the walls and spires of the Divide. The rainy weather Yates endured earlier had created an icy crust on the encompassing snowfields. Not much of the fresh snow was sticking to it. Instead, it was being swept down the slopes onto the lake. It wasn't collecting there either but skating along the ice to create a ground blizzard. The spindrift was so intense I lost sight of Yates when he moved farther than 20 feet away. For a while, I wasn't sure I was still going the right direction. All I could do was try to orient myself relative to the angle of the snowflakes streaming by until the outline of a familiar peak showed through a swirl of white.

Avalanches had thundered off the ridge between Grinnell Point and Mount Grinnell, swept over the goat cliffs on the southeast face, and fanned out onto the lake ice. Rock chunks and uprooted trees lay scattered halfway to the opposite shore. We skied between them. The ice was so thick most places that we could have driven a tank over it. Even so, there were weak points near the lake's edges and over upwellings. Always expanding or contracting with fluctuations in the temperature, the frozen surface was like a live skin, and it creaked, groaned, sang, shrieked, pinged, and gave off gunshot noises as it changed thickness. I couldn't help tensing up when fresh ice talk came *ka-zinging* through old seams and new cracks nearby. My subconscious insisted on interpreting each noise as another warning that I was someday going to step on the wrong spot and break through.

On glassy stretches, the storm skidded me around a little, but I'd learned the secret to making progress upwind where the ice was polished and slick. It was to chart a course like a sailor, tacking to port for a while, then to starboard, using the metal edges of your skis like a keel. You wouldn't have to beat into the weather forever, and you knew that when you were ready to return, you could hold your jacket open wide like a mainsail if you wanted, and start whizzing homeward so fast you'd scare yourself.

When we reached the head of the lake and started to deal with M1, trying to check his collar and condition, listening to him seethe, feeling him hit the front of the log box in a rush, my senses were buzzing so loudly that I couldn't string two thoughts together. He never calmed down. But I eventually did – at least enough to recognize that Big Daddy wasn't actually sucking all the air out of the woods. It only felt that way.

He wasn't truly huge for a dominant male wolverine. Nor was he glossy and sleek like a male in his prime. He was on the lean side at the moment and a little worn-looking, beginning to show the touch of age. Old scars marked his muzzle. When he'd bared his teeth during one of his snarling lunges, some appeared chipped and none too sharp. Despite the adrenaline flowing through me, this wolverine all at once seemed a lot more real – maybe one of the toughest animals in the world, maybe near-mythic in his deeds – but an animal nonetheless, dealing, like everyone must, with the challenges of time. Later, while we kidded about who was going to kiss M1 good-bye, I surprised myself by how much I did wish for good things to happen to him. Yet instead of being able to help him directly, all I had was this sham power to free him after interrupting his life.

<hr />

Upon our return to the ranger station, Yates went in the door first. I was still taking off my skis when he came back out, saying, "Fishy's going off." The trap by Fishercap Lake wasn't far. We were low on energy, and it cost a fair amount of calories just to keep warm in the storm, so we took the time to down a sandwich and a cup of tea before leaving. I asked Yates how many times M1 and other wolverines in the area had been caught altogether. In the four winter seasons since they began trapping in 2002/2003, team members had made something like a hundred captures involving 19 different wolverines, he replied.

Obviously, not every day was as busy at the trap sites as this one, but the project's success rate was extraordinary by wolverine-catching standards. Fur trappers have described these animals as the Holy Grail. By that, they mean that in addition to being the second-largest North American mammal that they can legally take in steel jaws nowadays (the wolf is the largest, where legal) and the one with the most fearsome reputation, the wolverine is legendarily mysterious, elusive, and above all, wary of traps.

Yates added that when he and Copeland fell into conversation with trappers and described the Glacier Wolverine Project, a common response was, "I don't believe you. Wolverines are experts at avoiding our sets even though we're careful not to leave a speck of human scent on them. They're the wiliest things in the woods. No way could you ever catch them a bunch of times."

The scientists had a reply, though they wouldn't always say it out loud: "But you see, there's a trick . . . We don't kill them."

Were we about to add to our wolverine capture total? On the way to Fishy, we punched in different frequencies on our radio receiver. The trap's signal came in loudly, but we couldn't pick up any electronic chirps from a tagged wolverine. Farther along where the trail led over a stream and on through lodgepole stands with an understory of serviceberry brush, we came on fresh coyote tracks. A hundred yards from the trap site, Yates looked down and announced, "Well, it's *not* a coyote."

He had intercepted a line of tracks twice as large. A wolverine's paw prints look a bit like those of a young grizzly bear, showing the five long-clawed toes and part of the heel. But in snow this deep and loose, all we had to go on were holes filled almost to the top with wind-driven powder. We couldn't be sure they weren't from the four-toed footsteps of a lynx. Of the nonwolverine species that raided Fishy, the worst offenders were these tufted-eared cats with big, snowshoe paws of their own. I expected to see one up close in a few moments.

When caught in our traps, however, lynx rarely growled. The big log box near Fishercap Lake was growling a bad-dream growl, the kind of foreboding rumble that in movies makes you silently shout to the character on the screen: Don't go in there! Whatever you do, don't . . . open . . . that . . . door . . .

We opened the box's lid. Yates sometimes called wolverines *werewolverines* or just *wereverines*, partly for the way they seemed able to disappear and rematerialize at will while we were tracking them, but partly for that growl. The wolverine in the gloom of the box wasn't one he recognized. It didn't have any of the colored ear tags we routinely put on captured and radioed animals either. Though it kept up its growling, it didn't rush at us to thrust its jaws through the slight opening. Yates guessed from its appearance and its reluctance to charge that this was a young animal – probably a yearling exploring the outer limits of its parents' territories and possibly a ways beyond. If he was right, this wolverine would become sexually mature in the months that followed. The time was coming for it to leave the area where it had grown up and try to carve out a territory for itself.

Downloading the computer chip in a GPS collar to collect information on recent movements. JACK NOLL

Yates rummaged through his daypack and pulled out an Argos collar, a very lightweight satellite radio device compared with the bulkier GPS units. It doesn't store data in its own circuits. Orbiting satellites record its locations and periodically relay the data in batches to stations on Earth. A researcher can tap in a code and download the information onto a personal computer from the comfort of a warm office.

The drawback was that this small device provided readings accurate to within only a few miles rather than a few feet. That was fine for following birds or whales that migrate thousands of miles, and it served well enough for other species when you only needed to keep tabs on their general whereabouts. It wasn't ideal for most wolverines, but Yates thought a yearling on the verge of dispersing to try to find a home of its own made a reasonable candidate for an Argos collar. We'd settle for learning roughly where our captive ended up – and whether or not it survived the journey.

We planted our skis upright in the snow like posts and strung a big tarp between them, fashioning a sort of lean-to shelter against the snowfall and wind. Once in a while, a burst would tear through the slight clearing so fast that it literally stole my breath away and I had to draw in hard to fill my lungs again. Yates sedated the yearling – a male – and recorded the usual measurements, then fitted him with color-coded ear tags and the Argos collar. For the second time in two days, he took off his jacket to cover a wolverine and stomped around shivering until he was sure the young male was coming out of the drug all right. We placed him back in the log box, locked down the lid, and skied to the cabin to warm up. Two hours later, we skied back to Fishy and let the fully recovered wolverine loose. Fare-thee-well, newly anointed M20. Keep in touch.

Accidentally captured in the wolverine traps, lynx were strikingly quiet and unaggressive by comparison.
DAVE MURRAY

CHAPTER THREE

Many Glacier, March 2006, Part III
Country Radio

When old age shall this generation waste,
Thou shalt remain, in midst of other woe
Than ours, a friend to man, to whom thou say'st
'Beauty is truth, truth beauty, – that is all
Ye know on earth, and all ye need to know.'

JOHN KEATS
from *Ode on a Grecian Urn*

Without supernatural assistance, our fellow creatures can tell us the
most beautiful stories, and that means true stories, because the truth
about nature is always far more beautiful even than what our great
poets sing of it, and they are the only real magicians that exist.

KONRAD LORENZ
from the preface to *King Solomon's Ring*

YATES HAD TO LEAVE SOON TO CHECK ON THE OTHER TEAM MEMBERS, who were
trapping and radio-tracking in different areas of the park. He also needed to pack
in new equipment and spare parts, try to troubleshoot malfunctioning electronics,
and help repair any weak points of the various log traps. Most of all, he wanted
to go home to be with his wife and son for a while. While he took a final day to
wrap up some Many Glacier chores, I skied to Fishy and Josey, dragging a frozen
beaver through the snow to each. This laid a scent trail for a wolverine to follow
to the log boxes, where I replaced the old carcasses that M1 and M20 had eaten.

Each trap site was also rigged with some really stinky meat in a burlap bag
dangling from a rope high in a nearby tree. There, the upper air currents would
carry the smell more widely. Not even a climber as lithe as a marten could get
to this food. But Steller's jays and their bold relatives the gray jays, commonly

called camp robbers, had pecked through the bags and made off with most of the contents, so I had to replace those lures as well as the beaver bodies. For spice, per Copeland's instructions, I added drops of either skunk scent or a puree of putrid fish and cow blood to the hanging bundles and dribbled a touch more onto the lip of the trap – ah, the glamorous lifestyle of the wildlife volunteer! Anything to pique more interest from passing *gulos*. Of course, we hoped that wouldn't include M1, at least not until his GPS data chip filled up.

The Many Glacier ranger station was the only outpost we used that had the luxury of electricity during winter. That evening, Yates turned on a computer and called up the park's weather site on the Internet. The instruments at Logan Pass had just recorded wind speeds of 107 miles per hour. Logan Pass stands on the Divide at 6,646 feet, just eight miles from the ranger station, which rests at about 5,000 feet. The gusts through the upper valleys around us must have been hitting hurricane strength at the same time.

The following day, dawn's colors turned to brilliant blue, and whatever didn't lie in shadow glistened. You could scarcely find sign of the three-day blizzard except for the cornices and snowfields that had puffed into fat snow pillows high in the lee of the crags. Tracks patterned fresh drifts here and there in the main valley, but most of what the storm gave in the way of white powder, the storm had taken away, sweeping it on east toward the prairies. The mountain goats up on the windward slopes of Mount Altyn were walking on bare rocks and dried brown grasses.

Yates headed out of the park. I kept him company some distance before turning back to radio-track F2. I found her signal coming from a hanging valley high on the side of Mount Allen. From the way that area had become the epicenter of her movements lately, I suspected she might have a natal den there. Late February through early March was the wolverine time of birth.

Given a light breeze at his back, Yates had chosen to ski down Lake Sherburne. When we got in touch by phone in the evening, he said he had followed wolf tracks much of the way. While he did that, F2 was possibly suckling days-old kits down in the hole she had dug 8 to 10 feet deep in the snow. If so, the white-walled sleeping chamber would be cushioned with shredded wood. Farther along, there would perhaps be another resting chamber, a feeding chamber, and at least one more side room that served as a toilet. Altogether, the tunnel might run for 20 to 70 feet at that depth and lead upward to an escape exit or two at its end. Her kits would have come into the world with fine, soft, pure white fur, looking like little polar bears.

◇◇◇◇◇◇◇◇◇◇◇◇◇◇◇◇◇◇◇◇◇◇◇◇◇◇◇◇◇◇◇

What drew me so strongly to Many Glacier, and to Glacier Park as a whole, was exactly that kind of perpetual beginning. Lovely in its contours, breathtaking in scale, the reserve spans a nearly 60-mile length of the Montana Rockies just south of the Canadian border. It's a million acres of Continental Divide topography, a superstructure of tilted rock layers, white, tan, gray, grayish green, wine red, and more than a billion years old. They have tales to tell of great forces at play on the planet, and their stories soar. They shine with alpenglow. They sing in your eyes. They make you want to stay strong for another century, because while you think you could maybe face dying, you can't deal with the idea of one day becoming too old and weak to ramble among these summits any longer.

The crags all around are beyond monumental; I'm a mote beneath them. They have endured for eons on end; my existence, by comparison, seems a passing glimmer, like the ring of ripples on a lake from the rise of a trout. The lesson from nature this grand, I would tell myself, is to at least have the grace to be humble. Then I started following wolverines around. They are smaller than I. Their life span is considerably shorter. Yet whatever they do, they do undaunted. They live life as fiercely and relentlessly as it has ever been lived.

If wolverines have a strategy, it's this: Go hard, and high, and steep, and never back down, not even from the biggest grizzly, and least of all from a mountain. Climb everything: trees, cliffs, avalanche chutes, summits. Eat everybody: alive, dead, long-dead, moose, mouse, fox, frog, its still-warm heart or frozen bones.

I will never really know what it's like to be one of these hunter-scavengers. On my best day, I could never even keep up with any for long. I feel humbled when I'm in the mountains, and I think that's as it should be.

Every day in wolverine country, bitter or bright, seemed to come freshly and powerfully made. Every hour of it brought new challenges and possibilities unique to the heights of the continent. And every life form, whose span seemed so brief next to the mountains', was determined to thrive and make more of itself regardless. Perhaps I needed this atmosphere more than I knew. I would turn 60 in 2008. The calendar made it plain that I was farther from the year of my own birth than from the year of my death. I had gone from truly and successfully ignoring this fact to merely resisting it, staring geezerhood straight in the eye and trying not to blink first while knowing in my bones that I had no chance of coming out on top. My body simply could no longer do what it had done in the past. Most of what was called for? Yes. All? Not any more, and this scared me.

When I'd looked at M1, I found myself identifying with him – not an up-and-coming contender but a veteran, fraying a little at the edges, working to hold on to what he had. I doubt he could afford to come up short on very many occasions. I could, because I had more alternatives. While I suppose he, too, could compensate by shortening the length of some treks or choosing gentler routes, I could cancel the trip if I didn't like the look of the conditions. I'd still find plenty to eat. No other guy was going to start pushing into my territory because I'd failed to mark the perimeter with fresh scent.

But I was on the verge of becoming bitter about having to look for easier options. I wasn't used to wondering whether or not I could get somewhere; I'd always just gone, trusting that I'd make it. Doing otherwise seemed to me like fudging, and yet I fudged more and more often and recognized that what I was doing marked the start of a long, ultimately terminal phase of drawing back. Before this broke my spirit one day, I needed to come to some sort of accommodation with aging. M1, F2, and our new acquaintance M20 would go pretty much full-on, the wolverine way, until they couldn't go any longer. I took heart from being near them in their wild, here-and-now world while I searched for the way of the two-legged animal with aspirin in a side pocket of his daypack and a nagging awareness of the passage of time.

◇◇◇◇◇◇◇◇◇◇◇◇◇◇◇◇◇◇◇◇◇◇◇◇◇◇◇◇◇◇

Through the next day, I tracked F2 under spotless skies as she moved about in the hanging valley and across the mountainside below it. After dinner, the signal from Swifty switched to rapid pulse. I skied out across Swiftcurrent Lake in the moonlight. A fine haze of ice was condensing around the peaks. It didn't obscure them so much as turn the top of the world luminous and send crystals so fine they were barely perceptible sifting down through the air around me while the stars shone overhead. In the trap was a lynx. Two women associated with the Rocky Mountain Research Station, Amy Boughton and Danielle Lattuga, had skied in from the gate to volunteer for a long weekend, and they were transfixed by the bright green reflection from the lynx's enormous eyes. They had never seen one up close.

Like most of its kind, the cat sat quietly inside the box staring back at us, stoically waiting. It scarcely moved a whisker. The contrast with a cornered wolverine, which by now would have turned into a dervish biting at the intruders, the air, wood . . . anything handy, could hardly have been more complete. But then lynx tend to be more retiring in general, perhaps partly because their lifestyle mainly revolves around hunting snowshoe hares and other small prey. It doesn't involve trying to bring down megafauna or arguing with other carnivores over the rights to a carcass, at least not as often as wolverines argue.

Whenever we caught a lynx, the protocol was to collect a tuft of its fur. The sample would be sent to a specialist at the Rocky Mountain Research Station, who would analyze its DNA and add the information to a study of Montana populations. To get the hair, I taped a small wire gun barrel-cleaning brush to the tip of my ski pole and eased it gently into the trap. Every once in a while, a lynx would bite the pole or bat it away. More often, the cat would only turn its head to watch passively as the brush stroked its side. This time, I held the lid open so Boughton and Lattuga could gather the sample.

I took very little about the project for granted, yet it was refreshing to see our work through their eyes. Watching their faces fill with excitement and hearing them talk about the experience after we turned the lynx loose reminded me of what an outlandish privilege it was to be doing things like kneeling in the forest

46

amid a ring of moonstruck mountains to pet an impossibly beautiful wild cat with a gun brush.

I hadn't picked up a cheep from M1 since Yates and I let him go, so I took the volunteers with me the next day to rebait the Josephine trap and activate it again. The hill between the lakes generally held quite a few tracks of snowshoe hares. During our trip, we found more tracks than I'd ever seen before. They crisscrossed nearly every square foot of the slopes.

"Looks like we missed a big party last night."

"The hares heard about what we did," Lattuga said.

"They caught Paws!" Boughton added. "Yay! The lynx is gone!"

Lake Josephine opened before us crisp and silent without a breath of wind, trading sunshine with the surrounding walls. I took off my coat and was still too warm skiing. We picnicked in shirtsleeves and sunglasses at the head of the lake. My pay may have been zero dollars per week, but I believed the women when they told me I had the best job in the world.

The day after that, I'd been tracking F2 again in her usual spot when I got M1's signal in the next valley to the west, Grinnell. Too soon, too soon! When was he going to cover the rest of his territory? Or had he already? I hurried back two miles to tell Boughton and Lattuga, who had been resting at the cabin, to get ready in case he triggered a trap. The signal showed him close to Swifty now. But then he went by it, continuing west. He was headed toward Fishy. As he passed through the valley bottom forest, the signal started bouncing around off the cliff walls and I lost his direction. Ten minutes later, I got a good reading again. He had skipped Fishy and was on his way west through the Swiftcurrent Valley at a steady pace. Within two hours, he had vanished up and over the Divide.

Boughton and Lattuga departed the next morning. The valley felt more vast and hushed in the aftermath of their company. I backtracked M1 and noted where he had marked the base of a couple of trees along the trail with his urine. En route, I happened on the perfect imprint of wings left by a ruffed grouse that had landed in the powder, and I meandered along the bird's three-toed tracks for a while. They led from fir sapling to young aspen to serviceberry shrub. At each, the grouse had paused to pluck off winter buds to eat. Winds had sculpted the snow into tall drifts with half-domes and deep hollows. This stoutly built bird was hiking through a scaled-down version of the surrounding topography, the difference being that when it got to be too much, the hiker took wing and set down a few yards away, leaving another bloom of feather marks in the snow.

Clouds formed over the Divide and drifted eastward in plumes and tatters. By late afternoon, storm light was tinting the alpine slopes copper and salmon. Skate-skiing over Swiftcurrent Lake to check the trap and make sure M1 hadn't gone in and depleted the bait, I looked round at the mountains and thought about why people commonly describe such landscapes as resembling a great cathedral. Wouldn't it have been the mountains and cliffs and giant pillars of old-growth trees and the angles and colors of the light on their crowns that kindled feelings of awe in humans first? Wasn't it possible that we strived to re-create those emotions closer to our homes through the construction of towering temples? It didn't seem especially important to come up with an answer. I was just gliding and wondering at the close of a dazzling Glacier day.

◇◇◇◇◇◇◇◇◇◇◇◇◇◇◇◇◇◇◇◇◇◇◇◇◇◇◇◇◇◇◇

I passed another day on my own and picked up the signals of two wolverines in the area besides F2. Flying overhead with a pilot and another radio receiver, Yates saw them both: F4 on the eastern nose of Swiftcurrent Mountain and F15 racing along a ridge off Yellow Mountain. We spoke by a park radio handset while Yates was in the air, and he told me that the locations from M20's Argos collar had stayed exactly the same for a while, which meant that the yearling must have already worked free of it. No wolverine would stay in one place that long unless perhaps it had discovered some lode of winter-killed carcasses. But even if it had, the scavenger would be more likely to eat its fill, cache a bunch of the surplus off to one side or another, and then keep moving on. That evening, sticking to my schedule of traipsing upstairs in the cabin to listen for the trap signals every half hour after dark, I finished dinner and made a 7:30 check. Hah! Josey was going off.

OK: sleeping bag and space blanket for spending the night. Extra flash-light, extra batteries, tarp for a windbreak, glide wax . . . oh, down booties and lightweight down jacket. Got to have those. And pliers and wire. Energy bars. Aspirin. Extra hat, gloves, socks. Park radio. Satellite phone. Spare batteries for them. Superglue, band-aids, antibiotic . . . candle; better have a candle. I won't take the rope I carry when traveling the lakes with a partner; no one to throw it to if I break through the ice. Gun brush for fur in case the captive is a lynx. What else? I know there's . . . Of course, red pepper bear spray.

Team members joked about what we were going to do when we finally caught a cougar. It was a possibility. Mountain lions were always somewhere around. The big cats like their meat fresh though. One wouldn't likely scavenge our bait unless it was old or ill and having trouble hunting. But that was the conundrum: If you do catch a big starving cat and open the trap to turn it loose, is it going to leave or eye you?

A worse problem would be coming upon a grizzly at a trap. Glacier is loaded with the great bears; the latest park count was close to 350, more than one for every five square miles. Although their denning period runs from November through March, a winter rarely goes by without a few signs of grizzlies out roaming around during thaws. They are opportunistic scavengers, and their nose for food rivals the wolverine's.

By habit, I always scouted out the tracks in the area as I neared a trap site. I was grateful that the largest I had yet found were those of a moose. When Marci

48

Principal investigator Jeff Copeland cradles a 10-week-old kit dug from its den high on the side of Mount Grinnell. RICK YATES

Johnson was working as Yates's assistant early in the study, she decided to shut down trapping on March 18th one year because the weather warmed so early. She skied to Swifty, moved the lid off, and pulled the bait. Five minutes later, a grizzly went into the box for a look, drawn by the residual smells. "It must have been sitting in the woods watching me the whole time," she recalled.

I put the lighter gear in my backpack and the rest in a duffel alongside the AM/FM radio – the first thing I'd loaded after I heard Josey's transmitter cheeping on rapid pulse. I had a feeling I'd be rendezvousing with M1. By the time I'd gone a quarter mile with the duffel strapped to my sled, I was almost sure of it, for I was skiing along fresh wolverine tracks on a route M1 regularly followed in his circuit through Many Glacier. Sure enough, they continued along the trail on the west shore of Swiftcurrent Lake. When I reached the hilltop between Swiftcurrent and Josephine Lakes, I took my straight shot toward the trap with the radio antenna and picked up M1.

The signal from the GPS collar's small VHF radio was double the usual rate, indicating that the unit's memory chip was full. Anticipating this, Jeff Copeland was due in Many Glacier early in the morning to be ready if we caught the male. He planned to download the chip onto a computer at the trap site, replace the collar's battery pack, and let M1 go in the hope that he might fill the chip with data again. With M1 in Josey tonight, it was up to me to make sure that he was OK and that the trap was secure. I hadn't gone through the formal training that would qualify me to sedate these animals. I was the wolverine babysitter, which was enough of a responsibility. The chip in M1's collar had secrets to tell, patterns to unravel. I couldn't afford to let anything go wrong before Copeland arrived to collect the results.

Anything: Though the drop down to the lake wasn't steep, I made turns to keep from building up speed, resisting the impulse to bomb down the slope. I kept in mind the volunteer who had shot down a milder slope on skis one night, fallen, and broken a leg in two places. The man was traveling with a partner who wanted desperately to help. But there was a wolverine in the Josephine trap, and the injured volunteer insisted that his companion go tend to the animal first. That, he said through clenched teeth, was the whole goddam point of being out here. Then he alternately crawled and poled himself along on one ski, back to the ranger station. Assisted by friends, he made it out of the valley without raising any alarms, determined not to be a burden to either the project or the park.

Viewed from Lake Josephine, Mount Allen fills a third of the night sky. The moon had a long climb to get all the way over the mountain's crest, and I didn't expect it to yield much light when it did. The cloud cover had grown too thick. Gusts off the Divide lifted scarves of snow off Josephine's surface and transformed some into dervishes that came spinning at me over the ice. The wind chill gave me a headache until I put a heavier hat over the one I was wearing. I wasn't gliding fast, but the effect of the flurries racing straight into the light from my headlamp was like being in a car speeding head-on into a nighttime whiteout.

Reaching the end of the lake, I put the bear spray within easy reach and advanced through the woods to the trap. The wind calmed among the boughs. The air smelled of spruce and fir needles and the sharp ozone tang of fresh snow.

Though my senses were on high alert, there were no surprises at the trap. I stood for a long time watching, listening. The winter forest stayed still as a painting. M1 didn't rumble until I began to wire down the lid so he couldn't jiggle it loose. I placed extra logs and some boards we'd hauled in earlier over gaps in the logs and wired them in place. Next, I packed snow over every crevice I could find. Since M1 would concentrate his efforts to escape at the brightest, most open-looking place, I was working to block any light as well as to reinforce possible weak spots.

The hardest part turned out to be picking the right radio station. Surprised at first by how many different AM programs came in over the encircling peaks, I spun the dial to find a channel that showed promise of staying on the air all night. While I planned to stay with M1 and talk him down or, that failing, bang on the box when he started chewing, the radio would serve as a backup if I nodded off.

A couple of talk radio programs came in loud and clear. When I brought the radio closer, M1 only seemed to get worked up and increase his growling and scratching. I couldn't blame him. No species deserved to be forced to listen to the kind of blather coming out of the speakers. I tried some country music stations, and M1 settled down a little. Either he was habituating to my presence and the radio noise, or deep down under that fur he was just another heart-broke, honky-tonkin', good ol' boy.

After he grew quiet, I tiptoed off, then skied into the open where I had enough sky overhead for the satellite phone to work. I called Yates. He told me that Copeland had got hung up in Missoula. Did M1 have enough meat left on the bait to help keep him occupied? Good. Yates's advice was to throw extra snow into the trap so the wolverine would have plenty of liquid as well. Stay until fairly late and keep M1 from chewing, he continued, but then I might as well head home for a decent rest and come back to the trap early, because I wouldn't see Copeland there until midafternoon at the earliest.

After triple-checking my handiwork on the trap, I settled on a Canadian country music station that offered the clearest sound and was presently playing some nice boot-scootin' music. "If it weren't for pickup trucks," the singer crooned, "there wouldn't be no tailgates." You can't argue with the truth, pardner, I told M1 as I enclosed the radio in a plastic bag and set it near the front end of the box, his likeliest choice for a possible exit. I huddled to keep off the chill as the hours and the songs about dee-vorce and drinkin' added up and more snow found its way in through the spruce branches. I couldn't feel my toes again until I'd skied halfway home.

The morning dawned with only scattered clouds. It kept clearing as I skied hard back to Josey packing one of the team's kits containing drugs and other equipment for Copeland to use. I found that I had nearly failed at wolverine babysitting. Rather than rip at the front of the trap as expected, M1 had been clawing and chewing away at the back end. When I got there, his head was sticking out of the hole he'd made. Another few minutes – a quarter of an hour at the most – and he would have been gone. We squared off in a bluffing contest, the wolverine and I, and it went this way:

"You want me to lose my job, furball?

"*Rawrr.*"

"Come on, man. Get back in there."

"*Rawrrrrrr.*"

"Get on in! Do it!" I waved my ski pole at him.

"*RAWRRRR. Rawk!*"

"Back off, you sumbitch. Gwan! Gyah! Hurry up."

"*GRAAAHHH – RAAAHHH!!! UNGH! UNGH!*"

He finally withdrew, and I was able to board up the hole.

The Canadian country music station had faded. I couldn't find many other stations during the daytime. M1 and I ended up listening to talk radio again. Bill O'Reilly was aggrieved about something and making sure we appreciated just how indignant he was. When the news came on, the lead story, as always that winter, was the war in Iraq. The announcer had new details about Operation Smoke 'Em or something. That was followed by reports of threats from North Korea, troubles in China, and . . . I turned the damn thing off. Whereas the sound of a human voice had offered some comfort in the dead of night, bringing the outside world's chaos into a brightening day at Josephine seemed like cutting a fart during a silent prayer.

I hunkered down near M1, wrapping myself in the space blanket to get through a windy spell. The wind eased to a light breeze. I wished I could shift my vigil from the shady forest to the sunny edge of the lake nearby, but I wasn't going to risk leaving M1 by himself again. I tromped back and forth from time to time, just often enough to let him know I was around when he started getting active again. Eventually, we reached a sort of détente, and he kept quiet for longer periods.

By afternoon, time was dragging more and more slowly. This was starting to seem a little like jailhouse duty. I felt bad for M1, confined in there hour after hour for reasons he could never understand. He was innocent. I almost broke into cheers when Copeland arrived, sweating and breathing hard, though not as hard as you might expect for someone who had just driven 300-some miles from Missoula to the far side of the park and skied nine miles carrying a heavy pack with scarcely a break. In his fifties and wonderfully fit, he was eager to get to work.

The procedure went without a hitch. The weather stayed fair, and he transferred the data from M1's collar to his laptop computer. For the next couple of

Give a *gulo* a few uninterrupted hours and it will chew and claw its way out of a trap made of 6- to 8-inch diameter logs (note the top log on the front of the trap). DAVE MURRAY

hours, we babysat together until the last of the drugs wore off and we could release the male. It was dark by the time we got off Swiftcurrent Lake, still half a mile from the ranger station. Copeland stopped a moment to lean on his ski poles. "I'm tired," he said. "I am really, totally, fucking tired." It had been a long day for both of us.

At the cabin's kitchen table, Copeland started looking over the GPS readings and perked way up. He let out a whoop. The chip had recorded 2,190 GPS data points in roughly one week. Due to insufficient satellite coverage or blockage of the signals when M1 was up against cliffs or under dense cover, not all of the readings qualified as solid locations. However, 1,215 did. That was as many locations as Copeland had acquired during a three-year study of an entire wolverine population in Idaho's Sawtooth Mountains using standard radio telemetry during the 1990s. He poured both of us a drink from the bottle of single-malt whiskey he'd carried in. We toasted each other and M1.

When Copeland mapped out those 1,215 locations days later at his office, they showed in detail how M1 had been covering his territory of close to 200 square miles. From the time track of his movements, it appeared that this male wasn't searching for food within that area so much as cruising the perimeter, presumably marking it as he went – outlining his holdings. This was probably the optimum strategy for a male to follow during the birthing season, when he had females rearing newborn kits with his genes inside that territory. Intruding males would compete with the females for scarce food.

Unrelated males also posed a possible danger to the kits themselves. To be sure the other males kept out, M1 was running himself ragged over the high ridges, down into river-cut canyons, and up among the glaciers again, going from one valley to the next, back and forth across the Divide, depositing his scent, and making side trips to check on the females' dens. Three feet long, he had traveled a minimum of 120 miles the past week and God knows how many thousand feet in elevation altogether. No wonder our guy looked lean and hungry. What a force he was. We toasted him several more times that night.

Born in late February or early March weighing less than 6 ounces and white as polar bears, wolverine kits grow rapidly and add darker fur. These captive kits are about four weeks old. DALE PEDERSEN

CHAPTER FOUR

Risks, Rewards, and Southern Polar Bears

They will soon be down
To one, but he still will be
For a little while still will be stopping
The flakes in the air with a look.

JAMES DICKEY
from *For The Last Wolverine*

THIS CLOSE TO THE 49TH PARALLEL, IT STARTS TO GET DARK before 5 pm during midwinter, and long evenings in the solitude of a snowbound cabin in Glacier National Park are made for musing. But then so are summer evenings in the park's high country, where the ruby embers of the day smolder on the peaks until well after 10 pm. The mornings and middays turn out to be pretty good for pondering, too. Even if you're not the reflective type, the sheer physical height and scale of the continent's crown bring extraordinary perspectives to the most commonplace thoughts. And if you are given to reflection, you might find in each panorama a kind of gateway to the four-dimensional universe where space is transfigured by time.

The passage of years – of ages – has height, width, points, planes, and edges here. Time takes on shape and volume. History stacks up around you nearly two miles high. Written in stone, it is the truth about the world, and it is beautiful.

Glacier's limestone and mudstone strata are the former beds of shallow seas warmed by the sun between 1.5 billion and 800 million years ago. As they were uplifted, a colossal block got pushed eastward over the rest, leaving ancient layers standing atop more recent ones. Some of the oldest, highest beds reveal patterns of ripples, mud cracks, and even raindrops, as if raised from ancient shores only yesterday. A few layers preserve mats and mounds of cyanobacteria mixed with silt, all turned to rock.

As fossils go, these marine microbe colonies, termed *stromatolites*, aren't especially striking. They look like smooshed cabbage heads. Yet they represent some of the oldest organisms on record. More important, they may have been the first to practice photosynthesis, manufacturing sugar for food with the help of energy captured from the sun. The waste product given off by this new process was oxygen. As it got pumped into early skies rank with carbon dioxide and methane, photosynthesis began to change the atmosphere. That in turn transformed the course of life.

Ultimately, the humble clumps of cyanobacteria and their successors made inhaling sweet air possible – made you and me possible, and the mountain goat nannies with young single filing along a blade-thin ridge, and the golden-mantled ground squirrels eyeing my trail snacks from nearby boulders. This is the sort of thing you ponder at 9,000 feet with your rump on an overhang built from primeval ocean bottom, a radio antenna for tracking wolverines in your upraised hand, and nothing around the rest of your body but blue, blue breathable sky.

You think about this, too: The hallmark of our particular era is the startling pace at which humans multiplied to the point of monopolizing much of the biosphere and altering its basic qualities. When Glacier Park was established in 1910, it had about 150 glaciers. Today, with human activities spewing carbon dioxide and methane as if we were intent on re-creating Earth's ancient atmosphere, a warming climate has reduced the number of glaciers to 25, and those are shrinking three to four times as fast as they were just half a century ago. The last one is expected to vanish by 2020. Disappearing icefields, an earlier onset of spring, higher soil temperatures on the slopes, and the march of forests uphill to invade alpine meadows - these aren't theories waiting to be proved or disproved. They are tangible events that have been measured in great detail by researchers. Comparisons of recent photos with historical ones tell the story to even the most skeptical in a glance. Such a clear and dramatic shift has made soon-to-be Glacierless National Park a sort of poster child for the climate change issue discussed at international forums.

It's some consolation to remember that the rock layers I'm hiking over have seen both warmer epochs and colder ones countless times during their rise from the seafloor. But during the miniscule slice of Earth's timeline that I've been given to see, I've grown attached to the way the glaciers ornament the peaks and brighten and sculpt them. The blue of the ancient ice glows from within like no other color in the mountains, and I relish the icefields' sharp and sudden coolness in summer breezes off the high slopes, all the more so because I know that the streams and rivers below rely on the glaciers' life-giving water in the hot season after other sources have run dry. Watching all this vanishing before my eyes has an ominous feel to it.

◇◇◇◇◇◇◇◇◇◇◇◇◇◇◇◇◇◇◇◇◇◇◇◇◇◇◇◇◇

I still don't really understand what makes wolverines tick. But I learned that they tick at a higher metabolic rate than other animals their size. If you were to picture them as organic cruising machines with a souped-up carburetor, you wouldn't be far off the mark. To hold in the heat of this internal engine, wolverines, like many northern mammals, wear a double coat – a dense inner layer of air-trapping wool beneath a cover of stout guard hairs, which add extra insulation. Textured to resist absorbing moisture, the long guard hairs that drape from wolverines are not only close to waterproof but also excel at shedding frost.

A *gulo's* crampon-clawed feet are enormous relative to its body, spreading its weight like snowshoes – a major advantage over most competitors and prey during the cold months. By contrast, long, harsh winters drain the energy reserves of hoofed animals postholing through the snow, leaving some dead to be scavenged and others weaker by the day, more easily overcome for dinner. In steep terrain like Glacier, heavy snowfalls also mean more avalanches, which claim their own share of mountainside grazers. If buried deeply, the carrion keeps like meat in an ice chest until it melts out for *gulos* to gorge on through spring and early summer. Many of the avalanches replace forests with vertical stripes and fans that start life over as meadows filled with wolverine summer snacks such as ground squirrels and voles.

In addition, wolverines cache food in snowbanks and in boulderfields with icy water running underneath. Bob Inman, who leads a long-running study of the species in the Greater Yellowstone Ecosystem, told me that supplies in such larders may keep not just for months but even from one year to the next. "I'm beginning to think we might have to consider tiny life forms like insects, bacteria, and fungi – the decay organisms – as some of the wolverine's main competitors for food," he said.

In any case, the list of adaptations that allow wolverines to make an ally of winter is impressive. Yet until scientists started to focus on climate change, no one gave much thought to how creatures with built-in snowshoes, a super-cozy fur coat, smoldering metabolism, and food cached in nature's refrigerators are supposed to handle swimsuit weather in our ever-toastier Age of Industrial Exhaust.

In February, pregnant females go into snow dens and prepare to give birth. Virtually all the dens discovered during the project and elsewhere in the Rockies were at high altitudes and dug 8 to 10 feet down into the snowpack. Though it may seem counterintuitive, snow, which traps a lot of air between its crystal lattices, makes a terrific insulator. The polar bear-white baby wolverines weigh only a few ounces at birth. They need every foot of that snow overhead for insulation, especially when Mom, their furry furnace, is away hunting. They also need to be too far under the surface for passing predators to find.

The kits won't venture out until sometime in May. Wolverine biologist Jeff Copeland and ecologist Kevin McKelvey created a continental map showing where snow lasts through the first half of that month. Then they charted the range of *Gulo gulo*. The two patterns were nearly identical. When Copeland took a closer look at the species' exact whereabouts, he discovered that the animals rarely occurred where the average maximum daily temperature in August exceeds 70 F (22 C).

Combined, these two key requirements – a deep, lingering snowpack suitable for denning plus low to moderate summer temperatures – largely define the wolverine's native range. Since much of the continent north of about 50 degrees latitude offers suitably frosty environments, the species is fairly widespread in the arctic, the subarctic taiga, and portions of Canada's boreal forest. Farther south, the animals have to go up in elevation to find heavy winter accumulations of snow, just as they must to reach more tolerable summer temperatures. This explains why the wolverines of the Lower 48 are confined mainly to western mountain regions. The species' relationship to cold and snow is what ecologists term *obligate* – it can't get by without these factors.

Wolverines are emerging as a far more sensitive and more important indicator of global warming than wildlife managers were aware of before. If you want to take this a step farther, you might even be justified in thinking of *Gulo gulo* as the land-based equivalent of the better-known polar bear.

◇◇◇◇◇◇◇◇◇◇◇◇◇◇◇◇◇◇◇◇◇◇◇◇◇◇◇◇◇◇◇◇◇◇

One early July day, while I was trying to get to Siyeh Pass from the alpine basin called Preston Park, I found the trail around the north-facing side of Matahpi Peak blocked by a snowbank. The wall of leftover snow wasn't wide, but it was scary-steep. I hadn't packed an ice axe. The day was hot, however, and the snow had softened even in the peak's shade. Having picked up two sharp rocks to use as makeshift axe heads, I was able to stab them deep into the snowbank at shoulder height to anchor myself while I started kicking steps toward the other side.

A dozen steps in, mountain time practiced another of its tricks on me. Instead of going by all too quickly, as time so often seems to do, it downshifted until everything was taking place in excruciatingly slow motion. My alternatives were stark: If I kept my footing, I'd reach the pass. If I slipped, I'd die on the rocks far below and feed wolverines and mountain ravens. I'd weighed the possibilities before starting across. Once underway, I hummed while thinking about anything I could to keep from weighing the possibilities again. The crossing seemed to take so long that I almost ran out of tunes.

Though I'm not much of a climber, I've done enough to understand the paradox of deadly serious risks making life sweeter. Existence is a gift; you know that to begin with. Yet it's human nature to forget and concentrate more on everyday problems and frustrations – on what you've lost or what you want rather than on what you have. Taking chances is an antidote for that. Mountains are chancy places that storm and avalanche and leave steaming fresh grizzly bear crap all

Mother wolverines typically move their kits from the natal, or birth, den to one or more maternal dens over the course of 10 weeks. Half the dens ever discovered south of Canada were found during the Glacier Wolverine project, all of them tunneled 8- to 10-feet deep in the snowpack near treeline. RICK YATES

over your safety and comfort zones. In return, they guarantee that you will never become one of those people for whom existence begins to feel stale. Now, you might find renewed joy in simply being alive through studying self-help manuals, falling in love, practicing yoga and diligently meditating, recovering from a terrible illness, or any number of other avenues. Most of them involve a long commitment. All I had to do was cross maybe 50 feet of sloping snow. It was a shortcut to bliss.

From the pass, I worked my way toward the head of the Otokomi drainage by following a narrow ridgeline with long drops to either side. This was the most direct route, one the wolverine F2 often used: not quite a knife-edge, more like a sidewalk-wide fin. When intermittent gusts had me waving my arms for balance, I continued on all fours. After a 100-yard stretch of quadruped travel, I angled down to a scree slope between two bands of rock. This felt like the more sensible route – before the scree suddenly gave way and I started sliding in a mini-avalanche of stone shards toward the lower rock band, which was the top of a cliff.

A lively imagination is not necessarily your friend on the mountain's edge. I'm the type of climber who can stay loose and capable on a tricky pitch when there isn't much exposure but is perpetually in danger of freezing up when the same type of terrain has a chasm yawning beneath it. Paralyzed on the talus at the lip of the cliff, I spent a terrible few minutes summoning the will to move.

For me, the predictable question – What am I doing here? – merged into the question of whether trying to get a little more wolverine data scribbled into a notebook is worth dying over. Hardly anyone out in the world below even knows what wolverines are. How many give a rat's ass about their future? The animals may not have much of one in this region anyway, given the pace of climate change on top of other modern pressures.

But I don't really believe that in my heart. I can't let myself. I have to think that what the project discovers is going to make a difference, that the smallest piece of information any of us collects could help nudge things in a better direction, just like I have to believe there's a sure way back from the edge of this drop. I know what the way is. I'm going to go all wolverine on this mountain's hide – windmill my arms and legs and scrabble up the scree faster than it can slide down past me. If that works, I'm . . . Screw ifs. Go.

It did work. I hit the ridge and hustled back along it on all fours the whole way. Finally, I stopped, reared up on two legs, and shivered with delight for no other reason than to be standing on a gentle slope. I dug a chocolate bar from the bottom of my pack just to raise the reward-to-risk ratio another notch. Closing my eyes, the better to savor each bite, I thought: wolverine research was fantastic when you knew for sure you were going to live.

Volunteer wolverine tracker and veterinarian Dan Savage about to put a new animal on the air with an implanted radio transmitter. RICK YATES

CHAPTER FIVE

Savage

Joy and sorrow
aren't two different feelings for it.
It attends us
only when the two are joined.

We can count on it
when we're sure of nothing
and curious about everything.

WISLAWA SZYMBORSKA
from *A Few Words on the Soul*

We all develop our own measures of risk and our own ways of balancing fear and pain against the goals we want to achieve. It is a subject I often discussed with Dan Savage, the project's vet. Before I really got to know the man, I'd made a midnight run into Many Glacier with him, Copeland, and other members of the team, skiing the miles to the Josephine Trap in a blizzard. The temperature had dropped close to minus 10 F. My hands were chilly inside heavy mittens. Doc Savage performed an implant by the light of a gas lantern while wearing thin latex surgical gloves, only twice walking over to briefly spread his hands over a little portable gas heater.

He began the operation by shaving a patch on the wolverine's belly and making a cut an inch and a half long through the skin. Next, he sliced through the underlying sheet of connective tissue. One slump of tired shoulders, one slip of cold fingers, a nick a fraction too deep, and it would all go miserably wrong. Gusts kicked sudden showers of snow off overhanging branches. Savage remained imperturbable.

Satisfied with the small incision, he inserted the radio, contained in a four-inch-long capsule with a sterile coating. His breath joined that of the wolverine and the steam rising from its opened body. Working in the same fast, steady rhythm, he proceeded to sew the innermost layer shut. Then he stitched together the subcutaneous layer. He sealed the epidermis – the skin – with a superglue so there would be no external sutures for the animal to worry with claws or teeth. And he was done. By the time the wolverine was carried back into the trap to recover, everyone else within the circle of lamplight appeared more exhausted from the tension than he did.

Another time, I watched Savage implant a wolverine in subzero weather on a January morning not long after dawn. I paced nearby to keep warm, grateful whenever I had something useful to do like break open more chemical heating pads to put under the patient or take another reading with a rectal thermometer to make sure the drugs weren't lowering the wolverine's temperature too far. Savage, meanwhile, removed his jacket during the operation, saying it was beginning to make him feel a little hot and stuffy. His mental focus was so intense that I think it rendered him immune to the elements.

Dan Savage is not a powerful-looking fellow. His strength lies hidden within a slender body and a pair of surprisingly delicate-looking hands. You wouldn't necessarily take him for a climber and vertical backcountry skier from his persona, either. He is altogether one of the most even-tempered people you could hope to meet. Although a reassuring style may be expected of doctors, his steadiness seems more noteworthy in light of the fact that both his parents suffered from severe bouts of depression.

Growing up in Kalispell, Montana, the heart of the Flathead Valley, his best days were spent with his father in the surrounding mountains. "Once those creeks started to settle down after the spring runoff, we'd head for the woods and go fishing together," he said. "I think that's what got me started exploring. I was always looking for the El Dorado of trout streams, always heading up the drainage to find another tributary or a better pool."

While Savage couldn't say that his father became truly relaxed and happy during their outings, the child could sense the man's troubled mind finding at least a measure of ease beside the flowing waters. "I especially remember one clear, blue-sky day, well into July – the air warm, the woods as green as they ever get. And the sunshine was pouring in, lighting up the channel. I still have a clear picture in my mind of all the sparkles it made on the ripples. My mom came up to me later at home and said, 'Your dad has never been sure whether there is a god or not. But he told me that after that day and the way the light was shining on the water, he thinks maybe there is.'"

Savage made a different kind of discovery. "I was pushing upstream as usual, looking for better fishing around the next bend. I went so far that I kept on going over the top of a ridge and came out at the head of another creek," he

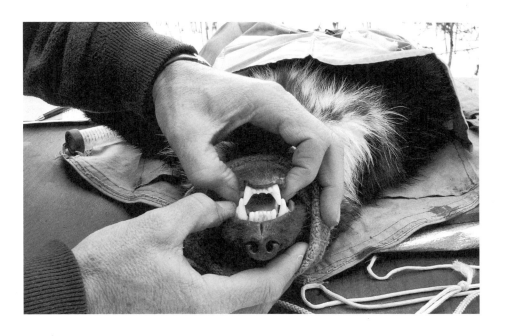

Though a young *gulo*'s teeth are not enormous, their bite force is. Scavenging wolverines regularly make meals of bones that larger carnivores leave behind. JACK NOLL

An expedition to a suspected den site at the head of the Grinnell Valley in May; good weather, but a risky time for avalanches. JASON WILMOT

said. "It was a creek I'd always thought of as being a world away because we had to drive for hours around the base of the mountains to reach it by car. I think that's the first real insight I had into how mountain topography works." He has been bushwhacking new routes and putting pieces of the Flathead backcountry together in his head ever since.

During his college years, Savage struggled with a debilitating back injury inflicted at the age of 19. He finally underwent surgery. It helped but didn't cure the problem. After graduating from veterinary school, he was offered a job assisting the sole animal doctor in Ketchikan, Alaska. Savage saw an opportunity to probe the northern countryside while training under the tutelage of a man who had been in practice for decades. Instead, the longtime vet showed Savage around the office and then basically vanished for weeks at a time, leaving the newcomer on his own to handle any animal medical crisis that arose in this area with some 14,000 human inhabitants and lord knows how many pets. Savage gained far more experience than he had bargained for in a hurry. But he reinjured his spine while in Alaska and had a second surgery after his return.

By then, Savage was frightened, not so much by the prospect of living with constant pain as of becoming unable to continue wandering the streams and mountains. In experimenting with methods of keeping the threat in check – medication, dietary changes, massage, stress reduction, whatever he could grasp at – he learned three invaluable lessons: First, a day or even a span of a few hours when your body is functioning without problems is a time of grace that may not be come again; don't take a minute of it for granted. I told Savage I understood, and I meant it quite specifically. I'd had a spinal fusion when I was 15, and the operating surgeon told me to plan for a desk job because I would never be fit for strenuous work. Second, various outdoor activities that stretched out and limbered up Savage's back seemed to cause the injured site to hurt less for a while. Third, hiking for the first time to Grinnell Glacier can help you decide what the rest of your life is going to be like.

"I hadn't spent that much time in the park," he said. "I was a local boy. And like a lot of local guys, I usually hiked and camped on national forest land, where you could avoid all the park-type rules, not to mention the tourist scene. But Grinnell was so beautiful it just floored me. In the space of a few miles, I passed elk, sheep, goats, porcupine, a fox . . . What didn't I see? I watched the biggest mule deer buck I'd ever come across in my life. There were marmots, bears – grizzlies and a black bear – and golden eagles. And then a meteor shower at night.

"With a quick climb up from the glacier to the Divide, I could have been looking west down into the Flathead. I'd visited rural Peru, thinking I might want to offer veterinary care someplace that had little or none. But in Grinnell, I thought: This region is my home, and Glacier is part of it. This is where I want to live and have my practice."

During the course of the wolverine project, he performed close to three dozen operations in addition to spending almost as much time radio-tracking animals as the rest of us volunteers did. Some of the surgeries were to implant kits (using smaller transmitters) at dens far up on the mountains' shoulders after exhausting climbs and more hours of digging through snow to find the young. There was never a crisis, never a loss. And of course never a veterinarian with a more perfect name for dealing with grizzly-fighting bone-crunchers in their untamed domain: What's that speeding along yonder slope? Is it a blur? A flame? No. It's . . . Doctor *Savage!*

Before a full day of work in his Flathead veterinary clinic, Savage might rise long before dawn, strap traction skins onto the bottom of his cross-country skis, and walk up the slopes of Big Mountain, the ski area at the valley's north end. Then, from the summit, he'll telemark down, drive 20 miles, and be in his office before the morning's first appointment. Or he might skin up the mountain after work instead and ski down in the dark. He'll do the same some days when the weather concocts a whiteout. He prefers conditions with the worst visibility, he told me, "because there's a better chance to experience that feeling of being the only person in the world." He works out on the rock-climbing wall at a local gym and sometimes goes to put his technique to the test on some serious rock walls in Utah's canyon country.

"I'm not trying to be twenty-five," he said. (He was in his mid-40s when we first met.) "And I don't consider myself a real climber. I'm just challenging myself. For me, it's like backcountry skiing and winter camping. Every time you do it, you get a little better at figuring out how to dress, how to move so you don't get sweated up or drained of energy, how to handle emotions when you're out there on the edge." What didn't quite get said is that this man is skiing and trekking and climbing for his life, moving hard to keep the aches at bay so that he can keep moving in the future. To some extent, it's something we all need to do. For him, it's crucial. Doctor Savage has prescribed this – being out there testing the limits – for his back and his happiness. It is his cure. His fear is of not taking risks.

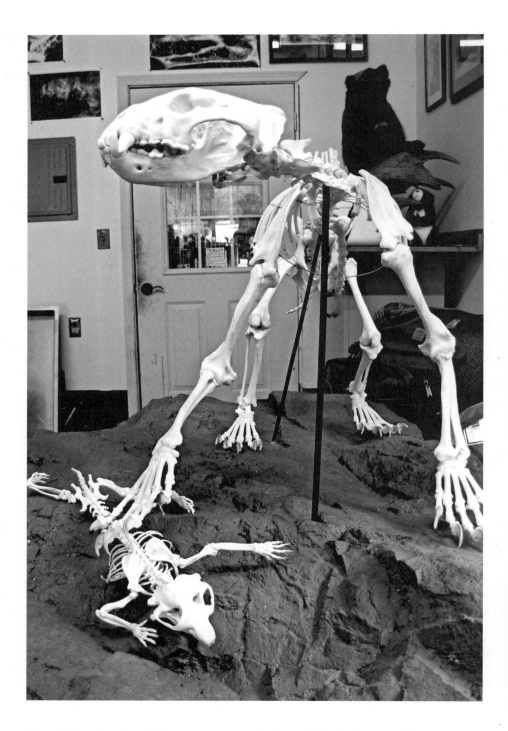

Stripped of flesh, the wolverine's frame seems to suggest that the rest of the animal serves as a life support system for a set of mile-devouring legs and feet. The victim on display is a mountain beaver, a distant, primitive relative of the true beaver. DOUG CHADWICK

CHAPTER SIX

The Glutton

Wherefore this creature is the most voracious: For he finds a carcasse, he devours so much, that his body by over-much heat is stretched like a drum, and finding a streight passage between trees, he presseth between them, that he may rid his body of flatulance and being thus emptied, he returns to the carcasse till he hunts eagerly for another.

SWEDISH ECCLESIASTIC OLAUS MAGNUS
from *Historia de Gentibus Septentrionalibus* (History of Northern People), 1555

The most remarkable circumstance relative to the economy of these animals, is the stratagem which they adopt for the purpose of alluring and seizing upon their prey. We are informed that they climb into trees in the neighborhood of herds of deer, and carry along with them a considerable quantity of a kind of moss to which the deer are partial. As soon as any of the herd happens to approach the tree, the glutton throws down the moss. If the deer stop to eat, the glutton instantly darts upon its back; and, after fixing himself firmly between the horns, tears out its eyes; which torments the animal to such a degree, that either to end its torments, or to get rid of its cruel enemy, it strikes its head against the trees till it falls down dead.

REVEREND WILLIAM BINGLEY
from *The Animal Kingdom*, 1877

HAVE ANOTHER LOOK AT THE INTRODUCTORY QUOTE BY WILLIAM BINGLEY. I've no doubt he thought he was passing along facts. I'm equally sure that the good reverend fell for a load of BS. No reliable naturalist has ever reported a wolverine providing vegetation to entice hoofed prey within striking distance. That's not to say that these hunters don't ever try to lure in a meal. They may not, but if they don't, we have the problem of explaining the dancing wolverine. Joachim Obst, a biologist with the Wildlife Management Division of the Department of Renewable Resources in Canada's Northwest Territories, described this episode to Jeff Copeland, and Copeland recounted it to me:

Rather than acting skittish and fleeing from the sight of a strange object or a predator, caribou commonly approach. We call them naturally curious. Naturally confident might be more accurate, the bottom line being that their long legs and oversize hoofs enable them to outrun almost any threat they encounter on the boggy, tussock-riddled barrengrounds of the North. They can afford to move in closer to gauge a predator's intentions and all but eliminate the possibility of a surprise attack. Obst noticed a wolverine making its way toward a caribou band, and as the traveler drew near, it began dancing and prancing on the tundra. That got the band's attention. The wolverine then dropped onto the ground and rolled around on its back waving its paws in the air.

"Obst said it was just acting crazy," Copeland told me. "The caribou kept walking nearer, forming a kind of crescent of interest." As the wolverine continued thrashing about on its back as though experiencing a seizure or the loopiest good time ever had in the arctic, a calf edged especially close. The wolverine whirled to its feet and made a dash straight at the curious young caribou. As soon as it became obvious that the calf was going to escape, the wolverine dropped down and went back to rolling and writhing and being *gulo* loco. Fascinated, the caribou gradually returned to watch, and the hunter made a second sudden rush at one. Again, no luck. The wolverine stopped, looked after the fleeing band a moment, turned, and padded on.

All kinds of animals dance. I'm not referring to stylized courtship displays with a lot of high-stepping, bowing, preening, and puffery. I mean loose-limbed, head-tossing, get-up-and-boogie-style dancing to the beat of a buoyant heart. In Glacier Park, I've watched elk, grizzlies, mountain goats, and deer break into dances on the mountainsides, both while playing with companions and while completely alone. Long midday rests seem to prime animals for this after they get up and stretch. Reaching a snowbank on a hot afternoon will set them off, too. They go slide-dancing away downhill in sprays of corn snow, and I know I'm not the only hiker who's done the same.

Dancing bears like to flop down all at once and wriggle-rub around on their backs. At other times, gamboling grizz will turn a dive for the ground into a somersault – or several. Some animals work themselves up from shaking to airborne frolicking after a swim. They also seem to fall into the mood during sudden changes in atmospheric conditions like the drop in barometric pressure (and perhaps the increase in ozone or static electricity) before the onset of a summer storm. Others dance for no apparent reason, and the only way we can relate is to remember moments when excitement welled up inside until we could no longer keep our arms still and both feet on the ground.

As for wolverines, I've seen an amateur video of a lone animal springing from side to side and spinning almost completely around as it bounded down a summer snowfield. I've listened to park visitors' reports of wolverines somersaulting downhill, and I watched another video that showed a pair of captive-reared youngsters making at least a half-dozen somersaults in a row down a steep tundra hillside. They looked like fuzzball versions of those fabled snakes said to take their tails in their mouth and roll off like hoops.

Now, no one can prove that a sudden mood swing or perhaps some captivating scent left on the muskeg wasn't what stimulated the wolverine Obst saw to start dancing and squirming on its back like a pent-up puppy. The chases of caribou could simply have been opportunities too good to pass up when the band pressed in to see what was happening. On the other hand, no one can prove that the situation wasn't precisely what it appeared to be: a case of a wolverine trying to catch a caribou by putting on a show – a dancing wolverine with a plan. Your call. Given how little is understood about wolverines even today, yours is as good as anyone else's.

<hr />

Here are the some of the basics of what we do know about wolverines:

They are first and foremost carnivores. In the most general sense, this term describes any organism that chiefly eats meat. Animals from spiders to birds of prey qualify. But when wildlife biologists talk about carnivores, they usually mean members of the *Carnivora*, a taxonomic order made up of more than a dozen different families of mammals.

They have robust skulls, which protect relatively large brains, and eyes positioned in the front of the head rather than on the sides, a trait common to hunters that rely on accurate depth perception. Their weapons include well-developed claws, sharp front teeth (the incisors), long fangs (canines), and check teeth (premolars and molars) specialized for cutting rather than grinding. On each side of a carnivore's mouth, the last upper premolar and first lower molar, jointly known as the *carnassials*, are arranged so that as the jaws close, they generate a slicing action like scissors or pruning shears.

Wolverines belong to the carnivore family known as the *Mustelidae*, more commonly called the weasel family after its most familiar members. From a public relations standpoint, this is a bit unfortunate, considering how corporate shills, spammers, faithless lovers, and hedge fund managers keep giving weasels a bad name. The best-known carnivores tend to come from the dog, cat, and bear families. Many of them rank among the most popular of all animals. Apart from fur trappers, people pay scant attention to the mustelids by comparison. Yet this is arguably the most successful carnivore family, for it contains by far the highest number of species – 56 – and they have expanded to fill the broadest spectrum of niches, from the arctic to the tropics and from mountaintops to jungles to kelp forests in the ocean.

Among the wolverine's kin in North America are pine martens, long-tailed weasels, short-tailed weasels or ermines, and least weasels. And minks, black-footed ferrets, badgers, fishers, and river otters. Plus, sea otters, known for using rock tools to break open shelled food and for having the densest fur of any mammal. Settlers along the coast of New England and Canada's Atlantic Provinces encountered what they called the sea mink. Whether it was a large, marine race of the more common mink or yet another species of mustelid, we may never know, for the fur trade quickly drove it to extinction. Worldwide, the *Mustelidae* includes Eurasia's sables (one of several types of martens) and polecats (ferrets), Southeast Asia's hog badgers, Africa's honey badgers and skunk-striped zorillas, and South America's fruit-eating tayras and six-foot-long giant river otters. To mention only a few.

Certain mustelids are gregarious – sea otters, for instance, float together in rafts of as many as a hundred – but the majority are semisolitary and largely active at night. Physically, the family is distinguished by having short legs that support an elongated body with one of the most flexible spines of any mammal. Their skull is also lengthened, with stout teeth and heavily muscled jaws.

The least weasel is the smallest member of the carnivora, weighing only a few ounces. Yet it has a more powerful bite than any carnivore in North America relative to body size. Only a few meat-eating mammals in the world can generate greater bite force on a pound-for-pound basis. One happens to be the fierce, toothy predator/scavenger dynamo known as the Tasmanian devil, a sort of marsupial counterpart of the wolverine. While I haven't found a measurement for the wolverine's bite force, it, too, has to be near the top of the charts. When a wolverine comes upon an elk or moose carcass that larger predators have worked over, it can crunch up the skeleton left behind, shattering massive bones that not even a grizzly would try to crack.

Recently assigned to a separate family of their own, skunks were long classified as mustelids. In addition to other shared characteristics, both groups have anal glands that produce the strong-smelling compounds known as musk. While skunks have taken this trait to a new level with a sulfurous spray irritating enough to repel enemies, the mustelids produce oily secretions with earthy undertones. Some commercial perfumes are said to contain a dash of mustelid musk, but it won't have come from wolverines, whose version has traditionally been derided as vile.

Natural history accounts seldom fail to highlight the wolverine's reputation for befouling woodsmen's cabins and supplies and even their own food caches with a smell so obnoxious no other animal will go near. This is supposed to be the wolverines' way of laying claim to things. Curiously, as far as researchers can tell, the discharges from mustelid anal glands are involuntary and, as with skunks, more for defense than for marking. In other words, when wolverines spurt musk, it's likely because they feel threatened or stressed, not because they revel in purposefully making stuff reek, as the popular lore implies. Even when they set out to mark territorial boundaries, it looks as though they mainly use urine and possibly some exudate from the skin of their bellies rather than musk. They also have patches of skin on the pads of their feet that may produce scent, though the tissue doesn't appear to be glandular.

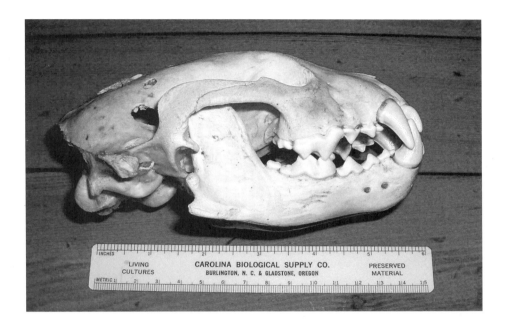

A carnivore's fangs, or canine teeth, are for stabbing, while the large upper and lower molars, called carnassials, are for shearing meat and cracking bones. Wolverines aren't just after the marrow inside, they consume the whole skeleton. RICK YATES

F4's slender, 2-year-old daughter F5, who later died in an avalanche. KEN CURTIS

Most mammals live amid a symphony of odors to which we are virtually deaf. We may not have much difficulty smelling wolverine musk, but we do have trouble interpreting it. From the way authors pump those tales of wolverines ruining everything they touch with a hideous odor, you'd think the animals' main goal in life was to help make outdoor writing more vivid. Wolverines don't musk that freely. Besides, nature operates on the principle that stinkiness is in the nose – and brain – of the beholder. Ask any male dog with his nose in a bush that a bitch has peed on.

If you come home to a shack musked by a wolverine – perhaps one startled by the clink and rattle of strange objects as it was tearing up the pantry – OK, you're not going to downplay how offensive you find the invader's smell to be. But if you're a wolverine groupie like myself, you might detect a smoky sweetness in the scent of the animals you're handling. Over the course of a capture season, our gloves and shirts became permeated with their rich, rank essence. I wasn't the only team member to admit missing it after we shut down the box traps with the coming of spring.

The aroma of musk derives largely from ketones and alcohols. According to Copeland, one of the ingredients identified from wolverine anal glands is also found in scotch whiskey, another acquired pleasure. He also mentioned that a class of chemicals often detected in their urine – terpenes, the basis of turpentine – can't be manufactured in animals' bodies. These compounds commonly come from conifers, and sure enough, evergreen bark and needles have been found in wolverine droppings.

On the subject of eating vegetation: I happen to believe that carnivore by birth or no, any mammal that would pass up plump serviceberries and mountain huckleberries warmed by the late summer sun is an ingrate as well as a fool. *Gulos* are neither. They leave purplish droppings full of fruit remains during berry time, as do the neighboring weasels, martens, coyotes, and wolves. And of course every bear in the woods, not to mention wandering volunteer researchers. Also like bears, wolverines may sometimes raid middens of pine nuts stored by squirrels and perhaps smaller stores of the nuts cached by Clark's nutcrackers and jays.

Along with the bear family, wolverines and other mustelids have an unusual reproductive sequence called embryonic diapause, or delayed implantation. After being fertilized during mating, the eggs don't continue to divide and grow. Instead, they remain in a state of suspended animation for months before they finally attach to the female's uterine wall and begin developing. Since the fetuses come to term rather quickly, delayed implantation allows mustelids to choose an ideal season for courtship and breeding and then bide their time waiting for conditions better suited to rearing young in the security of dens. Mind you, the strategy of postponed gestation might have originated as a response to completely different environmental challenges in Earth's past.

Mustelids, after all, have been around a long time. Fossils of martenlike beasts have been found in rocks that date back to the Miocene epoch, which began 23 million years ago. The family started radiating out to take up its unusual diversity of lifestyles in underground tunnels, trees, stony deserts, riverways, and saltwater. By 15 million years ago, recognizable forebears of modern mustelid species were showing up. They included the wolverine ancestor *Plesiogulo*. Arising in Eurasia, it spread via a land bridge to North America around 7 million years ago and was replaced during the Ice Ages by *Gulo schlosseri*, half again the size of the wolverine we know. Sometime late in the Ice Age epoch, the Pleistocene, *schlosseri* gave way in turn to *Gulo gulo*.

Today, wolverines form a circumpolar species, inhabiting high latitudes around the northern hemisphere. Their tracks cross boreal forests and tundra from Russia's Far East and Siberia to Scandinavia and continue south into Mongolia and other mountainous parts of Central Asia. In the New World, the animals range from Canada's Atlantic provinces to the Pacific coasts of British Columbia and Alaska. They dip south along mountain chains into America's western states and extend as far north as the barrengrounds of Ellsmere Island.

Taxonomists used to list Eurasian and North American wolverines as separate species. In keeping with the modern trend of giving less weight to slight physical variations, they are now considered merely different subspecies: *Gulo gulo luscus* in North America, *Gulo gulo gulo* in Eurasia. The wolverines of Canada's Vancouver Island have been isolated from mainland British Columbia for millennia by the Strait of Georgia. Some authorities think they have become sufficiently different to be assigned to a third subspecies, *Gulo gulo vancouverensis*. Whatever else they may be, the island's wolverines, together with the unique Vancouver marmot that shares its habitat, are on the edge of oblivion, pushed there by trapping pressures and widespread disruption of the mountain forest ecosystem by logging and road building.

Taxonomy, the formal scientific classification of organisms, has its tedious moments as experts split hairs and quibble over minute differences in the shape of bones. Still, it's the best scheme we've come up with for deciding exactly what kind of creatures we're looking at and for sorting out how they are related to one another. At the same time, the effort illuminates the difficulty of imposing order on the living world when life itself is all about flux and flow and transformation. Over the ages, local populations become distinct races become varieties become subspecies become species. The only constant is the becoming.

A specialized piece of anatomy, a unique behavior, a trick of body chemistry; each may serve splendidly to help an animal prosper in its environment. Then one day it doesn't because the environment has altered, maybe just a shade, sometimes dramatically. The molecular genius of the DNA double helix is that it gives every species the means to change as its surroundings do – to adapt. To evolve. At some point, the creature, while still thriving, is no longer the same species but something new on the face of the planet. Or, unable to keep up, its line is fading toward extinction while others are evolving to fill its niche. Trying to fit organisms into neat categories is like building sand castles in a rainstorm or grabbing gelatin tightly in your fist; things pooch out to the sides. While we struggle to neaten up edges, nature is doing the opposite, staying slightly messy, building a little slack into the system. It's how she ensures the resiliency of life.

◇◇◇◇◇◇◇◇◇◇◇◇◇◇◇◇◇◇◇◇◇◇◇◇◇◇◇

Dan Savage invited Rick Yates and me to his veterinary office on one of his days off. Amid the stainless steel tabletops and wash basins of the operating room where he typically worked on pet cats and dogs, he switched on strong overhead lights and began a wolverine autopsy. The subject, a male from the park study population, was young but nearly full-grown. Its skull had been punctured and broken by the bites of another carnivore. As Savage opened up the body cavity, the first thing he commented on was the heart. It struck him as large for an animal of 20-some pounds. He said the same about the lungs after he carved them loose. Working his scalpel forward, he came to the thyroid gland inside the neck and was really taken aback. The thyroid is the biggest endocrine gland mammals possess; even so, the wolverine's seemed huge in a carnivore this size.

Thyroid hormones regulate the body's metabolism and the workings of major systems, and mustelids have a higher metabolism than many other mammals. It's like having a motor tuned to run at a faster rpm. Looking at a weasel's movements when it's feeding, for example, sometimes gives me the impression of watching movie footage on fast-forward. Not surprisingly, the wolverine's basal metabolic rate measures above average for carnivores in its weight group.

Hyperthyroidism is the condition whereby an excessive production of thyroid hormones leads to overstimulation of the metabolism and the sympathetic nervous system, speeding up other systems in the body. Savage said that the hyperthyroid cats he deals with in his practice were restless and constantly ravenous, no matter how much they were fed. Could having a notably large thyroid gland yield any of the same results but without the long-term ill effects? Our speculations about how wolverines might have evolved to stay cranked up an extra notch or two didn't lead far, but they helped keep the dissection of a wild young mountaineer from getting depressing.

The stomach exposed on the table beneath us seemed extra large as well. This wasn't as unexpected. It's an advantage for a predator or scavenger to be able to pack in as much food as possible before competitors, fierce weather, or something else forces an end to the feast. Eagles sometimes gorge themselves until they're temporarily unable to take off. Wolves can eat 15 to 20 pounds of prey at a time and then go days without hunting. Least weasels are so revved up that they have to gobble their own weight in meat every few hours. And while most of the derogatory labels pinned on the wolverine have little to do with fact, this mustelid wasn't nicknamed the glutton for no reason at all.

Gulos come ready to consume supersize helpings and to cache what they can't finish in one sitting. They don't miss many meal possibilities to begin with. In Alberta's Jasper National Park, I was told, rangers searching for missing climbers from the air look for a concentration of incoming wolverine tracks on snowfields to lead them to the bodies of those who fell, froze, or were swept away in an avalanche. Well, sooner or later, one way or another, we all get reprocessed. You could do worse than help build wolverine muscle and blood when your turn comes around.

Savage palpated the stomach and raised his eyebrows. "It's like a sack of gravel," he said. "Feel it." We did, and found the organ loaded with chunks and splinters of bone – a rubble of skeletons. Bone marrow, where the body manufactures new blood cells, is a trove of concentrated nutrients. Excavations of middens in caves suggest that it was an important food for early humans, judging from how systematically the larger bones of prey animals were broken open. The crushing strength of wolverines' jaws allows them to exploit this rich resource as well. Though the bones themselves contain oils and other lipids (fats), very few animals actually go on to consume those, least of all the thickest ones. But wolverine turds show that at least one mammal does, and the stomach Savage examined made the fact even more obvious. The wolverine's bone-shattering bite force is an important aid in chewing through frozen meat as well.

◇◇◇◇◇◇◇◇◇◇◇◇◇◇◇◇◇◇◇◇◇◇◇◇◇◇◇◇◇◇◇◇

An acquaintance hired an expert to completely clean the bones of a captive wolverine that had died and to mount the skeleton like a museum curator would for display. With just a few barely visible support rods and wires, the man produced an extraordinary, gleaming white angel-of-death *gulo* posed in midstride. Ironically, the moment I saw this fleshless thing, it brought the species to life for me in new ways. Due to the long, plush fur that normally hangs from a wolverine's sides, I'd never quite grasped how different the conformation of the body was from that of its short-legged kin. This specimen's upper and lower limb bones were surprisingly stout and long, especially for a mustelid. The feet underneath sprawled almost three-quarters the length of my outstretched hand. Together, these features so dominated the animal's frame that the rest of the skeleton started to look like a light carriage atop them. My mind called up goofy images of monster trucks with their little cabs rocking over four enormous wheels. I left thinking of a wolverine, with its big heart and lungs and souped-up metabolism, as a life support system for a set of legs.

Discussing the wolverine's restlessness, volunteer Alex Hasson once said, "You keep covering enough country, you're gonna find something to eat." Now, I thought he might have summarized this predator-scavenger's strategy in a sentence. With such legs, and claws for crampons, the wolverine can certainly go

A captive wolverine amid musk ox and elk leftovers. DALE PEDERSEN

far distances across practically any terrain. And it doesn't matter if all that turns up during a circuit of the peaks is a months-old carcass stripped of its last tatters of sinew and gristle. A bone-eater can still fill its stomach. That may be what carries some through the leanest times when the mountains ask in a harsher voice every hour, Who among you is fit to survive? How wolverines manage to flourish on the continent's heights amid 100-foot snow drifts and plunging escarpments was still far from clear to me, but I felt I was steadily gaining more clues about what allows them to try.

To deal with the mix of snowbound stretches and wind-cleared ground, seasonal project assistant Lacy Robinson devised a set of rollers for our sleds and skis on a winter foray into the Two Medicine Valley capture sites. DOUG CHADWICK

CHAPTER SEVEN

A Stranger's Sojourn

Of human life the time is a point, and the substance is in a flux, and
the perception dull, and the composition of the whole body subject to
putrefaction, and the soul a whirl, and fortune hard to divine, and fame
a thing devoid of judgment. And, to say all in a word, everything which
belongs to the body is a stream, and what belongs to the soul is a
dream and vapour, and life is a warfare and a stranger's sojourn,
and after-fame is oblivion. What then is that which is able to
conduct a man? One thing and only one, philosophy.

MARCUS AURELIUS
from *Meditations*, Book Two, Number 17

I'D WANTED TO BE A BIOLOGIST SINCE I WAS IN GRADE SCHOOL, so I became one.
After finishing graduate research on the behavior and ecology of mountain goats
in another part of northwest Montana, I was hired by Glacier Park's chief biologist to take the first in-depth look at the goat population in this preserve. Each
month from spring through fall during the next three years, I hiked a series of
valleys to locate the shaggy, white climbers high on the mountainsides. I identified the different age and sex classes, which appear much alike from a distance,
and kept track of their activities. Officially, I was a seasonal technician. In reality, I was more like a horseless cowboy roaming the range to check up on the
herds – a goatboy. I say that with pride.

I loved the scientific work, loved the clearer picture of mountain goat biology
that emerged from prime natural habitat where the animals' numbers had never
been pared by hunting. Most of all, I fell in love with the setting, where I was
simply one of many life forms moving within the huge, unsullied sweep of the
Great Divide day after day. Between the capricious weather and the wheeling of
the sun, shadows, eagles, and seasons, I never saw the same mountain twice, no

matter how often I looked. And yet with every outing, I gained a surer grasp of the rhythms and moods of that utmost landscape. Glacier pushed in through my senses and seeped in through my pores until it woke up all the parts of me that tended to go dormant in the tame world beyond.

Once mountains lodge in your soul, the need to have real peaks around you becomes almost a physical itch. After I finished my studies in Glacier, my wife and I lived for 11 years in a cabin on the west bank of the North Fork of the Flathead River, a federally protected wild and scenic waterway. The park began on the opposite shore and rose upward from there. I turned from research to journalism, reporting on wildlife and conservation. Though my assignments took me from Siberia to the Congo to undersea reefs, I didn't feel as though I'd made a major career transition, since I was almost always following biologists in the field to gather the information I needed. But I often wished I were doing the field studies myself.

Back home, I spent much of my free time traipsing around Glacier. On top of the usual hiker's craving to put on new miles, I had a grizzly bear-dependency problem – and a pretty serious one. Whether I'd just finished diving among great whales or chasing after jaguars, the year wouldn't seem complete if I didn't get in enough days basking in the aura of power and freedom that radiates from *Ursus arctos horribilis* on an open mountainside. It prevents smugness.

While volunteering with the Glacier Wolverine Project, I scribbled down notes – an automatic reflex when I hear new facts or ideas about animals – but I had no intention of writing a narrative of the work. It was a delight to be directly involved with a study in the park again and take part in the events and discussions without feeling any obligation to distill them into some kind of journalistic end product. If anything, my wolverine time was a vacation from reporting. Or so I told myself, and I clung to this opinion for a long time. In the end, obviously, I gave in and started writing this account.

It wasn't only the wolverines' struggle for survival that changed my mind. The amount of effort required to learn the slightest detail about the creatures was a tale I could no longer resist telling. Then there was the rare band of people who had committed to making that effort in the face of the formidable high-country odds. Counting myself lucky to share their company, I felt that their stories deserved to be told as well. Though from a strikingly diverse array of backgrounds and strongly independent, they somehow found their way to wolverines and coalesced around them, perhaps drawn, consciously or subconsciously, by a quality they and the animals shared: As they say in Montana, these are folks who don't have any quit in them.

There were periods in volunteer Dave Murray's youth when he had no other choice than to be on his own in the backcountry. The self-reliance he developed in order to cope shaped the course of his life, which began in the little mining village named for his Irish grandfather: Murray, Idaho. Dave Murray's father worked the mines there in the silver-laced Coeur d'Alene Mountains. He died of silicosis – miner's lung – when Murray was 11. The disease incapacitated the man long before that, and the family moved so he could try to find other work. Wherever they wound up, they struggled to make ends meet and lived in part off what they could hunt and gather from the surrounding mountains.

After the father's passing, Murray's mother married a man who made a some-times living dismantling machinery at abandoned mining operations for parts and scrap iron. Often drunk and occasionally brutal, he would deposit Murray and his brother, two years older, at some remote site among old mine carts, rails, and a rusting mill that had ground the ore. He left the boys with tools, cases of dynamite, and instructions to take the place apart. Then he would drive away and stay lost in the bars.

"He always said he was going to town to bring us back supplies, but we might not see him for a month," Murray told me. "We hardly knew where the hell we were. He didn't leave us any food. We starved our asses off, trying to live on fish, rabbits, a deer if we were lucky, anything we could find. But we had fun blowing stuff up. Nothing better than dynamite for a couple of young teenagers."

Murray's mother finally left his stepfather about the time Murray turned 14. As a single mom now living in Salmon, Idaho, she worried about her youngest son getting in trouble hanging around town once school let out for the year. So she sent him off to find a hermit uncle living somewhere in the wilderness along the Middle Fork of the Salmon River. She couldn't provide directions, but she knew this man was locally renowned for the braided ropes and halters he made from deer and elk hides. Backcountry horsemen prized them and carried in goods to trade for his leatherwork. They could tell Murray where the cabin was.

Murray never found the place that summer, nor during any of the next three summers when he was told to try tracking down his uncle again. I don't know how hard Murray tried. What he would do is travel deep into the wildlands, wandering until he found a setting that called to him. There, he would fashion a little shelter, throw up a sweat lodge from bent willows and a piece of plastic, and live on his own until fall with the help of a fishing pole and .22 rifle.

There were times when he came close to starving again. Once, when he was camped in a steep-walled canyon, the river flooded. His route out lay along the bank, which was underwater. The cliffsides were too high and steep to risk scal-ing. Trapped in place, with the game fled or swept away and fish impossible to catch from the muddy rapids, Murray moved upslope to a boulderfield and lived on tough, starchy roots of the sunflower called arrowleaf balsamroot for two weeks before the Salmon receded. Despite the obstacles he faced, those summers camped along unpeopled creeks and rivers were the most fulfilling he had yet known in his young life and in many respects the most dependable. The wilderness was always there for him, and he has held it dear ever since.

"I went back this summer with my son and father-in-law, looking for my old camp where I got walled in by the flood," he said. "I was surprised by how much everything had changed, but I guess I shouldn't have been. I mean, it had been thirty-some years. Brush was standing fifteen feet high in places I remembered being bare ground. But I found some boulders that looked familiar. Then I saw where I could crawl in under one for shelter, and I did, and it all started to come back. When I scraped down into the dirt that had built up over the years next to the boulders, I found the ashes and charcoal from my old campfire, even little bits of burnt tinfoil. Oh God, I started bawling. I must have sat there and cried for half an hour."

Murray worked at odd jobs as he grew older, including a stint fishing in Bristol Bay off Alaska's coast. He wound up in construction, making wages as a roofer around Missoula, Montana. As time went by, he decided he could run a crew and do a better job than the outfits he was working for. He started his own roofing business, sleeping in his truck on the job site to start work earlier than anyone else. He expanded into the scaffolding supply business. These days, the former feral child owns and runs Industrial Technologies Corporation, which builds schools, warehouses, factories, highway bridges, and the like. When business is going full tilt, boss Murray is responsible for making sure everything gets done on time and within budget by a labor force that exceeds 200. Yet he keeps skipping out to come chase around after a bunch of *gulos*. Who says America isn't the land of opportunity? Helping people learn more about these animals is a passion for him. To tell the truth, I think he has become addicted to what he calls "those fuckin' awesome little guys."

Everything about wolverines calls to Murray – the unfettered scope of the country they roam, the way they muscle over the ridges and cols and precipices and overhanging snow cornices day and night, and the fact that those fuckin' awesome little guys act willing to chew off your head and rip out your lungs when you try to stop them long enough to attach a transmitter; he sensed a kind of rock-bottom dignity in that. In his day-to-day dealings, Murray is easygoing and considerate. He'd been donating weekends to help reconstruct a small local church and also to build a home for the family of one of the men who worked for him. But within every person's soul lie provinces that refuse to be governed and for freedom's sake ought never to be. Deep down, Murray wanted to be a wolverine. I think this was true of all of us on the project to a greater or lesser degree.

◇◇◇◇◇◇◇◇◇◇◇◇◇◇◇◇◇◇◇◇◇◇◇◇◇◇◇◇◇◇◇◇

Wolverines don't unnecessarily complicate their lives. They won't equivocate or trade in partial truths; I call this the wolverine pledge. Would that it were a

Dave Murray moving a captured animal. Immobilized by drugs and unable to blink, the wolverine requires a blindfold to protect its eyes from light, drying air, and freezing temperatures. DOUG CHADWICK

policy more widely followed. More than that, wolverines are the ultimate role models for not taking crap from anybody or anything. But they aren't always easy to emulate in Glacier. When hikers here see you coming down the trail with an H-shaped radio antenna, an awful lot of them stop you to ask what it's for. The nervous ones quickly get around to asking whether you've, um, happened to find any grizzlies close by. Glacier's biggest carnivores are much on visitors' minds. The trailheads have signposts warning everybody to "Be Alert – You Are Entering Grizzly Country." At times, an additional notice, printed on a red background with a drawing of an ornery-looking bear in midstride, instructs hikers to use extra caution because "This Area Is Currently Being Actively Used By Grizzlies." When you explain that you're tracking wolverines, you get a variety of expressions: surprise, relief, enthusiasm, curiosity. Comprehension would be somewhere toward the bottom of the list.

"Wolverines! Cool. What are they?"

"About this high? I think we saw some eating those purple flowers in the meadows."

"They're sort of like little wolves, right?"

"Omigod. I heard they're really ferocious. What should we do if one comes close? If you run, does that just make them more likely to attack?"

"Wolfy reens?"

To be fair, the name wolverine not only sounds wolfish but springs from the same Old German word: *wolver*. And the high-elevation habitats that wolverines favor are home to colonies of flower-munching megarodents: hoary marmots. These alpine versions of woodchucks, or groundhogs, can weigh as much as 20 pounds, and they have bands of contrasting colors in their fur and a fairly long, thick tail somewhat like wolverines do. The fact that one is a roundish vegetarian with chisel-like buck teeth for clipping plants and the other is an elongated, shaggy hunter with sharp incisors, stout canine fangs, and those special molar teeth called *carnassials* designed for shearing the flesh off victims such as marmots isn't always obvious at a distance. I'm trying to be generous here. As for the woman who saw a wolverine with a dead ground squirrel in its mouth on the moraine below Grinnell Glacier moments before I did and described a muskrat taking some kind of chipmunky thing for a ride? All I can say is that it must be fascinating to live in her world.

We wildlife types can get pretty snotty about people's misconceptions of creatures, forgetting how we ourselves would sound asking questions of, say, a locksmith or financial analyst. Once in a while, bored with giving out the usual answers, I might tell the next group that asked about the antenna: "The Red Sox and Yankees have a big game this afternoon, and I don't want to miss it." At other times, I'd wordlessly use the wand to scan hikers' packs and pockets like an airport security guard, then point my chin down the path and tell the subjects that they were free to continue. A couple of guys nodded in understanding about the baseball game, but almost no one else fell for this stuff. Besides, I would start talking about wolverines partway through.

I liked sharing natural history facts with visitors. To me, the opportunity to do this during fieldwork was a perk of the project. The most rewarding aspect was discovering, once the hikers better understood what a wolverine was, how many had actually seen one. Not a marmot snoozing on a boulder or a muskrat taking its chipmunky friend on a trip to the lake, but a wolverine on the move – or two, or a mother with kits – often just minutes before we met. There were days when it seemed as though everybody coming or going along the trail had been watching real wolverines except the great Dr. Knowitall, keeper of the antenna, who happened by a little too soon, or too late, and couldn't find anything except cheeps on his radio receiver.

Only 40 to 50 wolverines make their home in Glacier. Their individual territories are as big as the home ranges of grizzlies, but, unlike the bears' living spaces, wolverines' don't overlap. Although the territory of a male typically does encompass the territory of one or more females, it excludes all other adult males, just as each female excludes other adult females from her domain. Thus, while the park might see well over 10,000 tourists a day in the peak of summer, the number of wolverines that can squeeze into the reserve's 1,500 square miles may never exceed more than a few dozen. Those 40 to 50 current inhabitants nevertheless represent the single largest, most significant concentration left in the lower 48 states.

"When we started establishing national parks in the U.S.," Copeland said, "we didn't set them aside because we thought they would be great places to protect wolverines. But today if someone were to say 'Let's create a wolverine reserve,' it would be Glacier National Park." Wolverines may not exactly be thick here, but their territories elsewhere are even larger, which means the animals are spread out even more thinly.

Readily accessible during the warm months and directly connected to a sister reserve – Waterton Lakes National Park, across the border in Alberta – Glacier has a superb trail system with more than 700 miles of well-designed, well-maintained routes. The majority of them wind through alpine and subalpine terrain, where open slopes offer excellent visibility in prime wolverine habitat, and a few of the resident animals tend to frequent areas along some of the most popular day-hiking routes. Casual visitors probably have a better chance of glimpsing *Gulo gulo* in Glacier than anyplace else on Earth. In particular, I'd guess that our acquaintances M1, F4, F7, and their offspring were within view of more people more often than any other wolverines alive over the past several years.

Few if any visitors ever saw M3, a burly young male sired by M1. I didn't meet M3 myself for years. But he'd developed a reputation among the team as the King of Attitude compared with other wolverines in a trap, which is really saying something. In true imperial style, His Majesty also appeared bent on expanding his influence, conquering an ever-larger territory north of his father's realm. M3's name kept coming up in interesting contexts during fieldwork, usually as an icon of audacious behavior.

When trying to decide our next move, we sometimes weighed the possibilities from a "What would M3 do?" perspective, more often than not when we were just horsing around, trying to keep ourselves entertained on another all-day march. For instance, when one of us suddenly held up a hand in warning because he'd heard a noise in the brush, the conversation might go like this:

(*Whispered*) "Movement over there behind that line of trees."

"Got it. Ahh, it's only some hikers coming off the slope. Looks like two couples."

"Humans! Good. Let's go take all their food. I'm starved."

"That's extremely insensitive of you."

"Come on. We're wolverine guys. You think M3 would have an issue with this?"

Another time, after several days of tracking, basing out of a trailer that Yates scrounged from a government surplus of emergency housing for hurricane victims, Dan Savage and I decided to add some class to our lives by dining off fine china at a park-edge lodge. We paid the check and were on our way out when a nicely put-together, vivacious woman intersected our route and said, "I saw you two earlier coming back to the road carrying radio antennas. I'm vacationing by myself, getting to know Glacier Park for the first time. Are you studying the wildlife here?"

"Yes. We're trying to learn about wolverines."

"That sounds fascinating. I'm sorry, wolva-whats?"

This wasn't about wolva-whats. Savage was once featured in *GQ* (*Gentlemen's Quarterly*) magazine because, well, I guess the editors wanted a strikingly handsome veterinarian from the West in that issue. Quick as he was to recognize predatory behavior in the wild, he seemed oblivious to the signs of it here indoors.

"Wolverines," Savage enunciated with care. "There aren't very many left, but they're holding up fairly well in the park."

"Really! I didn't know that," she replied. "I was on my way over to the bar for a drink. Is that where you're going? I'd love to learn more about wolva-rings. So they're kind of like wolves?" she asked, turning to escort us toward the lounge just off the lobby.

"A little like wolves, yes," said the good Doctor Savage. "But they're in a group of animals we call mustelids. Wolverines are the largest type that lives on land." Seeing her baffled look, he added. "The mustelids are the weasel family.

Wolverines are like big weasels."

"Oh," she said, and, "My goodness, I just noticed the time. It's so late! I shouldn't be keeping you up like this. I'm sure you've got a long day ahead tomorrow. I know I do. Hey, good luck with your studies. Ciao."

"Au revoir."

"Nice to meetcha.

I shook my head at Savage and muttered, "We finally get a fan, and you tell her we're studying weasels. Big weasels."

"Well, wolverines are mustelids, so we are studying big weasels."

"No. You say, 'Ma'am, we're just a couple of true Western he-men studying the most vicious, deadliest, grizzly bear-shredding carnivore in the Rockies.' Nobody likes big weasels. M3 doesn't tell the ladies he's a big weasel."

<hr />

I stopped for a morning cuppa at Montana Coffee Traders in my hometown of Whitefish, a 30-minute drive from the park. A local electronics engineer named Rocky came over to tell me about a Glacier wolverine he'd seen. Only one road, the Going-to-the-Sun Highway, traverses the park from west to east. Open for barely four months of the year, the route crosses the Divide at Logan Pass. Rocky had hiked from there up the busy trail that leads to Hidden Lake Overlook. At the top, he found a ranger intently watching the lakeshore through a telescope. She stepped aside and waved him over. Through her lens, he made out a grizzly standing on a path near the water. Then he noticed the agitated wolverine close by on a pile of sticks.

At first, he took the pile for a beaver lodge, but the sticks may have covered a carcass. Bears often heap dirt, snow, or branches atop leftover food to hide it. Wolverines have been known to do the same with a bounty, though they more often carry chunks off and hide them. As for whose cache this was now, negotiations were in progress. The bear pressed closer. Rather than give ground, the wolverine scrambled forward and made jerking motions as if preparing to lunge, and the bear backed down. This sequence was repeated several times. In the end, the grizzly turned away and went around the lakeshore by a longer path.

Rick Yates once witnessed a wolverine on a boulder near a food cache forcing a nosy grizzly to detour. Several different accounts from biologists describe cases of a wolverine coming upon a grizzly that was feeding on a carcass and driving the bear off it. This, we can all agree, is a badass thing to do when you weigh maybe 30 pounds. In a couple of cases, observers said they saw a wolverine run up onto the bear's great back and start working over its head.

Wolverines come preloaded with what looks to us like an insane amount of attitude. But to back it up, they have powerful limbs to go with those impressive claws and exceptionally powerful jaws to open and close those formidable teeth.

Glacier Park has the highest density of grizzlies south of Canada – more than one per 5 square miles – and they compete with wolverines for prey and carcasses. Sometimes the 30-pound wolverines succeed in driving off the giant bears. And sometimes they die trying. DAVE MOSKOWITZ

The combination makes them considerably bigger and more dangerous in deed than in stature. In their role as scavengers, the northern equivalent of hyenas or jackals, they have been competing for carcasses with larger carnivores for many thousands of years. Earlier in the Ice Age, the large, ancestral wolverine named *Plesiogulo* was doing the same with immense short-faced bears, dire wolves, and saber-toothed cats, not to mention giant northern hyenas. Wolverines that were slightly weak, momentarily slow, or intimidated by a superior force were not the ones that wound up passing on their genes.

Natural selection led to wolverines capable of outsize success in hunting, too. It's not unusual for wolverines in Canada and Alaska to take down grown caribou. Domestic reindeer, which belong to the same species, are the wolverine's main prey in parts of Scandinavia. Single wolverines have even been reported overcoming full-grown moose, which can weigh anywhere from 600 to 1,600 pounds. In terms of weight ratios, that would be like a housecat nailing a deer. Although I suspect the moose chosen were ailing, injured, mired in deep snow, or vulnerable in some other way, this still counts as a frighteningly lethal accomplishment.

F2 was first captured at the start of 2003 and many times thereafter, especially during the early part of the study. Though barely two-thirds the size of M3, she was every bit as much of a berserker in the log boxes – the kind of wolverine that made it easier to picture one coming upon a hefty grizz and thinking, "Yeah, I can beat up that wuss." If someone cracked the trap's lid, F2 rushed the opening without fail, snapping, snarling, wildly defiant even though the worst that usually happened to her was that someone simply let her go since she was already carrying an implanted radio.

When Yates did need to sedate this animal one time, he gave up trying to jab her with a syringe-tipped pole. Instead, when she charged again trying to tear off a chunk of him through the crack, he sprayed the drugs directly into her open mouth. I think F2 was one of the chief reasons he always insisted that females were feistier than males when captured. Although she never stopped going into the log boxes for a meal now and then, she learned to take bites with a light enough touch to keep the lid from falling and so developed into an expert raider. She could be savage, and she could be sneaky-smart. Either way, there wasn't any quit in her.

Wolverines are built for winter with frost-shedding double fur coats and a fired-up metabolism: a pair of captive animals. DALE PEDERSEN

CHAPTER EIGHT

Good Mother Wolverine, Her Boys, and Bearhat Summit Girl

People usually consider walking on water or in thin air a miracle.
But I think the real miracle is not to walk on water or in thin air,
but to walk on earth.

THICH NHAT HANH
from *The Miracle of Mindfulness*, translated by Mobi Ho

FROM TRACKING F2, PROJECT MEMBERS LEARNED that she and the next adult female to carry a radio implanted by Dan Savage, F4, had adjoining territories. Their common boundary ran down the middle of the Grinnell drainage from its headwaters to where it merged with the main Many Glacier Valley. F2 claimed Grinnell's eastern half and several adjoining valleys, while F4 roamed the lands to the west, continuing across the Divide into the McDonald Creek drainage. When busy lab technicians finally got around to analyzing DNA from hair samples taken when the animals were handled at traps, the team learned that the two females were related closely enough to be either sisters or a mother and daughter.

F5, also captured in Many Glacier the first winter of the study, turned out to be the year-old daughter of F4. In the meantime, F2 had denned in the Boulder Valley on the eastern face of Wynn Mountain, overlooking the Great Plains, and given birth to kits also fathered by Big Daddy M1. Yates led a couple of attempts to get to that high-elevation site in May, a month when so many snowslides and rockfalls were thundering down the warming slopes that Blackfeet Indians called it "the time of the mountains talking." The team didn't reach the den until early June. By then, F2 had moved out. Examining the area, they found the remains of mountain goats and blue grouse.

Two years later, when Yates and Savage inspected another of F2's dens, they turned up feathers from a swan and a duck and wondered how those birds ended up in a wolverines' alpine pantry during the snowbound months. Perhaps they got lost among the stormy peaks during migration and made a forced landing on the snow. They might have washed up dead on the edge of a high-country lake before the water froze, or they could have been catching up on sleep some distance out in the lake when a wolverine took them. Everything is possible with these opportunists. *Gulos* often patrol shorelines. People have observed them chasing fish and frogs in the shallows, and they swim readily and well using their big paws to good effect as paddles.

At Wynn Mountain, the team started to scrape together some clues about what sort of food had fueled a mother wolverine and her growing young at a den. But they couldn't tell anything about how many kits F2 was rearing. That was the kind of number the project needed to start piecing together the population's size and rate of reproduction – the dynamics that lead to success or failure over time. However, when the team trapped a new female the following winter, they learned that at least one kit had survived from the den on Wynn Mountain, for F7, as they called her, was a year old, and DNA revealed her to be F2's daughter.

The researchers knew that F5 had shared her mother F4's range as a yearling while gradually exploring neighboring terrain. Now F7 appeared to be doing much the same thing, basing her activities within her mother F2's territory. F5 eventually found a place of her own just south of her mother's. As F7 got older, she leapfrogged the territories of both those females and established a territory immediately south of F5.

I realize that the tale of so many F's can sound slightly confusing, but stick with me. This little slice of life in a wolverine neighborhood has huge implications. Wolverines, remember, had been defined as intractable loners – too irritable to tolerate one another's company longer than is absolutely necessary for mating and rearing babies. According to the traditional view, a female drove her offspring away for good soon after weaning when they were a half year old. Should the young linger instead of taking off for parts unknown, she might even harm them. If she didn't, the male whose territory encompassed hers would. Although it was still early in the Glacier study, a pattern was beginning to emerge that contradicted those notions and made a good deal more biological sense.

Radio locations from the project offered regular proof that while the kits did separate from their mothers around the age of six months, most were still tolerated within her territory – and the resident male's – for the better part of another year. This would allow the youngsters to continue gaining size, strength, and experience within a familiar setting where they knew the travel routes, secure resting spots, and favorable locations for finding food. Equally important, they wouldn't have to risk fighting for living space with older, battle-tested animals; Mom and Dad would see to that in the course of defending their territories. The juveniles could gradually begin to probe other areas and get a feel for the lay of the land outside. But if they weren't having much luck finding meals or got chased off by resident wolverines, they could always return to the safety of their parents' turf.

Over the years, the study animals' radio signals, along with track patterns in the snow, would also show young males as well as young females that had separated from their mother occasionally reuniting with her and traveling with the older animal. Still more intriguing, both sexes of juveniles also did this with their father, possibly as often as they did with their mother.

Examples of growing juveniles becoming independent of Mom's care only to go off and spend a little time with Dad are virtually nonexistent among other mammals, including most primates. We didn't record a great many of these temporary reunions, but the ones the team gathered shed light on a unique young-rearing system based on social relationships more complex than almost anyone except Copeland had suspected before. Words like *family ties*, *cooperation*, and *affection* had never been put together with the word *wolverine*. They were the last terms most naturalists would have picked. Yet it was beginning to look as though they applied. That didn't make wolverines any less fierce, just more fascinating.

As the juveniles approached two years of age and the onset of sexual maturity, departure time was finally at hand for any that hadn't already struck out on their own. The flush of new hormones in their bodies may have provided most of the incentive they needed. In addition, they might have begun to experience serious friction when they encountered either of their parents, with whom they would soon be competing as adults. These same tensions drive a variety of adolescent mammals to disperse in search of new ranges and new opportunities. We're not all that different ourselves.

<><><><><><><><><><><><><><><><><><><><><><><><>

During the days and nights I spent interacting with M1 in March of 2006, I already felt like something of an old hand on the project – a bona fide wolverine guy. I'd got involved almost exactly two years before when, in March of 2004, I arranged to meet field team leader Rick Yates in Many Glacier, where he'd been for most of the winter. Before I left my home in Whitefish and drove around to the other side of the mountains, his wife gave me a new radio receiver to take to him.

I reached the closed gate at the park boundary and started marching atop a hard snow crust into the usual east side headwinds. I'd only crossed a couple of drifts before I found Yates's assistant, Marci Johnson, waiting on the other side with a truck. It had been a light winter. The wind was keeping most of the road scoured bare, allowing the team to continue driving some distance inside the closed gate. We still got plenty of fresh air, for most of the pickup's rear window was missing. Johnson said a wind storm had shot a rock through it two weeks earlier.

Yates was glad for the new, upgraded receiver. Signals detected from the implanted radios had been the most valuable source of information about wolverine activities from the beginning of the project. As of 2004, they remained the sole practical means for keeping abreast of the animals' movements through winter. Trying to physically follow the tracks of individuals up and over the winter peaks would have amounted to an endless expedition across unstable avalanche slopes and icebound cliffs in worse-than-awful weather.

Yates and Johnson had tried putting satellite collars on two wolverines. Both were the kind that would record precise GPS locations and store them on a memory chip in the collar's on-board micro-computer. Neither collar was working. It was a disappointment but not a surprise, given the chronic gap between technicians who design devices that perform splendidly in the laboratory and biologists who require that they also function after being soaked during river crossings and repeatedly frozen and thawed.

The young male M3, the King of Attitude, had been fitted with a different type of unit tied to the Argos satellite system, which stored the locations aboard orbiting spacecraft and periodically beamed them to data banks on Earth. Less bulky than the GPS collars, this type was less accurate, but it was still operational. For that matter, Copeland phoned the ranger station from his Missoula office to say that the real-time readout on his computer was showing M3 atop Apikuni Mountain, adding, "He's probably looking down at you guys right now."

We rushed off with a receiver to get a fix from the VHF radio M3 was also carrying, but we couldn't pick up its signal. M3 had moved on, probably dropping behind the peak on his way back north. Captured the previous winter as a yearling, he had remained largely within the ranges of his parents, M1 and F4, through the rest of 2003. As the months marched on, he began shifting his movements farther and farther north. That took him into the territory of M1's northern neighbor, M6, who made his home in and around the drainage of the Belly River, which flows north from Glacier into Waterton Lakes National Park.

The last wolverine trapped in 2003, M6 was a fairly old male. His strength and ability to maintain an exclusive range were likely fading. Nevertheless he had fathered a son, M8, who was in good condition when caught in 2004 as a yearling. When M6 was recaptured at Lee Creek near the northeastern edge of the park during 2004, he looked worse for the wear of another year and badly in need of a good meal. He went into the Lee Creek trap again for a bite of beaver. The team that skied there to turn him loose was startled to find M3 nearby and signs that he had been clinging on the outside of the log box, chewing his way in. If M3 wasn't expressly trying to get at M6 and rip him up but was after the bait instead, he certainly wasn't intimidated by the fact that the old guy was in there with it. The scene reinforced the researchers' opinion that M3's incursions into M6's territory had escalated into a full-on invasion and takeover. Indeed, the next time M6 was located, he was well south of his old territory, apparently driven into exile. It was the last time he was ever found.

His son, M8, continued to poke around Many Glacier. Johnson watched him come up onto the porch of the ranger station one evening and investigate the

Good mother wolverine F4 carries a Columbian ground squirrel back to her kits waiting hidden at a summer rendezvous site. BILL GARWOOD

firewood pile. Captured again not long afterward, he bore a fresh, deep wound that ran from his eyes toward his muzzle. Having mostly occupied his parents' territory to the north since birth, he, like his father, may have been under assault from M3, who was a year older than M8 and big and brawny even compared with older adults.

The evidence against M3 was far from airtight. For all anyone knew, M8 got his face slashed tangling with a different wolverine or some other predator. Yet soon after the crew salved his wound with antibiotic and released him, he was back in the trap – several times – apparently ravenous and also unable or unwilling to search for food in his old homeland farther north, where M3 was patrolling. At one point, M8 simply refused to budge from the trap when Johnson tried to release him. Then he, too, departed the region.

He most likely traveled southwest across the park's Lewis Range, which forms the Continental Divide, then the park's Livingston Range farther west. His next radio locations came from Teakettle Mountain overlooking the town of Columbia Falls, then from the south end of the Whitefish Range less than 10 miles away and overlooking my hometown. After pausing for a month, he resumed his journey. Moving northwest, he must have headed into the Salish Range, continued over those mountains, reached the Purcell Range, and made his way across them, because his signal showed up again on the Purcells' western edge where Montana borders Idaho and British Columbia. There, roughly 100 miles from Many Glacier, the wayfarer at last showed signs of settling in to a new home. Before winter was out, he was dead in a steel-jawed trap set for bobcats, and M3 ruled the northeast section of the park that M6 and his son had once called theirs.

◇◇◇◇◇◇◇◇◇◇◇◇◇◇◇◇◇◇◇◇◇◇◇◇◇◇◇◇◇◇◇◇

Toward the close of April, 2004, I hiked along McDonald Creek on the park's west side with Alex Hasson. His family was Lebanese, and some of his older kinfolk lived in Jerusalem. Growing up in eastern Montana, he'd acquired the nickname "Buck" and the skills needed to ride, rope, rodeo, and handle strings of pack horses in the backcountry. Hasson had started a career in railroading in his teens and retired early. His time these days was entirely his own. Since he liked nothing better than roaming the park's farthest reaches and climbing its peaks, usually solo, it seemed natural that he would find his way to the Glacier Wolverine Project as one of its first volunteers. He also volunteered for part of the year with the Missionaries of Charity, founded by Mother Teresa, in settings from Poland to Nepal. While distributing medical supplies in Ethiopia months earlier, he'd nearly died in a car wreck that took the lives of two others. His face still bore healing scars where attendants had dug fragments of glass and steel out of his flesh. He was 50 years old.

From this side of the Divide, he oversaw the trap site near Avalanche Creek below Mount Cannon. Hasson covered enough ground through the winter to keep partial track of F4 and her daughter F5, now 26 months of age. He was also monitoring F2's 14-month-old daughter F7. As we proceeded up the McDonald Creek Valley, we passed elk herds among the brush grown up in old slide areas. Spruce trees along the floodplain bore fresh scars where grizzlies emerging early from their dens had clawed away the bark to get at the cambium layer underneath—the only fresh green food above the snowpack.

Hasson pointed to a higher slope, and we got out binoculars to scan a copse of trees where he thought F5 might be holing up to den. We couldn't detect any signals, but while we were swapping stories over lunch, Hasson brought to life a memorable day earlier that month when he had homed in on cheeps from F5. They came from the east, he said. Yates was flying overhead at the time, taking advantage of calm winds and open skies to locate as many of the radioed animals as possible, searching hardest for individuals that hadn't been heard from by anyone on the ground for a while.

"I told Rick, 'I think I've got F5 up Avalanche Creek,'" Hasson recalled. "He radios back from the plane, 'Which direction?' I tell him she sounds like she's somewhere near Bearhat Mountain. 'OK,' he says, 'we'll go try to get a fix.' A few minutes later, he tells me, 'I got her signal pinned down. Whoa! I can see her.' 'On Bearhat?' I ask. 'Yeah,' he says. 'She just summitted.'"

Bearhat Mountain is a sharp, solitary peak – a monumental fang rising alone between Hidden Lake and Avalanche Lake. Too sheer-sided to even hold much stunted alpine vegetation, it is almost entirely bare stone, open to the weather on every side, encased by ice and snow well into May. I can't think of any animal that would possibly qualify as wolverine food living within 2,000 vertical feet of the summit. Nor do I know of a route up Bearhat that leads anywhere but right down another side with more steep cliffs.

I kept wondering what F5 had in mind making the long, exposed climb to the very tip-top in late winter/early spring. How could that fit into any creature's survival strategy? Was this another attitude thing like facing down grizzlies – the sort of outrageous feat that might seem routine to a beast that combines a near absence of fear with a superabundance of strength? Or could F5 have gone up to take in the view – not through her eyes, as we would, but through her dominant sense organ, the wolverine nose? Was she up there surveying grand vistas of scents?

Hasson shrugged. I was beginning to notice that people on the project did that quite a bit after they described something a wolverine had done. To me, it meant that we had no end of opportunities for discovery ahead, and I was getting more intrigued on every outing. Summiting Bearhat in April! Because . . . well, because you can. Who imagined wolverines were that hard-core?

F4, surprised at her den near treeline, racing around researchers while they excavate the tunnel to find and radio-tag her kits. JEFF COPELAND

Earlier that winter, F4's movements became concentrated in the headwaters of Alder Creek, a tributary to McDonald Creek. Her restricted movements were a sign that she was preparing to den there and give birth. Wolverine kits grow remarkably quickly. By the first or second week of May, they would be robust enough for the team to capture and implant with a scaled-down transmitter. Yates flew to see exactly where F4's tracks converged, as that would mark the probable den area. To his surprise, he found M1 right next to the site, apparently checking on his family, possibly even bringing them a share of his food.

On the 6th of May, when the kits would have been at least two months old, Yates, Hasson, Marci Johnson, and Savage made their way up the snow-buried mountainside toward the den. By the time they reached the locale, it was midafternoon. They couldn't detect F4's signal at first. Whatever tracks she might have left earlier were hidden beneath fresh snow. F4 had already moved once, carrying the kits from their natal den to a maternal den. This second site, so plain when Yates had flown over it, was nowhere to be seen by the team on the ground.

The crew spread out to search for sign while Yates crisscrossed the slopes with the radio receiver, covering an ever-widening grid without luck. When he finally picked up F4's electronic cheeps coming from directly below in the snow, there was still not the slightest sign of an entrance hole above. Daylight was fading behind the peaks as the crew began excavating the snowpack to find the wolverines' burrow somewhere in its depths. Once they broke into the tunnel around eight feet down, they turned to shoveling horizontally, like miners following a vein or archaeologists exposing a long-lost royal chamber.

By then the hour had grown so late that F4's implanted radio shut down, as it was programmed to do each night to prolong the battery's life. No longer able to judge where the female was within the den, Yates wormed his way forward through the hole until he heard the mother growl at last. He was relieved – her reaction probably meant he was nearing the kits – but not quite thrilled, knowing that he was presently blocking her possible escape route with his face. He eased away and widened the tunnel with more strokes of his shovel. Shortly afterward, she shot out and began circling not far off, intently watching the invaders. And not long after that, M1 materialized from out of his vast territory. Like F4, the father stayed close by, not threatening but not especially intimidated by the pack of shovelers, either; just watching as the night deepened and his eyes became disembodied blue-green sparks in the light from the team's headlamps.

More hard digging was needed before the kits were found. F4 had been nursing two of them, both males. After using his shovel to shape part of the snowpack into an operating table, Savage went into his zone of absolute concentration on the chill, towering night slope and implanted the pair. The team tucked the young wolverines back in a chamber of the tunnel and waited for both to come around from the drugs. Midnight passed before the men could pack up and start dragging themselves a couple of miles farther along the side of the Divide. Their destination was Granite Park, one of two stone chalets in Glacier's backcountry, perched on a side ridge and boarded up for the season. They shoveled their way into the maintenance quarters beside it and fell asleep sometime around 3 am. Upon arising the next morning, one of the first things they did was check the radio receiver. The new signals came in clearly from the direction of Alder Creek. Glacier's wolverine population had two more members on the air: M9 and M10 – F5's younger brothers, though they might never meet.

Three months later, in August of 2004, Hasson invited me along as he searched for radio signals on the Highline Trail. It was a path I loved to ramble. Paralleling the Divide, the Highline winds for miles through alpine meadows and krummholz (weather-dwarfed copses of subalpine fir and spruce marking the upper edge of treeline) below a steep stone rim known as the Garden Wall. The wall's top is the continent's top. Blossoms overflow the wild gardens at its base. After four and a half miles, Hasson picked up cheeps from F4 and her kits near Alder Creek. He was trying to home in on their location when he put down the receiver and started waving frantically to me from a bend in the trail.

Thirty feet away, the three wolverines were drinking from a seep among yellow monkeyflowers, purple penstemon, and a crimson array of Indian paintbrush. It took a moment to grasp that the smaller wolverine with silvery streaks running along its sides was the mother. M9 and M10 were a darker, chocolaty brown with bronze side streaks. Mom looked gaunt beside them, but then she was doing all the work in the family, still going off to hunt and carrying back the take to her offspring. Hidden away at various rendezvous sites among boulders or dense krummholz, those strapping young males passed much of each day idle. The family continued to drink their fill at the seep before descending toward a rock outcrop. From the moment they got going, the brothers acted intent on drawing F4 into a play session. They took turns jumping to put their forelegs up onto her back, nudging and nipping her and each other.

Hasson's thoughts and mine were running along the same lines:

"Look at those big galoots. Hey, isn't it about time you boys went out and got a damn job?"

"Yeah. How long do you think you can just goof off and keep ordering in?"

"Probably another month at least. Might as well enjoy it."

"She really is a good mother, isn't she?"

The trio braided their way downslope like a single large, furry animal with all kinds of bulging, squirming parts, separating only when they paused to test the winds rising from the vast countryside spread below. These were handsome, exuberant creatures, agile and strong in equal measures. And although most everything on a flower-lit day atop the continent seems to exude vitality, the wolverine family so unexpectedly close gave off bursts that burned an afterglow into my brain. I hiked back that evening well and truly hooked on *gulos*. To be honest, I'd already been drawn into the study, but now I was infatuated. Wolverines kept introducing me to unsuspected layers of wildness. Soon afterward, I was radio-tracking on my own whenever I had free time and often when I really didn't.

On the Highline Trail days later, I picked up F4's frequency from below the path. The usual cheeps had become sharp chirps with a slight reverberation, indicating that the source of the signal was quite close. I ran down to the top of a cliff band for a look, thinking she might be traveling across the meadow full of ground squirrels below. I couldn't catch sight of her. While I stayed to keep watch, my son, Russell, hurried ahead on the trail with the antenna and receiver in case she turned that direction. Sooner than I expected, he came trotting back to join me.

"So?"

"I went around the corner, and F4 was loping right down the trail. She practically ran over me." He was grinning as though it would have been an honor if she had. This was his first wolverine sighting.

We carried on two miles to Alder Creek and picked up cheeps from her sons in a boulderfield. Strewn wide and heaped high, the boulders were big chunks of granite from an intrusion of molten rock between layers of the old seabeds. The boulders were light-colored, granulated with shining quartz crystals, and animated by pikas, or coneys, the littlest members of the rabbit and hare family. With small, round ears and short rear legs built more for scurrying and climbing than for hopping, they are also known as haymakers for their strategy of harvesting vegetation and stacking it to dry in the sun. After it cures, they haul it to larders deep within the rock piles to serve as winter food.

M9 and M10 were sitting tight in their rendezvous site somewhere equally deep within the stone jumble. We looked for half an hour while I tuned the receiver strength lower and lower so that I would have to be almost on top of the brothers to detect their transmissions. Perhaps that's where I ended up, though the signals kept bouncing among the boulders, indicating slightly different directions with each step I took. The best I could do was declare that the kits were very close and tucked away in a crevice so securely that I couldn't possibly get to them, which is exactly how rendezvous sites were supposed to work.

The next time I made the 11-mile trek along the Highline from Logan Pass to the part of the Going-to-the-Sun Highway called The Loop, I was with Yates. He wanted to investigate a rendezvous site he had narrowed down earlier. Not far from the one I'd explored, it was situated beneath the largest boulder in the whole rockslide. Yates wanted to see if he could find any droppings, telling me, "We've picked up a fair amount of winter scat, but we hardly have any to show what the wolverines have been eating in summer." After wriggling down through a crack between the massive boulder and a smaller chunk wedged beneath one side, he noticed a lower opening with fresh dung left on a slight ledge.

He could have grabbed it with one outstretched hand, but he chose instead to try to pick the stuff up with two twigs, chopstick-style. Yates is not a fastidious fellow. Working on his family's small farm and dairy as a young man, he butchered livestock and regularly collected dead animals, hides, and offal from other farms to haul to a rendering plant. Give him moose droppings, and he'll mash them in his palm to see if he can identify the plant parts. But he didn't want to handle wild carnivore poop if he didn't have to, because there is a remote chance that it will contain microscopic eggs or larvae from a potentially dangerous parasitic worm that invades membranes covering the brain. I've never heard of anyone becoming infected, but that's practically beside the point. Once you learn of the possibility in wildlife courses, an image of worms wriggling on the brain is pretty much with you for life.

Crawling among boulders nearby, I heard a long explosion of curses issue from the labyrinth that held Yates. Then came a long silence, then scuffling and grumbling, followed by another burst of cursing. When Yates finally emerged, his face was clouded with frustration. Mumbling that he had muffed the chopstick technique and dropped his prize out of reach, he stalked around in a black mood for several minutes. The man took solving the mysteries of wolverine food habits seriously. He kept telling me – telling himself, really, "I should have just picked it up."

"We'll find more."

"I already did. I collected older scat while I was down there. But the wolverines were using this rendezvous site in June when the big boulder was the only thing sticking out above the snow. What I got looks like old winter-type food. *ARGHH!!* I should have just picked that fresh piece up."

And so it went for some time on down the trail. I had never seen anyone that upset about dropping somebody else's feces. He actually hiked back another day on an outing with his son and devised a way to collect that sample.

The Highline Trail became something of a regular commute for me, as I was particularly keen to see how autumn and the coming time of separation would play out in F4's family. Through late August, I found the brothers still mostly together but separated by as much as a quarter of a mile at times. They seemed to be moving around more often, possibly doing a bit of hunting on their own as opposed to waiting quietly at a rendezvous site. I would start wondering if they were going to rendezvous with their mother at all whenever she stayed away a good part of the day. But F4 always returned. Then, during the first part of September, something changed. After the 10th, I picked up the brothers' signals far apart from one another and far from hers.

F4 stayed west of the Divide more often than not and gravitated toward Haystack Butte to hunt Columbian ground squirrels. The colony there had emerged late from hibernation, burrowing up through lingering snows. While other ground squirrels were already asleep for the winter, these needed to stay out feeding into the frosty fall days if they were to put on sufficient weight to get them through another nine months underground.

I couldn't locate either kit until the 2nd of October, when I got M10's signal from the Highline Trail. The following day, I picked up his brother, M9, across the Divide, high in the Swiftcurrent drainage at the head of the Many Glacier area. By midmorning, M9 had moved about five miles east down the valley onto the bighorn sheep and mountain goat range on the south face of Mount Altyn. That put him just beyond F4's turf and also just outside the limit of M1's territory.

M10 reappeared on the airwaves October 8th. His signal came from the head of the Grinnell Valley just at the outer edge of F4's territory there. My readings converged on a gold and burgundy field of autumn brush between the base of a soaring stone rampart called Angel Wing and Grinnell Lake, colored turquoise by the finely ground rock flour off Grinnell Glacier and shimmering under the low-angled sun. He was in a perfectly beautiful place. I never heard from him again.

Yates did weeks later. Or, rather, he heard a mortality signal from M10's radio, programmed to switch to a rapid beat when an internal sensor failed to detect movement for a long spell. The transmission came from Boulder Ridge, leading east off Wynn Mountain. This was well beyond F4's territory now but still within the borders of where M10's father, M1, roamed. By the time Yates was finally able to reach the site, all he could find was the radio in its protective capsule. No bones, no fur. Nothing. The capsule lay partially buried in a ground squirrel's hole. Yates said it looked like the work of a scavenger trying to hide an item to chew on later. He reasoned that M10 was taken by a predator that scattered his remains. Which kind of predator was most likely to have caught him? Yates shrugged.

In a reserve such as Glacier, the predator possibilities are as varied as they were centuries ago, ranging from grizzlies to golden eagles, which do some of their best hunting in partnership with the winds over open ridgelines. I ran into George Ostrom, a longtime local resident and keen outdoorsman, on the Going-to-the-Sun Highway one morning. As we talked, he pointed up toward Hay-stack Butte, where golden eagles regularly nest on the cliffs, and recalled seeing one swoop down into the meadow below and come up carrying a wolverine, probably a young kit. As if having second thoughts about the sort of quarry in its talons, the bird dropped it.

On the 31st of October, I recorded five locations for M9, the last of them at 3:42 pm. It was on the eastern edge of Mount Altyn in Many Glacier, and it was the last signal I would ever get from him. As the days grew shorter and colder, he continued eastward out of the park onto the Blackfeet Reservation. A local man encountered him there during the winter. He was a trapper and hunter, and he happened to be out running cougars with his pack of dogs. The dogs drove the young wolverine up a tree, and the man shot M9 dead.

The winter that M9 and M10 died, F4's previous offspring, F5, their older sister, conqueress of Bearhat Mountain, was swept away in an avalanche that carried her over a 300-foot cliff and deposited her remains below Bird Woman Falls. An inveterate traveler, she must have crossed a thousand snowbound slopes in her brief life. That was the wolverine way: to keep moving, keep pushing forward. For a few minutes of one day, she happened to be crossing one more slope when frost cracked a rock loose, or the temperature rose a degree and sent a trickle of water down to lubricate an underlying cliff ledge, and a few crystals began to slip. Megatons of them followed. All of her strength and courage and ferocious will were useless against a mountainside coming loose. Nothing she had learned in her few years could keep the tumult from swallowing her. Yates and Hasson picked up her body from the rubble. Her organs were crushed, her bones broken in a score of places.

Wolverines roam the peaks at will, scale them, summit them, scavenge in their snowslides, shelter in the crannies of their boulderfields, hunt their cliffs, and intimidate their largest inhabitants. They may be the toughest animals in the world and come as close as any I know to truly mastering the mountains. But in the end, nobody masters mountains, not every time. You don't overcome country like this. You try not to let it overcome you. You win by keeping even. Before I joined the project, I'd had no idea of what an achievement it was for a wolverine to grow old.

Known for his bird portraits, John James Audubon painted this odd-looking version of a wolverine in the 19th century based on a stuffed specimen. In keeping with a tradition that continues today, he depicted the predator in a ferociously bad mood. JOHN JAMES AUDUBON, courtesy Arader Gallery, Philadelphia, Pennsylvania

CHAPTER NINE

Kwi'kwa'ju

Through the pages of this book stalks the mightiest
of wilderness villains, a freebooter and a bully,
a bandit who knows nothing of fear.

from the cover of *Carcajou* by RUTHERFORD G. MONTGOMERY, 2001

DURING THE LATTER HALF OF THE ICE AGES, wolverines encountered a potent new force in the environment: humans, spreading from Africa into the northern latitudes of Eurasia and from there into the New World. Used to contending with other meat eaters for prey, carcasses, and caches, wolverines wouldn't have hesitated to follow their keen nose directly to game the newcomers had downed and to the supplies of meat and oils they stored. Animals caught in snares or other traps would have been treated by wolverines wheeling through the neighborhood as drive-in food. As soon as post-Ice Age societies began domesticating prey in the form of livestock, wolverines would have tried for that, too.

Agent of natural selection, sculptor of prey animals' strengths and senses, competitor of carnivores many times its size, carcass remover, recycler – you could give a wolverine any number of neutral titles. Hardly anyone ever did. Some Scandinavians knew the wolverine as the fell (mountain) cat, rock cat, and nasty cat, but most of the old European names for the animal were variations on *glutton*, among them *fat belly* and *devourer*. Even *Gulo gulo*, the Latin label chosen in 1780 by the German taxonomist Peter Pallas, means glutton – twice. And gluttony had by then been on the church's official list of the Seven Deadly Sins for almost 1,200 years.

In keeping with the universal pattern of making certain predators out to be larger and more dangerous than they really are and the people who slay them more heroic, stories were told of wolverines hunting people alone in the woods and seriously injuring or even killing those who confronted them over food.

Native American perceptions of the creature are harder to summarize. Depending on which tribe and which one of its legends you focus on, the wolverine was a creator, brother, enviable powerhouse, trickster, fiend, or just a plain pain in the ass. Some groups told the tale of the fourth cub, the runt of a mother bear's litter, who went off alone to become a wolverine. To others, wolverines were skunk bears. Micmac Indians, an Algonquian tribe, named the wolverine *kwi'kwa'ju*, a malevolent spirit. French fur traders interpreted this as *carcajou* and spread the label more widely.

To say that French voyageurs and other whites in the first waves of colonization were predisposed to portray wolverines as diabolical is putting it mildly. Trappers back in the Old World already had a long tradition of describing the animals as demons or devils, and most everyone in the New World fur trade would have liked to send them back to hell. Not that wolverine pelts lacked value. They were highly prized, especially for the lining or trim of parkas and other coats because of the hairs' water-repelling and frost-shedding qualities. But the gluttons' knack for taking other furbearers from traplines, sometimes leaving only the stench of musk and a torn paw in the steel jaws, was as infuriating as it was costly. As the fur industry swept westward across North America, the wolverine's reputation as a ruthless plunderer was inflated by each new tale of brazen break-ins at camps and of carcajous that learned to follow snowshoe tracks and rob every successful set in a long string of traps.

Reviling wolverines wasn't fundamentally about wolverines - no more than condemning wolves through the centuries as sadistic spawn of Satan was about the wolves themselves. Denigrating other races and ethnicities of people as disgusting, shifty, sinful, brutal, and so on *ad nauseum* isn't about them in particular, either. How could it be, when the same slurs have been applied to almost every animal and every variety of person ever perceived as an enemy?

This is about the psyche of *Homo sapiens*. We react strongly to any threat of competition for resources and dominion. That impulse is old, deep, and consuming; a territorial wolverine could easily relate. However, we humans also have a spectacular ability to maneuver images and thoughts in our minds and to think symbolically. And Shazam! Our enemies are no longer ordinary beings. Inside our heads, they have mutated into evil things, flaws in the world's proper order that deserve to be rooted out. This mental ploy seems to come as naturally to us as dreaming or carrying talismans for luck.

I could go on at length about the brilliant and compassionate sides of humanity, which are just as real. But I'm trying to explain more fully how a species as tough and unyielding as the wolverine, superbly adapted for survival in demanding environments, could become imperiled or extinct so suddenly in so many places. My view of its frontier history often resolves to the account I read of one wolverine that kept tearing its way into a shed and making off with the meat stored there.

The men at this winter encampment laced the place with traps. When evening came they heard a disturbance and ran out to discover the source. Sure enough, it was the *gulo*, come in search of protein, remembering where the best sources lay, trying to extract sustenance from the frozen winter landscape, exactly as it was designed to do. The animal was heaving and tugging at the icy bulk of a carcass many times its own size. Steel jaws gripped three of the wolverine's legs. Undeterred, drawing on the fire in its metabolism and straining every fiber of its muscles, trailing chains broken off their anchors, that wolverine kept dragging the bulky carcass away toward the woods until the men caught up and ended its story.

Once firearms and steel traps joined our arsenal, the death toll of carnivores as a whole soared. Not all that many generations later, societies had the technology, institutions, and mind-set in place to attempt mass extermination. Local, state, and national bureaus were putting bounties on competing meat eaters' heads. Government agents were hired to not only knock back predators in conflict areas but to completely eradicate their populations, tracking down every last holdout in the backcountry. Poisons – strychnine, cyanide, and then, after World War II, the tasteless, odorless, devastatingly lethal compound 1080 (sodium fluoroacetate), developed by German military chemists – were broadcast over the landscape inside carcasses and balls of meat.

Wolverines had evolved over millions of years to excel at locating any scrap of a meal left lying around the countryside. Overnight, that adaptation turned into a ruinous liability in the fantastical new age of chemical genocide. Wolverines also suffered indirectly as other carnivores dwindled, because larger hunters had always provided an important percentage of the carcasses available to scavenge. An intact predator community such as the one protected within Glacier Park may be among the most vital and overlooked elements of the wolverine's niche. Such communities were becoming more and more rare.

Gulo populations in Europe shrank northward toward the most remote and rugged refugia. Today, Norway and Sweden each hold 300 to 350. Finland, where more than 6,000 were killed over the past 150 years, has 50 to 150 left. Russia is believed to support the most wolverines. It ought to, considering that this northern nation spans 11 time zones. But the total there is unknown and the fur trade poorly regulated.

Eastern Canada's wolverines are now considered rare or endangered. The species vanished entirely from the lower 48 states during the first half of the 20th century. Although sporadic reports continued to come in from the Glacier Park area, they probably represented wanderers from the Canadian Rockies, not evidence of a viable U.S. group. It's possible that somewhere in Glacier's sturdy heart, one small enclave – one extended family, one clan – held out decade after decade, with a wayfaring Canadian *gulo* occasionally adding a shot of new blood to the line. But it's unlikely. Wolverines move around too much, and too many poisons were spread right up to the outer edges of the park for too many decades.

But during the 1960s and 1970s, as both Canadians and Americans began to limit the use of predator poisons, wolverines returned to the Lower 48 on their own, coming south down the spine of the continent. Their first solid foothold was, fittingly, Glacier National Park and the surrounding national forests. From there, they recolonized other mountain chains in Montana and portions of Idaho and Wyoming.

Montana's wildlife department responded by instituting a "harvest," becoming the only place in the United States outside Alaska where you could legally get yourself a wolverine hide. The state had several thousand registered trappers at the time, and each was allowed one wolverine in the winter season. Prices for pelts over the past few decades have varied between $200 and $400. Some wolverine hides with arresting patterns of white fur on the chest or around the base of the tail occasionally fetch a premium. No one kept track of the annual take at first. Later, game managers began to make guesstimates based on reports from sample areas. The total one year came to 50, they reckoned.

It wasn't long before Montana's marginal wolverine population was no longer expanding. If anything, it was thinning out fast. In the face of growing criticism, officials started to put an upper limit on the legal take, but they fought to keep it generous, citing the importance of "providing recreational and economic harvest opportunities" and "preserving our frontier traditions." In 2008, the state finally dropped the kill quota to five. Whether it stays at that level or is reduced even further is less relevant to the wolverines' future than the number of traps spread throughout the same habitats to catch coyotes, bobcats, otters, and the like. Those jaws maim and kill unintended victims every year, wolverines included. Managers refer to these as "nontarget" or "incidental" captures. How many occur is unclear, because not all of them get reported.

◇◇◇◇◇◇◇◇◇◇◇◇◇◇◇◇◇◇◇◇◇◇◇◇◇◇◇◇◇◇◇◇◇◇

Remember the wolverine pledge: No equivocating and no trading in partial truths? Trying to understand wild animals' lives is hard enough without having to sort through a clutter of official pretexts and euphemisms. At this point, no wolverine death south of Canada is "incidental" to the species' future here. Although game managers can't say how many wolverines inhabit Montana, a realistic estimate would be 100 to 150, tops. Idaho might support a similar number, primarily in its wilderness areas. The ecosystem that includes Yellowstone and Grand Teton National Parks could have another 50 animals. Washington's North Cascades ecosystem hosts a handful. And that's pretty much it for Lower 48 *gulos*. The fragmented total is nowhere near high enough to "provide recreational and economic harvest opportunities" or "preserve our frontier traditions."

While Michigan calls itself the Wolverine State, one recorded there in 2004 was the first in nearly two centuries. None has been seen since. During 2008, a marten researcher set up automatic camera traps in forests around California's

Even where wolverine trapping is tightly limited or banned, the animals get caught in steel jaws set for coyotes, bobcats, and other midsize carnivores. JOEL SARTORE

Lake Tahoe and was astonished when one snapped the portrait of a wolverine, the first documented in that state since the 1920s. Genetic tests on hairs left at the site indicated that the animal came from Idaho's Sawtooth Mountains population, 600 miles distant. The next winter, he showed up again in the same area.

In June of 2009, as I was writing this book, a young male wolverine radioed during December 2008 in northwestern Wyoming was crossing into Colorado to become the first of his kind recorded there since 1919. According to Bob Inman, who has led a wolverine study in the Yellowstone/Grand Teton area since 2001, the wanderer followed the Continental Divide south along the Wind River Range and then continued through the rolling sagebrush expanses of southern Wyoming. From there, he headed back up among the peaks and was last reported above 10,000 feet in northern Colorado's Rocky Mountain National Park, having covered around 500 miles.

These kinds of expeditions – these wolverine firsts by bold young males following the urgings of hormones, scents borne on breezes from afar, or their wolverine dreams – would be a heckuva lot more rewarding if there were just one more wolverine, a female, anywhere on those new horizons. Several years earlier, Inman and his team tracked another young male from the Grand Teton area nearly to Pocatello, Idaho, then back, then up to the northern end of Yellowstone and from there westward into the Centennial Mountains of Montana. Altogether, he traveled 550 miles in seven weeks. A line drawn around all the routes he explored would encompass more than 7,000 square miles. His last route took him into the steel jaws of a trap, where he died.

Since the 1990s, conservationists have filed several petitions to list the wolverine as imperiled in the contiguous states under the Endangered Species Act. Each time, the U.S. Fish & Wildlife Service (FWS) reviewed the requests and concluded that there was not enough known about the remaining population to warrant protecting it. This was sort of like a lifeguard deciding not to help a swimmer in trouble and sinking beneath the water because the guard can't see that person very well anymore. How do you collect detailed population data when the animals are too scarce to be counted in most places? Some accused FWS of stonewalling.

When Copeland, a federal employee, made some public comments to the effect that denning wolverines might need more protection from human disturbances in the backcountry, he received calls from a top-ranking official in the Bush administration who told him to *think very carefully* about what he was saying. But after FWS denied a petition in 2006, a federal judge ordered the agency to go back and take another look. The issue wasn't that FWS hadn't been given relevant information, the court ruled; the issue was that FWS had ignored it. Before long, leaks from within FWS, together with the work of probing reporters, revealed that there was more to this than bureaucratic inertia.

The following is a December 15, 2008, news item from "Washington Watchdogs," a periodic feature of the Washington Post's Investigations blog, prepared by Derek Kravitz: *"Political meddling at the Department of Interior into the designation of imperiled species and habitats was more widespread than previously thought, investigators found, according to a lengthy inspector general's report released today. The report focused on 20 questionable decisions made by the U.S. Fish and Wildlife Service, finding that Julie A. MacDonald, former deputy assistant director for fish and wildlife and parks, had a hand in at least 13 of them. But the report also found that MacDonald, a senior Bush political appointee, had help from others at the agency who 'enabled her behavior' and 'aided and abetted' her. MacDonald resigned under pressure in May 2007 after investigators found that she had tampered with scientific evidence, improperly removed species and habitats from the endangered species list, and gave internal documents to oil industry lobbyists and property rights groups."*

One of the 20 questionable decisions referred to was the 2006 denial of the petition to list wolverines. Late in 2008, during the waning days of the Bush administration, FWS finally issued the result of its court-ordered second look at the petition. It was another thumbs-down. This time, the agency argued that wolverines didn't warrant protection because they were related to populations in Canada, and those seemed to be doing all right. Had this line of reasoning been followed before, it would have prevented the listing and successful recovery of wolves, grizzlies, and America's symbol, the bald eagle. All of those species, by the way, were granted Endangered Species Act protection when their numbers in the Lower 48 were substantially higher than those of wolverines now.

Endangered or not, species need champions these days to secure their future. They also need public opinion in their favor. But the public can't develop a connection with an animal it's scarcely heard of, and what little people have heard about wolverines is the same old-same old: a blend of prejudice, fantasy, and overblown campfire stories from the boondocks, reeking of musk and testosterone. Out of every 100,000 American citizens, 99,999 haven't seen a wild wolverine to decide about the animals for themselves, and most never will. Granted, they haven't seen polar bears or tigers in the wild, either, yet those carnivores have legions of fans. The difference is that they're in the news, in magazine stories and children's books, and all over televised nature programs.

Wolverines rarely register on the public's radar. Even if you were inspired to pore through scientific journals, you couldn't come up with much of a sense of wolverines' daily lives. No one has observed them that closely and continuously in the wild for the simple reason that no human can move that far, that constantly. In fact, I can't think of any animal that could, not in the mountains. Well, maybe a snow leopard. Which is why its ways remain equally mysterious to us.

Marci Johnson, a field assistant early in the study, sets out across Josephine Lake toward the Great Divide.
RICK YATES

CHAPTER TEN

Why We Go
A-Wolverining

Time is but a stream I go a-fishing in. I drink at it; but while
I drink I see the sandy bottom and detect how shallow it is.
Its thin current slides away, but eternity remains.
I would drink deeper; fish in the sky,
whose bottom is pebbly with stars.

HENRY DAVID THOREAU
from *Walden*

ON THE LAST DAY OF OCTOBER ONE YEAR, my wife and fellow volunteer, Karen Reeves, and I walked up the Grinnell Valley in Many Glacier following radio signals from F2. The first snowstorm to coat the lower elevations had blown through just days before. Since then, the weather had cleared, bringing hard-frozen nights but strong afternoon sun. The snow was melting away in open areas. Autumn's asters re-emerged, withered but still showing purple among the dead grass stalks, and bright orange clusters of mountain ash berries clung to bushes at the meadows' edges. Wherever the trail led into forest shade, though, it disappeared beneath seven inches of white. Treading the cusp of fall and winter made us want to absorb the last warmth as if we could somehow store it up against the days to come.

We stopped for lunch where the woods opened onto the pebble beach near Josephine Lake's outlet. A newborn breeze from the white divide stirred the blue waters. The air came filled with high musical notes that at first had us looking around for a passing flock of crossbills or pine grosbeaks. Once our eyes adjusted to the sundazzle off the lake, we saw that thin panes of perfectly clear ice had formed along the edges during the night. Wind and waves had broken them apart and pushed the shards down to collect at Josephine's base. Between the shore at our feet and the open water 50 feet out, the surface resembled a gigantic, floating glass chandelier. Each wave that undulated through it caused the pieces to bump against one another and ring, setting off another bright arpeggio.

I gazed southwest along Josephine's length to Mount Gould, Angel Wing, Mount Grinnell; to the spindrift clouds flaring off the peaks' lee side like pennants; to the glaciers cupped in between – Grinnell, Gem, Salamander; to the waterfall pouring from them toward the valley floor like pure electricity jumping an arc. It was just scenery, but the scene was an ode to heaven and earth. I said my good-byes to autumn. I ate a peanut butter and jelly sandwich. I listened to the chiming of the ice. It was just a moment in the mountains, but enough moments add up to a life.

◇◇◇◇◇◇◇◇◇◇◇◇◇◇◇◇◇◇◇◇◇◇◇◇◇◇◇◇◇◇◇◇◇◇◇

Winter always comes, and spring forever follows, but not all at once. You know how climbing a steep scree slope goes: For every three steps up the mountainside, you slide two back down. Sometimes three or four. Spring comes to the Continental Divide like this. It's a string of broken promises. First, the spell of soft weather. Then the blizzard that has you drawing back into your parka hood, frosted and fugitive amid deepening white drifts.

Yesterday, April Fool's, 2008, brought another snowstorm. Today, as Karen, Dave Murray, and I ski toward Bowman Lake, perched up in a basin in the park's northwestern corner, we have to sidestep newly bare ground. There are juncos picking fallen seeds from the soil and flocks of cedar waxwings in the cottonwoods, whose buds are beginning to swell and ooze pungent sap.

The sky is overcast, and more snow is falling. But it's token snow, a flake here, a flake there. Safe passage snow; Canada geese are flying northward through it. Disappearing-on-contact snow; within half a mile, we're taking off hats and gloves. I lift a ski to avoid running over a spider picking its way among the dissolving crystals. To travel closer and higher toward the continent's crown – ever deeper into the throne room of temperamental mountain gods – and encounter more welcoming weather is rare. The snow has stopped altogether by the time we reach the lake six miles farther up the valley. Massive, white mountain shapes rise from the shores, packed in vapors and often inseparable from them. When a summit appears through a wreath of clouds, it looms so high when seen from the lake that it looks as though the peak has come loose from its stone shoulders and started to float.

Six and a half miles long and not quite a half mile wide on average, Bowman Lake stretches like a fjord in the channel Ice Age glaciers scooped out between the mountains now named Rainbow and Numa. Moments after our skis intersect wolf tracks on the shore, we see some of the pack out on the lake's frozen surface, just as we did on two earlier trips this year.

During our first trip, the ice was wind-polished in between ripples of drifted snow. We moved over it scouting for places to chop through and set a tall post in the hole. First, we bolt a deer leg atop the wood and screw small, cylindrical gun-cleaning brushes into its sides. The post then becomes a passive device to snag wolverine fur for DNA analysis. Murray was preparing another of these bait posts by himself when four wolves came trotting his direction from the opposite shore. They were clearly coming to see what was going on. As Karen and I watched from a distance, the group – three grays and a black – drew closer, while at least a dozen more wolves began singing in the surrounding woods.

"Cool. After they kill him, let's take his stuff and tell everybody the wolves carried it off."

"Where'd Murray go? I can't even see him now."

He was hiding behind overhanging branches, not because he was nervous but because he was trying to get a photo and didn't want to scare his curious visitors. The four of them stopped about 75 yards off. They stared his direction for a few moments, turned and went half a mile toward the head of the lake, veered from the edge to the center, and lay down to relax there on the ice, rulers of all in view.

This afternoon, there are three gray wolves and a black on the ice again, though they're a mile distant. We ski out to inspect a deer carcass 200 yards from shore. The body lies in pieces, stripped to smooth bone. According to the footprints in the trampled snow, ravens and eagles did most of the clean-up. Fresh otter tracks from farther up the valley skirt the remains and continue to open water around the lake's outlet.

Pressing on, we check our two posts. Placing a series of such hair traps in various parts of the park is an attempt to add information about the wolverine population's makeup without directly intruding into the animals' lives. We're hoping that setting the posts out on lake ice or open shores will keep the bait from being eaten by other climbing predators such as martens and lynx, which generally stick close to forest cover. It also helps that the scavenging birds seem to avoid the raised deer legs for some reason.

Not surprisingly, wolf tracks circle the posts. But we find no wolverine tracks or fur. I guessed from a distance that we wouldn't, because I could see the bait just as we had left it. At stations in other drainages, wolverines had not only coated the gun brushes with hair but also grooved the wooden post with their claws and made off with the legs we'd attached by heavy bolts driven through shoulder bone. British Columbia biologist John Krebs documented a wolverine dragging the carcass of a mountain goat for nearly two miles. For animals with this kind of strength, ripping loose one of our bolted-down deer legs was probably like trying to open a bag of airplane snacks is for us – an absurd annoyance no one wants to hear you fuss about.

We'll check again in two days and then take those posts down for the season before a grizzly bear does it for us. I thought we might cross the tracks of a grizz or two on the trip in today since males are already emerging from their dens. Tomorrow, we'll ski to remove a post at the lake's far end. Bowman's surface is smooth, its snow cover less than an inch thick, granulated and good for gliding. The clouds are staying high through late afternoon. I'm looking forward to a fast 13-mile round trip with open weather and fresh wolf tracks to read along the way.

Before the light fades, we open up the small patrol cabin that serves as our quarters, chop wood to get a fire going so we can melt snow for water, and settle into an evening routine of dinner and talk around the stove. As always, the snowmelt tastes of spruce and fir needles, lichens, bark, and smoke – the flavor of an evening in the woods. The first person to head out the door for a nighttime pee returns saying, "It's snowing again, coming down pretty heavy." When I go out with my headlamp for a look, the air incandesces with so many flakes that I can barely make out the trees close behind. Two hours later, it's snowing harder. Our trip to the upper end of Bowman won't be so quick after all.

I fall asleep almost instantly and set off wandering the busy dream world I often enter the first night after leaving home for a different location. Upon awakening, I see Karen silhouetted against a deep red glow. It takes a moment to register that she is feeding wood into a cabin stove to bring coals back to life. An early riser, she admits to being a little worried that she might have overdone it this time and apologizes in case the hour happens to be closer to midnight than to dawn.

"Anyone know what the time actually is?"

"*Ungh. Nunh-uh.*"

"Me neither."

Of course not. None of us ever seems to be wearing a watch out here. It's almost an unspoken pact. If we're to be ruled by any schedule, let it be calibrated by the levels of strength in our limbs and degrees of light in the sky. Right now, the time is quarter after beginning-to-stir-in-the-dark.

Karen proceeds to make coffee and fetch more snow to melt and fill our water bottles for the trip ahead. "Still coming down," she announces on her way back through the door. I tromp outside in camp slippers. They disappear into seven inches of new snow.

Ah well. In theory, each of us will only have to break trail a third of the way. That's part of the point of working with a team of three; that, and having two people to haul on the end of a rope if the lead person breaks through the ice. This time of year, it is bound to be weakening badly at the lake's head, where two open streams discharge mounting currents. Grabbing an armful of lodge-pole logs from the woodbox, I return to the warmth and candlelight and good companions inside.

126

To gather genetic information, we set up tall posts with bait, such as a leg of a road-killed deer, atop them and wire brushes on the sides to snag wolverine hair for DNA samples. ALEX HASSON

Dawn arrives an hour or so later. The snowfall dwindles as the brightness grows. From the lower branches of a spruce, a varied thrush, the North Woods counterpart of the robin, whistle-trills a song that says, "Snow or no snow, spring has sprung." Ground mist – usually a sign of clearing skies above – stretches across the lake ice, hovering, constricting to wisps in places, rolling like a fog-bank in others, always reconfigured the next time you look. Once again, it is the vast expanse of the lake ice that appears solidly moored while the mountains above seem adrift on the vapors.

Murray makes a few final preparations under the porch roof and leaves with a light backpack, saying he'll break trail for a while and we can catch up. From the spark in his eye, I doubt it. When Karen and I ski onto the ice, he's already a small, black, distant figure in a universe constructed in shades of white. He enters a tongue of mist and dissolves within it, as if his presence had been an illusion all along.

"He's got a lead of more than a mile."

"My guess is we won't see Murray again before the head of the lake."

"No, he's built for going, not stopping and waiting."

Karen and I depart hauling one sled for the two of us. We fall into a rhythm of pausing every so often to switch the load. Not to brag, but we're good at this kind of routine – reading one another's energy level, wordlessly sharing tasks in the field. We ought to be; when we got married, I think Elvis was still doing shows in Vegas and newly formed Apple had just introduced something called the personal computer.

No animal has been out on the ice since the storm ceased. The fallen snow passes by completely unmarked, the miles absolutely silent. I'm thinking of how I've seen city dwellers react when wilderness quiet enfolds them. They look around themselves, uneasy, then awed, listening carefully. Many have never heard no-sound before. As the forest on the shore behind us blurs to a low, dark horizon, the wide plastic sled creates what looks like a luge path to infinity through the snow in its wake. Karen and I have a sense of being the only people in a freshly forged part of the continent – except for Murray. Blazing the track, he must be feeling like the first and last creature on Earth.

It's been two hours since I saw the trailbreaker, but I can envision his path. I know he never sees his skis through the first half of the journey. He simply swings his feet through the downy cover of snow, and his body slides forward over it without so much as a whisper. It isn't like walking on a cloud, but it may be as close as a person can ever get outside of a dream – or heaven, if the place is half as white and fluffy as it's cracked up to be.

As the day warms, the snow imperceptibly settles until Murray at last notices not the upturned tips of his skis, not quite yet, but the twin lines they start to etch three feet in front of him as they tunnel just under the surface and cause crystals on top to cave in. I wonder if Murray entertains himself by pretending,

128

as I sometimes do, that it isn't his hidden skis cutting those lines but some mysterious force showing the path toward his destiny.

Bowman Lake bends toward the northeast from foot to head. To set the straightest course, you orient on a conspicuous point about three miles distant on one side. After passing that, you switch your aim to a point on the opposite side roughly two miles farther on. Each becomes your sole objective on the flat, unchanging field of no-color. Trouble is, so long as you're watching, neither point ever seems to get closer. Whatever you do, don't start counting: step, pole *One*; step, pole *two* . . . Hauling several-hundred-pound loads on their sleds, polar explorers knock out this kind of white mileage before breakfast. How do they divert their minds from the march?

Eating sandwiches on the edge of point number one, we hear our first noise of the lake trek: a subdued raven mewl, issued over and over, sounding like a question rather than the usual raucous commentary these birds voice. We're in a shadow thrown across the basin by Rainbow Peak, but sunlight is blazing on the ice ahead. The topsy-turvy weather pattern continues with skies growing brilliant blue toward the heights and brewing storms over lower elevations behind us.

A half-mile beyond point number two, we hear the journey's second noise: thunder that lasts for more than a minute. It comes from an avalanche about 200 feet wide sweeping down a sunstruck, south-facing chute. More slides rumble as we follow Murray's approach to the lake's head. His track parallels the shore now. He chose to keep close enough to the edge here that he could shatter his way to land if he fell through the ice.

<hr>

Karen and I find our teammate lying in the sunshine at the bared base of a Douglas fir on a mattress made of his coat and rain shell. Stripped down to a T-shirt, he's half asleep and totally at home. Just getting to Murray's Nest, as we name the spot, our ski tracks instantly fill with water behind us and turn to slush. We know that the ice has grown even more perilously thin between us and our post, which stands about 200 yards farther, wired to a large root of driftwood on shore at the very head of the lake. There are already narrow strips of open water along parts of that beach. A lone, lost-looking mallard swims in the widest one, a gap of about 15 feet around the mouth of one incoming stream.

We don't have to traverse this final stretch of ice if we don't want to. We could get to the post by circling on land around a small bay. But that would involve crossing the other incoming stream. Murray has scouted it and tells us we would probably end up wading at least waist deep.

My idea of a solution begins with leaning back against a tree to rest, eat, soak up sun, and watch light play across the geometries of the peaks. We've made good time and have more hours than we'll need to get back. Finally, I tie one end of the safety rope around my chest, pass the other to Karen and Murray, and start straight for the post over the ice. Halfway there, I'm probing and stabbing ahead with my ski pole every step, testing the thickness. Thirty feet from shore, it seems to be the night's snow as much as the soft ice underneath that's spreading my weight enough to still hold it. Water is beginning to seep into my tracks. I call for slack in the line, pick the only snow bridge left where the shore ice meets land, and race for it with all the speed I can muster. It's not cross-country skiing and not quite water skiing. Let's call this hybrid *glooshing*. It gets me to shore. The others gloosh routes close to mine, and we all arrive at the post with moderately dry boots.

The last time Murray and Karen were here, they uncovered the local phenomena known as larch balls – clusters of larch needles tightly compressed by the action of waves washing them up and down the sloping shore through late autumn. They form ovals and spheres ranging in size from swan eggs to beach balls. After setting up the bait post, Murray and Karen spent an hour rolling larch balls across the ice toward targets, or, as they called it, Bowling for Wolverines.

Unfortunately, it didn't help bring any in, at least none that touched the bait or left hair on our post. Studying a carnivore that naturally exists at extremely low densities, you get used to what scientists euphemistically term *negative data*; that is, you learn a lot about where they haven't been lately and what they weren't doing, and you tell yourself that this is an improvement over not knowing a blessed thing. I log the no-data in my notebook. The post comes down and we turn for home, gliding easily now in the trail we made through the snowpack.

The luge track to infinity guides our skis straight, making it easier to look around at the slopes to either side and the big cumulus clouds billowing and squalling over the Whitefish Range far to the west. So much space, so many colossal shapes, and yet I'm keenly aware of immediate details and patterns, the slightest breeze or change in snow depth close at hand. My eye catches a dark fleck amid the crystals: an early mayfly – way early. Then a winged ant with soaked and crumpled flight gear. Did these individuals have a slightly different chemistry that fired them up to emerge long before their insect peers? Were their biological clocks haywire? Could it be that they simply misread cues from the environment? Warm day; downright hot here in my miniscule niche on shore. Must be time to take to the air, go prospecting for mates. Bet it's Action Central out there . . . somewhere . . . a little farther . . . Whoa! What *was* my bug brain thinking?

How my consciousness can be so absorbed by the enormity of these surroundings and laser focused on minutiae at the same time is a mystery. I only know I'm in a state of awareness more all-inclusive than I recall experiencing before, and I like it. Instead of casting about for mental escapes, I want to take in everything about the march now, too – the motion of boots and bindings, the friction chafing my toes and heels, the pull of the sled against the rope coiled like a harness across my shoulder, the complaints of muscles and tendons forced into repetitive motion mile upon mile – take them in and accept them. Accept that tiredness is what happens when you're on the move, and that it happens after fewer miles as you get old, and that I qualify as old. So what? In your finest hour afoot, you were never a wolverine anyway, Chadwick. But then you already know that. Just keep going and keep doing it, old fella. Don't waste a perfect tabula rasa like the frozen surface of Bowman by complicating life with coulda-done-this and wish-I-were-that. Just be what you are. Just be.

<hr/>

Evening brings purplish clouds on the mountain contours and a higher cloud cover lit by an early moon. I eat two fairly crummy freeze-dried dinners and fall into bed. Karen is up early again, stirring the fire's embers. Either I'm still tired from the trip, or she's really early this time – weird mayfly early. My groggy brain stumbles toward another thought: Didn't I throw a wristwatch into a ditty bag I packed months ago, just in case I had to time a rendezvous with another volunteer? I rummage among wires, fish hooks, duct tape, et cetera by headlamp and find the thing.

"Oh boy. 4:18. I'm going back to the rack."

"Did you ever change your watch to daylight savings time?"

"Ah. Right. It's 5:18. And I'm up."

A cup of coffee later, Karen steps outside. During my second candlelit mug, it occurs to me that she has been gone in the darkness for quite a while. I'd thought she was listening for wolves, but when I go out to follow her tracks, I find her down at the lake's edge looking up at the sky. The night's clouds have vanished, and the great summit-rimmed bowl is aglitter with stars. If a march through the mountain gods' throne room doesn't put a human life in perspective, an unobscured view of the universe framed by peaks certainly ought to. The Milky Way is a torrent. Constellations stand forth as if someone laid an illustrated guide to them over the rest of the faraway suns. I can't imagine they would look much brighter through a spaceship window, but I'm freezing and soon turn back for the cabin. Karen quietly says she's going to stay a bit longer.

Dawn's light reveals new depths to the ranks of peaks under an immaculate sky. While the colors brighten on high, ground mist condenses over the lake ice. It settles in thicker than it did the morning before and seems to concentrate the cold. As we take down the bait posts and remove the metal brush hardware, our fingers grow numb and our faces sting. But by the time we've packed up the sled to depart Bowman, sunlight bouncing off the high slopes seems to be warming the air a degree every few minutes. Before we ski off the lake ice for the last time this year, we pause at some coyote tracks. Turning to examine their pattern, backlit by the sun just coming over Rainbow's shoulder, I find myself looking at countless tiny sparks dancing through the air in front of my eyes.

Galaxies within galaxies, invisible imps cavorting with miniature sparklers; they're ice crystals so fine they are virtually weightless, some gliding in spirals, others rising like dazzling confetti in an updraft. We're passing through the fast-evaporating remains of one of the bands of ice fog that clung to the lake earlier. It's all magic, this mountain world – natural magic. Enough to enwild you – rewild you, renature us all. As if that weren't wonder enough, it's spring. Oh, and there are wolverines out there loping their wolverine lope, following their wolverine noses, thinking their wolverine thoughts, whatever shape those take, and crunching up bones. Just don't ask me where right now.

A younger Jeff Copeland, during his earlier study in Idaho's Sawtooth Mountains, where the biologist discovered an unexpectedly sociable side to these animals. JEFF COPELAND COLLECTION

CHAPTER ELEVEN

Copeland and Socks

We have a habit of writing articles published in scientific journals to make the work as finished as possible, to cover up all the tracks, to not worry about the blind alleys or describe how you had the wrong idea first, and so on. So there isn't any place to publish, in a dignified manner, what you actually did in order to get to do the work.

RICHARD FEYNMAN
from a 1966 Nobel lecture

SOME CARNIVORES SPECIALIZE IN HUNTING A PARTICULAR SPECIES or category of prey. Others are generalists. Hunting, scavenging, and occasionally berry picking, wolverines patrol the length of the generalist spectrum. Copeland has seen where, like bears, *gulos* tore apart fallen logs to get at the grubs inside and rolled over rocks in order to lick up ant larvae in the colonies underneath. An hour later, they might be raiding eggs from a bird nest or sizing up a massive bighorn ram with an injured leg – whatever comes next.

It pays a generalist to be curious, and wolverines being wolverines, their curiosity is fierce and unrestrained. That's part of what Copeland so admires about them. Inquisitiveness is our birthright too, but Copeland's brand is hard-earned. Honed during a long journey toward becoming an expert in his field of biology, it involves continually learning to ask better questions. I'll never be able to explain all the things that impel him and a small cadre of other scientists to investigate *gulos*. I only know that it is part of the human desire to know more and know truly, and that at this juncture of history it is as vital to the animals' existence as their own extreme nosiness.

Over the years, I had hiked with Copeland, weathered blizzards with him, and taken sedated wolverines from his arms during trapping operations. We'd shared meals and free-ranging discussions many a cabin evening. I'd hung out

135

in his Missoula office to paw through his files of scientific publications and look over computer-generated maps of wolverine movements. But while I had often talked with my fellow volunteers about what led them onto the wolverine way, I never quite got around to asking the boss man. That began to seem like a lopsided view of the project, and I found myself wanting to fix it.

After all, Copeland was the one who had made a conscious decision to dedicate his career to the study and conservation of this species. Had he chosen otherwise, most of the rest of us would still have been out exploring Glacier, but not with the intensity and fascination that carried us down the trail while radiotracking these animals.

Where we'd barely paid attention to the existence of wolverines beyond crossing the odd set of prints or glimpsing one every few years, we now followed the beacons of individuals we could plainly picture in our minds. We knew them by the spit that had hit our faces at traps, the fur we'd stroked when they were tranquilized, the toes of the paws we'd spread to examine the partial web of skin in between. We cared about how they and their young and mates were faring. We marveled at their abilities and the scope of their journeys. Our awareness of the life-and-death dramas being played out within natural communities around us expanded apace, and the mountains seemed that much wilder, that much fuller, and that much more vibrant as a result. We had Copeland to thank for this. And he thought he was the one getting the bargain from those of us working for free.

Copeland set time aside to sit down with me and talk for several days to satisfy my curiosity about how his mind came to be wrapped around all things *gulo*. I've quoted his words at length here. He'll probably never see them in print. One of the things he told me is that he dislikes reading about himself and his research; he just likes the work. I figured he'd say that. Copeland, an ex-farmland kid from the Midwest, ex-serviceman, and ex-game warden of a socially and politically conservative stronghold in central Idaho, is the anti-Flash. He may be overseeing very cool investigations of the coolest of carnivores in the opinion of the rest of us on the project, but you're not going to catch him all dressed up in Important Scientific Expert clothes.

◇◇◇◇◇◇◇◇◇◇◇◇◇◇◇◇◇◇◇◇◇◇◇◇◇◇◇◇◇◇◇◇

Copeland doesn't remember being more curious than other boys growing up in Indiana farm country. "I did some hunting and a little trapping, and I was fascinated by fossils," he said, "but I didn't have any special commitment to understanding animals. From high school, I went straight into the Air Force. I got to be friends with a master sergeant who was an amazing outdoorsman. He took me on trips into the swamps of South Carolina, where we were based. I think that's when my interest in nature really developed. After I got out of the military in the midseventies, I enrolled at the University of Idaho to study wildlife.

"I made my beer money doing scat analyses [*picking apart the droppings of animals to see what they have been eating*] for the wildlife department. It was predator scat – mostly coyote, badger, and bobcat. Maurice Hornocker [*of the Idaho Cooperative Research Unit, affiliated with the University of Idaho*] and his colleague Howard Hash had just started the first study of wolverines in North America in 1972, up in Montana. My best friend was analyzing scat from their project. One day, he comes over and hands me some reddish hairs attached to a piece of skin that he got out of one wolverine scat and says, 'Tell me what you think this is from.'"

Red fox? Red squirrel?

"I knew the answer right away; there's no mistaking the structure of human hair. I sat there stunned. Was I looking at a piece of a long-lost hiker? A redhead from some plane that vanished in the mountains? A murder victim? The whole mystery of it sort of seared the image of a wolverine into my brain."

Hornocker and Hash's pioneering study took place in the Swan Mountains, which mark the western edge of the Bob Marshall Wilderness south of Glacier Park. Not many of the radio collars the men attached to wolverines stayed on for more than a few weeks. The other reason their subjects proved hard to track over long periods was that so many were being taken by fur trappers. Despite those obstacles, the researchers determined that the animals were traveling an average of nearly 20 miles daily in territories that encompassed the heights of the mountain range.

Copeland continued: "In my undergraduate years, I lived to hunt and fish. I think another reason wolverines intrigued me – I sort of hate to admit this now – was that I really got into trapping for a while. I *loved* marten trapping. I couldn't wait to get back up to the country martens live in around the upper edge of tree line. I never allowed myself to imagine what one was going through hanging there, flailing in a trap for hour after hour until it froze to death.

"What I loved was that subalpine and alpine setting. It took me a while to realize this. For some reason, it's where I'm most at home," said the man who grew up surrounded by cornfields. "I've never felt better in my life than I did when I went to Alaska and Norway later to visit other wolverine researchers. It's like our high country everywhere – dwarf trees, rolling tundra, rock, and scree for as far as you can see. When I did my study in the Sawtooths, I'd fly over some little basin way up among the peaks, and I'd say, 'I just have to hike there. I have to be there.' But I'm getting ahead of myself.

"The more I learned about martens, the more interested I became in mustelids. And wolverines are the kings of mustelids. For me, they represented a consummate predator. I was taken by their legendary ferocity. A lot of this was still kind of tied in with my hunter and trapper mind-set – you know, matching wits with animals, killing stuff.

"I remember the instant things started to turn. I'd shot my share of deer. One day I shot a handsome big buck, and it fell down dead, and I asked myself: Why did I do that? Maybe, I thought, I don't have to do that any more.

"By seventy-eight or seventy-nine, I was trying to get into the University of Idaho's wildlife graduate school. But funding for the mustelid project I wanted to do never came through. So instead of going to graduate school, I hired onto an elk and moose study near Elk City [*in the remote Clearwater Mountains east of Grangeville, Idaho.*] During our field surveys, we kept noticing sign of fishers in the area. They were getting caught by marten trappers, who were selling the fur on the black market back East. Because fishers were really rare regionwide, this got my attention. I started my own little fisher study on the side, livetrapping them and putting on ear tags, trying to get a better handle on the population."

A mustelid intermediate in size between martens and wolverines, the fisher favors dense forests and is one of the few predators able to successfully hunt porcupines. Often referred to as the American sable and heavily trapped for its plush, dark fur, the species all but disappeared from the contiguous states early in the 20th century along with the wolverine. An extensive program to transplant animals from Canada and surviving enclaves in the Great Lakes region reestablished fishers in the upper Midwest and Northeast. They never recovered in the West and remain one of the rarest of forest carnivores in this region, despite reintroductions.

"Then a wolverine came in and demolished one of my fisher traps," Copeland continued. "What the . . . ? We weren't even aware we had wolverines around. Here was this long-lost, mystical beast appearing out of nowhere, and it just ripped my trap to pieces. My next experience with a wolverine was in the Gospel Hump Wilderness. I cut tracks and followed them to a hole in the snow. When I poked my head in, I saw that the hole corkscrewed down for five feet to reach part of a frozen deer carcass. That was the work of a scavenger with one amazing nose.

"My interest in wolverines was getting fired up. But I needed a job, and I took one as a game warden. I wardened for the next eleven years – about eight years longer than I should have. It takes two or three years to learn to be a game warden. After that, you just sort of are one."

Copeland stands a bit above average height. His chest is solid and his arms well muscled. He bears himself with squared shoulders and a level gaze. It wasn't hard to picture him handling situations that called for bluff and bluster, and he was in plenty of facedowns. The hard part wasn't the physical risk involved. For him, it was having to listen to poachers' lies and excuses. Endlessly.

"I worried that the enforcement work was making me an angry, cynical person," Copeland said. He missed the truth-telling of science. He could see more clearly now that the kind of connection to nature he needed lay not in fur trapping, not in hunting, and not in protecting wildlife by playing gotcha with game hogs. He wanted the challenge of research.

Back in the 1970s, a fox trapper near Stanley, Idaho, killed the first wolverine anyone had heard of in the area for decades. Agency biologists decided they'd better look around to see if they had any others. They carried out occasional surveys, mostly by airplane, flying in winter to search for tracks. That was about the extent of Idaho wolverine research for many a year. In 1992, money became available for more intensive studies on the Sawtooth National Forest, and it provided the opportunity for Copeland to do graduate work on *Gulo gulo* at last. The start of the Glacier Wolverine Project was still a decade away.

"Back in the early nineties, the deal was, 'OK, Copeland, nobody knows much about wolverines yet. There are the mountains. Go figure it all out.' Maurice Hornocker gave me the live traps made from metal barrels that he'd used in the Swan Mountains. At the same time, he warned me I might never catch a wolverine. He suggested I consider studying something else to be sure I could collect enough data for a master's thesis.

"I found a river guide and cross-country skier named Sparky Easom who knew the country and could get to just about any part of it in a hurry. Then I hired Beth Bratlie, a Stanley local and a snowmobiler. She knew the area well, too, and was looking for work. I needed her to help run the traplines. Right away, she proved indispensable in just about everything we did, from putting in a temporary camp to fixing whatever broke down on our snowmachines. Before long, she was in charge of all the logistics of our fieldwork. I picked a drainage, and we laid two lines, setting out a trap every mile for between 10 and 20 miles along each one – the fur trapper's approach. Four days into the study, I caught my first wolverine.

"It was in the last trap at the head of a valley. You can imagine what a 35-gallon steel drum with a wolverine inside it is like. That barrel was vibrating like a bomb about to blow. What the hell do we do now? I had a fiberglass jab stick for injecting the immobilizing drug. I open the jab hole in the barrel, and this slobbering, growling head comes shooting out. It was a female. She was absolutely ferocious. She eats the jab stick. Well, shatters it. The jab stick's gone. The syringe is gone. Finally, after an hour, I get the drug in her. We put a VHF collar on. She wore it for a week and took the thing off 15 miles from the trap.

"Hornocker had experimented with making it easier to handle a wolverine by adding a squeeze chute arrangement to a barrel trap," Copeland went on. "He gave me the model. That didn't work. The second animal we caught was an old, old female. A sweet gal, much more calm. She made it through the rest of the winter but was pretty much on her last legs. She died that spring. The third and last capture we made that season was another old female. I'd brought a blowgun – my latest bright idea for getting a drug dart in these critters. But we had a wildlife veterinarian along this time, and he used the jab stick with no problem. From all our work the first year of the study, we ended up with exactly one antique wolverine on the air.

"But I also met Socks. Indirectly. We had automatic cameras set up at many of the traps, and I could easily recognize him on film from the white on his paws. He'd come up to the barrels, knock them around, tip them over, and never go in. Like M1 when we first caught him in Glacier, Socks was a big, stout, handsome guy in the prime of life. He was clearly the resident male in that drainage – the Man.

"I got convinced that if I just had a mirror set up inside one of the traps, he'd see himself and think it was another wolverine and go in to do battle or whatever. I found a Miller Beer mirror like they hang on the walls of bars, not that I ever visit such establishments. It was dark inside the barrel, so I also convinced myself that I needed to light the mirror. I got hold of a neon Christmas decoration, and I wired that inside. That has to have been the most ridiculous trap ever put in the woods. There's no punch line to this story. Socks didn't go in. I'm just telling you how desperate I was.

"I went back to Hornocker and said, 'This ain't workin'.' He referred me to Clint Long, one of the most amazing people I've ever met. Clint came out of the Scripps Research Institute in California. He was a microbiologist, but he'd become fascinated with wolverines at an early age. Now he was living in Boise and keeping a group of captive *gulos* at his place. He'd built a very controlled facility called the Carcajou Research Center – concrete floors so clean you could eat your lunch off them. And he was devoting a big part of his life to recording the wolverines' activity cycles, reproductive condition, marking behavior, types of locomotion; you name the subject, he was keeping daily records of it.

"When I'd started, I knew these animals were supposed to have big home ranges, but I didn't know how much they moved – not really. I thought, heck, I can keep up with them. Two days of trying that, and I was a humbled believer. Yet I went right ahead stringing all my barrel traps along one key drainage when what I needed were just a few traps that worked, spread out through the study area to cover more wolverine territories. Clint told me about a trapper in Canada who used log boxes to catch wolverines. I went for a visit, and his boxes looked like the answer for us. I spent the summer picking sites and building a dozen of them. I tweaked the design slightly. We had success right from the start our second winter and went on to catch a total of eight different animals. And one of them was that damn Socks.

"Three other scientists besides Hornocker had put radios on wolverines: Audrey Magoun, working up in Alaska's Brooks Range; Craig Gardner, near Talkeetna, Alaska; and Vivian Banci in the Yukon. Two more biologists – John Krebs and Eric Lofroth, both in British Columbia – started projects around the same time I did. But the only dens ever documented in North America were a handful that Audrey had found. No one had captured and marked any kits. We still didn't know when the young separated from their mother or how. Was it gradual or were they booted out all at once? What did they do next? I was determined to find out.

"Scandinavian researchers had tried gluing transmitters to wolverines. Otherwise, the only alternative seemed to be to keep putting on radio collars and hoping the animals didn't get them off right away. Then Wayne Melquist of the Idaho game department suggested that we try implanting transmitters, since this technique had recently been tried successfully with river otters. We switched to doing that. The automatic cameras we installed at all twelve traps were another great technology to have. We got photos of two wolverines pulling bait out of the same trap together. One was Socks. The other was a transient two-year-old male – later caught, implanted, and labeled Number 333 – that stayed in Socks's home range before moving on to establish his own territory the following winter. A resident male cooperating with a subadult male – and an unrelated one at that? I'd never even heard of such a thing among wolverines. Nobody had.

"Toward the end of winter, I flew to locate one of the females we'd implanted, hoping to find her den. This was way back in the Frank Church Wilderness. Clint, Sparky, and I went in. The night before we started into the high country, Clint broke his toe in the cabin where we were staying. He snowshoed around for the whole week with that toe sticking out at a wild angle. Our plan was to check out the den and put a data logger by it to automatically pick up the female's radio signal and record the pattern of her comings and goings. The data logger was one heavy, bulky piece of equipment to be packing around. About five miles along, I was crossing a lake when exhaustion hit. I plopped down on the ice to catch my breath. After a little while, I look over one shoulder, and there, a hundred yards off, is a wolverine going by. I can still picture that effortless, beautiful lope out in the middle of the big mountain basin.

"It was Number 333. He made my day. Good thing, because when I humped the data logger up to where I'd located the den from the air, there was nothing but an unbroken layer of fresh snow. I started digging through it and found the entrance hole but no other sign of the female's presence. She'd moved out. I climbed to a high ridge at the head of the basin and picked up her signal. It was coming from a bowl on the opposite side. I could make out her tracks and what looked like a den hole in the distance, but there was a vertical cliff at my feet. I couldn't see a route down that was even half safe.

"After we returned to town, I went flying again to check on our female. She'd moved to yet another basin. It would be a long slog from a different direction to reach her, but it was doable. We went partway and set up camp. I snowshoed on to the den for a look and found tracks of the female and kits around the entrance. Bingo! The next morning, we went together to dig the kits out. The wolverines were gone again. I think Mom got spooked by my tracks.

"The Scandinavians knew something about disturbance. What they'd do was track a female to her den, mess with it, then back off and wait for her to bring the kits out to move them. Then they could kill them all. Their goal was to protect domestic sheep and reindeer herds. What we didn't know was that even when there's been no disturbance, females will move from a natal den to a maternal den after a while. And they may go on to move from one maternal den to another as the kits grow older. The other thing we didn't know was when they'd all leave the den for good. April was shot. We were into the beginning of May now. But I still wanted to try for those kits.

"Back to town, back up in the air. I found the female. She'd moved again and was within the official wilderness. We would have had to get special permission to land there. I decided to give it one more try after that, and we flew by helicopter. We found her and the kits out on the snow right by the edge of the wilderness. They took off running from the noise of the chopper. Suddenly, all three vanished into the snow. Put this bird down and let me out. I ran to the hole and stood over it until the others joined me. We blocked the entrance and started digging on different sides. The mother must have felt cornered because she came bursting right up through the snow like a Titan missile from a submarine.

"We got the kits – two females. They were tiny things, small for their age, but we didn't know that then. Hell, we didn't know that Mom would flee and we'd end up bottle-rearing two orphan wolverines. But she came right back and watched from not far away. When the vet finished implanting the kits with small transmitters, one cried and cried. I wish Clint had been there. He'd have recognized the difference between real pain and ordinary distress at being handled. That kit later died. Something must have gone wrong during the operation. I'm guessing the discomfort led either the kit or the mother to chew open the sutures. I found the kit's body later in a small depression scraped into the ground. Pieces of wood had been chewed off a log and laid over her. It was almost certainly the work of the mother, and she hadn't disturbed the site since. I was looking at a wolverine burial site. I wanted to quit. That little grave was unbearable."

◇◇◇◇◇◇◇◇◇◇◇◇◇◇◇◇◇◇◇◇◇◇◇◇◇◇◇◇◇◇◇◇

After the country melted out, Copeland flew once a week to get radio locations. "Then we'd go in on the ground to try to follow the animals," he explained. "The wager was that I'd buy a steak dinner for anyone who could stay with a wolverine for 24 straight hours of tracking. Our local gal from Stanley, Beth Bratlie, won it one time. That was the only time. I wanted to collect as many radio locations as possible, define the habitats where animals spent time foraging, and see what kind of places the mother and her surviving kit, labeled Number 203, were choosing for rendezvous sites. Beyond that, I didn't have any great study plan.

1

2

3

4

Climate change at a glance: Grinnell Glacier in 1938, 1981, 1998, and 2009. About 150 glaciers were tallied in Glacier National Park when it was founded in 1910. The last will vanish between 2020 and 2030 according to current projections. T.J. HILEMAN/GNP ARCHIVES, CARL KEY/USGS, LINDSEY BENGSTON/USGS, DAN FAGRE/USGS (clockwise from top left)

Heading into Many Glacier on the closed road, the crew is prepared for a variety of traveling conditions farther up the valley. ALEX HASSON

Another day at the office: volunteer Rebecca Hadwen radio-tracking wolverines along the backbone of the continent. RICK YATES

Remarkably agile, wolverines are adept climbers of trees as well as cliff faces. DALE PEDERSEN

A captive wolverine stretches after waking up from a nap. DALE PEDERSEN

A captive wolverine shows off a healthy set of teeth during a yawn. DALE PEDERSEN

Huntress of the marmots and ground squirrels that abound during the warm months, F4 closes in on one of the rodents in a boulder-strewn meadow. BILL GARWOOD

As a yearling, F5 remained in the territory of her mother, F4. By age 2, she was gradually carving out a home of her own in the adjoining high country to the south. KEN CURTIS

The popular comic book superhero, Wolverine, about to dispense justice to evildoers. Wolverine™ & ©2010 Marvel Characters, Inc. Used with permission.

The original legend for this painting was "Hungry wolverines, cousins of the weasel, wait in ambush to seize a calf or sick straggler from a caribou herd." Certainly wolverines hunt caribou of all sizes, but whether or not they put quite as much forethought into the hunt as the original caption hints at is unknown.
WALTER A. WEBER / National Geographic Society

Rick Yates prepares a drug syringe at the tip of a jab pole near a trapped wolverine. MARCI JOHNSON

Jack Noll cooking breakfast at the Two Medicine patrol cabin. ALEX HASSON

In the light from a headlamp, the eyes of a lynx caught in a wolverine trap take on a sapphire glow.
RICK YATES

Created by wave action on the beach of a mountain lake, balls of larch needles are put on temporary display by a volunteer in no particular rush to be doing anything anywhere else. ALEX HASSON

A wolverine near Boulder Pass covers the miles in its tireless lope. KEN CURTIS

A captive mother and her kits, born the color of snow. They will begin to darken after their first week.
DALE PEDERSEN

A Russian wolverine skims over the snow with its large snowshoe feet. Like humans and bears, but unlike dogs and cats, *gulo*s have a plantigrade locomotion, meaning that they walk on their heels as well as the toes. IGOR SHPILENOK

F5 stalking ground squirrels in an alpine talus field. KEN CURTIS

The author looking on as Rick Yates removes M3 from the Boneyard trap. ALEX HASSON

An East Side storm complete with hurricane-force winds. RICK YATES

Seated bear-like, a captive 2-month-old kit brings to mind the native legend of the wolverine as the fourth bear cub – the runt of a grizzly's litter that went off to live alone. DANIEL J. COX

Based on readings from the satellite collar he was wearing, this map depicts a typical week of movements by M1 through his territory along the Continental Divide. Though the Google Earth map depicts the topography in

162

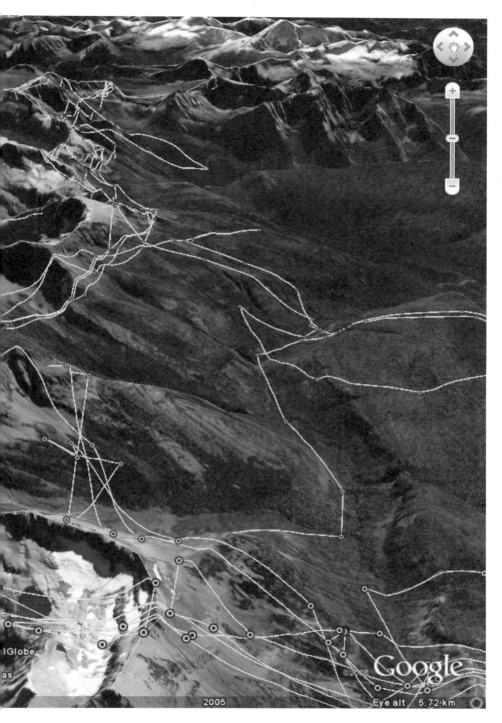

summer, these travels actually took place in winter when the landscape was buried in snow and ice. Courtesy of
Google Maps

Mating Relationships of Wolverines in the Glacier Park Study

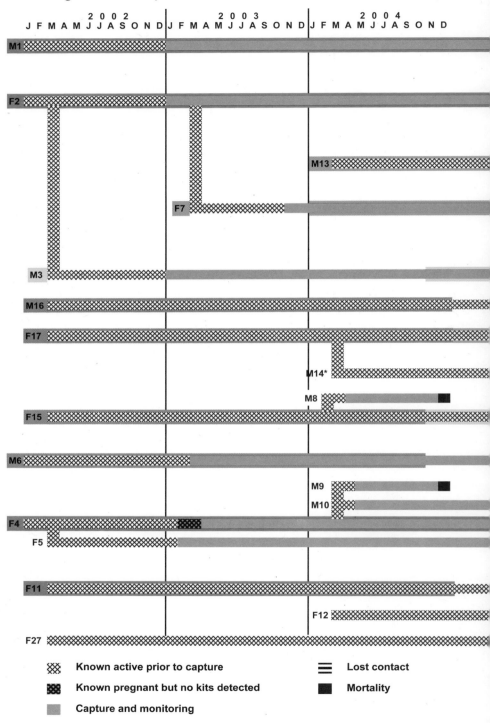

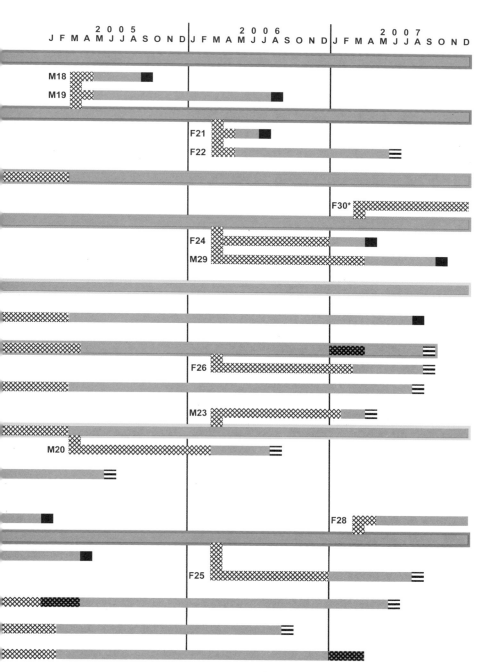

Like colors denote mating based on DNA from fur samples. The Glacier National Park study overthrew previous assumptions about the species by finding that juveniles remained within their parents' territories into the second year, and continued to travel with adults at times during that period. Even so, the harsh forces within their niche – larger predators, climbing accidents, avalanches – combined with trapping beyond the park's borders claimed many of the young animals before they reached maturity. *M14 is likely, but not confirmed, to be the offspring of F17 and M16. *F30 date of birth uncertain. Data courtesy of Jeff Copeland

Bearhat Mountain in early June. F5 climbed to the summit in the winter conditions of early April. Rick Yates watched her final push to the summit while flying in a light plane to locate radioed animals. What was she seeking at the top? We have no better explanation than we have for why human mountaineers climb the tallest, hardest peaks. RICK YATES

"The trend in wildlife biology was toward statistics and computer modeling. But you need a lot of data to work with, and that didn't exist for wolverines. This was old-time natural history – a real dinosaur of a research project: Go out there, tough it out, and see what you can see. Most of the time, you don't get much for your sweat and sore muscles. But anything you do learn could be something no one ever saw or even thought about before.

"During the summers, I was living with my family in a cabin at an old sheep ranch. When I went to investigate den sites or rendezvous sites, my daughter Maggie was small enough to crawl in among the rocks on talus slopes and tell me what she was looking at. My other daughter, Jodie, was with me on a rock pile in the timber one day. We'd been tracking an old female, and her signal had vanished. We were sitting on the boulders taking a rest and talking when I noticed a wolverine head poking through a crack. It was sniffing Jodie's leg.

"Kits were supposed to be on their own after a few months, but I'd found a yearling with an adult female several times, and I was at a loss as to how to interpret that. In October, the mother of Number 203 died. We found her ripped to pieces. So here's the surviving kit going into her first winter. Her sister's dead, accidentally murdered by us. Her mom's dead, torn apart by some big predator or predators. On her own, 203 finds a trap and goes for the food in it. Over and over, even when there are only scraps left. We're catching her four times a week. At camp, Cheryl [*Copeland's wife*] says, tongue-in-cheek, 'Maybe her dad will come take care of her.' The next day, Sparky is flying and radios us. 'You're not going to believe this,' he says, 'but 203 is traveling with Socks about eight miles from the trap.'

"On snowshoes, I found where the two of them had gone to an abandoned outfitter's camp and dug up an old hide to gnaw on. The next day, I followed their tracks to a deer carcass. They'd fed on it, then dragged it into a hole they'd dug and laid down next to it. Before they separated, I'd recorded them traveling together for three days over thirty miles. After that, I noticed that when I got a radio location for 203 and marked it on the map, there would often be a dot already there representing Socks. Apparently, she was visiting places she had learned about from him. She might also have been following his trail. I saw them together more than half a dozen times that winter while flying. This wasn't indirect evidence from radio signals of a dad traveling with his daughter. It was visual confirmation.

"The third winter, I tried to catch more kits but didn't have any luck. Pretty soon, it was late enough in May that the young were out following mom around. You still have a chance of running them down on the snow at that age. Up in B.C., John Krebs was doing this with a salmon net. One day on a helicopter flight, I saw two kits below. We set down and I jumped out and went chasing after one. I kept breaking through the crust, but I finally gained on the kit enough to leap. Between the time I left my feet and the time I planted my face in the snow, the kit juked aside, and I wrapped my arms around empty air. The other kit was running away from Beth and scrambling in my direction. I grabbed it, and it grabbed me with its teeth. All I could do was keep holding tight, trying to ignore a bunch of little daggers sunk into my arm.

"The other one escaped into a rock pile. I crawled under a boulder after it. Clint stayed up on top. He moves a small rock, and the rock growls. Clint sees a tail and grabs it. The kits were brother and sister. We named the male Popov and the female Nadia after an old girlfriend [*not her real name*] who smelled really bad. It was a wild day, a totally miraculous day. Both of them lived through the duration of the study. After they became independent of their mother in the fall, they'd be with each other for a while, then go separate ways, get back together, split up again. And then I'd find one or the other with Socks. I even saw Popov, Socks, and Socks's daughter 203, who was by that time becoming a two-year-old, traveling in a group – three generations of a family. After 203 left, Socks and Popov went 35 miles and met up with Nadia."

<hr>

So picture Copeland out to understand wild wolverines by trying to follow them through territories of as much as 200 square miles for females and 400 square miles for males. He was discovering extraordinary behavior, but his glimpses of it were brief and mostly through an airplane window. The rest had to be extrapolated from distant radio locations, and many an Idaho mountain and river valley stood between him and the next scrap of information about any one of his subjects. He eventually expanded the study to take in approximately 3,500 square miles. Yet even that vast countryside held only 50 or 60 adults, each one traveling without letup, often quite far. For example: Socks and the female that gave birth to Popov and Nadia had produced a son two years earlier. About the time of his second birthday, this male left the Stanley area, went to the confluence of the Lochsa and Selway rivers, and was back 13 days later, having completed a round trip of 220 miles.

There are, however, other routes to knowing a species. Peter Krott, an Austrian-born naturalist, raised some 30 young wolverines at his home in Finland over the years. Many were allowed to roam the household and interact with his young children. He wrote about his family's life with the animals in magazines and books. One volume, *Demon of the North*, published in 1959, includes the saga of a young female that left for the wild and then returned, as he saw it, seeking help. She had been traveling for three weeks through the winter woods on three legs. The fourth had a trap clamped onto it. She came carrying the steel jaws in her mouth and collapsed on Krott's porch from exhaustion.

Written in a folksy style common to popular outdoor literature of the period, much of Krott's work is richly anecdotal and infused with emotional interpretations. Which is another way of saying it's not always easy to draw out biological facts from the wolverine dramas presented. Nevertheless, he was the very first to offer a fuller portrait of *gulos*, including descriptions not only of their tolerance for one another but also of what he took to be a capacity for affection. "Indeed," Krott wrote, "the bad name these animals enjoy rests not so much on the actual damage they inflict on man, but rather on the fact that they are so difficult to catch or kill; for we detest what we cannot subdue."

In addition to visiting Clint Long's animals at the Carcajou Research Center, Copeland developed a relationship with Dale Pedersen, a Northwest area businessman who also owned captive wolverines. Pedersen kept the majority in two large, carefully constructed outdoor compounds complete with boulders, ponds, and logs set at various angles. At any given time, there were nearly as many wolverines loping around those yards, splashing through pools, balancing along tree trunks and branches, digging among roots, and napping in cubbyholes, as existed in the entire Sawtooth National Forest.

Like Krott, both Long and Pedersen had become acquainted with a quite different beast from the one depicted in legend and lore. On breaks from fieldwork, Copeland was able to spend hours talking with those men while watching animals that would come trotting over to undertake their own studies of him. Then the wolverines would begin romping together, wrestling, and otherwise mingling right at his side. A number of them had favorite companions and finetuned their level of aggression even while scuffling and scrapping, so that they could continue interacting.

At some point when you're keeping close company with a creature, you're likely to begin projecting yourself into its skin. It's a natural tendency, but it needn't lead to the kind of anthropomorphism that converts animals into storybook characters with human personalities. It can be an experiment in which logic teams up with two other extraordinary human qualities, empathy and imagination, to try meeting the world with that creature's eyes, its feet, its urges, its perceived concerns. Our ancestors used this skill. Tribes around the globe still do, and so does every good pet owner at times. I wish field biologists felt more free to mentally pad around on all fours – practice a little identity transfer, a little rational shamanism – without fear of being criticized as having gone mushy in the brain.

"I started out with all the conventional views about this species that every other carnivore biologist had," Copeland told me. "Getting to know Clint and Dale gave me a whole different set of expectations." To spend time among their animals and go away thinking of wolverines as unrelievedly antisocial became almost impossible. That wolverines would have developed capacities such as he'd seen on display in captivity and yet have no purpose for them in natural settings defied logic. For Copeland, it became a matter of finding out when and in what form these behaviors appeared among wild populations, and he was already getting a few answers.

"Socks was a frightening presence in a trap. It was as if he was indignant about being caught. Outraged. He filled the air around him with his ferocity. He snarled and gave off guttural warble-growls, and he snorted. I don't think I've ever heard another wolverine snort like Socks did. You were aware that this is a different personality, and I'd better pay attention. Yet of all the animals, it was Socks who led the way to an epiphany about sociality in wild wolverines. All those years, everyone kept saying 'Adults are solitary. They only get together for long enough to have sex. If a male goes into a den, it's to steal the food there and eat the young.' And what do I find? Socks hanging out in a den with a female and her babies, telling us we're full of it.

"At scientific meetings, I'd sort of whisper, 'I think males might form long-term attachments to the females in their territories. I think they associate with those females and their offspring in the denning season. And it looks like they keep associating with their offspring as juveniles, at least now and then.' Geez, I felt like one of those talk radio guys promoting bizarre conspiracy rumors.

"But in the evening after a meeting, when the mustelid biologists were sitting around having beers, the stories would start to come out: 'Well, now that I think about it, I did see a pair of grown wolverines together outside the breeding season once,' or 'You know, I came on these tracks of a group of three full-size wolverines I never could figure out . . .' Even though the Scandinavians have found a lot more dens than we North Americans have and observed wolverines longer, they were sure that resident males went into dens and ate the kits. My friend Jens Persson studies wolverines in Sweden. For years, I kept telling him that something else was going on, and now he's starting to see it."

To be fair to Copeland's skeptics, the kind of joint custody arrangement he was describing – with young of both sexes leaving their mother at the age of around seven months, but then going on to spend some one-on-one time with Dad and also occasionally returning to reconnect with her – was virtually unheard of for mammals of any kind. And the last one anybody would expect to find practicing a complex family relationship was *Gulo gulo*. The old concept of a solitary North Woods devil had its teeth locked hard onto people's imagination. When researcher Audrey Magoun hung a photo on her wall that showed a female lying on her back and cupping two kits within her arms while she nursed them, people who saw it didn't believe a mother wolverine could be that tender. Some thought it must be a trick picture.

A male wolverine invests nigh-incalculable amounts of energy defending a huge territory and its food resources, keeping close track of the two or three females within it, and courting and mating with them. For him to do all this only to turn around and devour his offspring – his genetic legacy – doesn't seem like a plan nature would sign off on – any more than nature would design a female mammal too surly to apply every caregiving skill in her repertoire toward rearing the relatively small number of young she can produce in her lifetime. Biologists were confusing the resident male with neighboring or transient males, which may come in and kill the young in dens if the resident male dies or becomes unable to defend his territory. Insofar as the invader is eliminating a competitor's genes and stands to promote the eventual spread of his own, such a strategy does fit within nature's guidelines. Grizzlies, wolves, lions, and other top predators practice similar behavior. If that seems ruthless compared with the way we do things, you haven't been reading the chronicles of war, slavery, and infanticide better known as human history, which one sage aptly defined as the violent misuse of time.

◇◇◇◇◇◇◇◇◇◇◇◇◇◇◇◇◇◇◇◇◇◇◇◇◇◇◇◇◇◇◇◇◇◇

"Every wolverine field biologist in North America was at a furbearer symposium in 1995," Copeland said. "We got together – all five or six of us – and talked about how to raise research dollars ourselves instead of always relying on government funding. As an outgrowth of that, Clint Long and I started the Wolverine Foundation. My own Idaho project had run out of money by 1995. The foundation held a raffle in Boise and managed to raise enough for me to fly once a month and keep the study going into 1996.

"In midwinter, I learned Socks was dead. His remains, including the transmitter, were scattered. I never would have found the main part of his body if other wolverines hadn't dug it up out of the snow. It looked as though he had died sometime in the fall. Socks was ten to twelve years old, which is about the maximum for wolverines in the wild. The fact that he was lying a dozen miles beyond the limits of his territory would have seemed odd, except that this fit a pattern I'd begun to see. Wolverines approaching the end were going off somewhere else to die." Some probably had no choice, having been driven out as they became too feeble to defend their turf.

As a rule, state wildlife departments employ at least a score of game biologists to manage the relatively few types of animals that sportsmen hunt. One or two additional biologists oversee the thousands of native species, from bats to salamanders, lumped together with the somewhat dismissive title of "nongame." In 1996, Copeland became Idaho's first nongame field biologist. He made surveys of eagles, peregrine falcons, and trumpeter swans, looked into the distribution of rare reptiles and amphibians, gave talks to local nature clubs, taught field courses, and helped university students with research projects.

"An eclectic, interesting job," as Copeland phrased it. He made it more personally interesting by patching together a study of wolverines in the Teton Mountains. "Since there was no legal trapping of them in Idaho, they qualified as nongame rather than furbearers. A guy who owned a Teton ski hill offered logistical support. We had kids from the 4-H Club checking traps and a local veterinarian who volunteered to do the radio implants. We caught three wolverines and almost one grizzly bear. This wasn't intended to be big-time research. It was a great community project – good fellowship and curiosity leading to some more information, another piece of the puzzle. Folks raised enough money for me to fly and monitor our radioed animals through the winter of ninety-seven–ninety-eight."

In June of 2000, Copeland took a vacation to join Audrey Magoun and two young wolverines at a camp in the tundra of central Alaska. The kits had been born to captive Alaskan wolverines at Dale Pedersen's facility. Magoun took them to this remote spot in the Far North to observe their development in a natural environment. "They sure gave me more insight into a mother wolverine's responsibilities," Copeland said. "They'll run you ragged. You finally sit down, and you've got a wolverine chewing on your pack, squirming around in your lap, climbing up your back to chew on an ear. Then they're gone, nosing through the tundra tussocks and playing with each other. Just when you think they're perpetual motion machines, suddenly it's nap time. And I mean suddenly. One second they're going full tilt; the next, they lie down almost in midstep wherever they happen to be, like somebody hit an off switch. Pretty soon, though, they're up and racing around again. You're trying to keep pace, looking around at the country, and all at once there's a wolverine hanging off your fingertips with its teeth."

Magoun produced a delightful video, *Wandering With Wolverines*, from her experiment that summer. A viewer can't help but notice how quickly baby *gulos* become large *gulos*. This reflects a metabolic rate that, for the first few months, is off the charts compared with mammals of similar size. The video also offers constant proof that *gulos* grow up relating to almost everything with their nose and teeth. They see a stick on the ground, they sniff it and then bite it. What's that? A box someone set down? Sniff, snuffle, chomp. They scoot into the cooking tent, and they're up on the shelves going completely dental, even biting metal containers. A bush plane lands, they climb up onto the wing struts and start biting those.

Out on the tundra, with no new objects close by, they go back to nipping each other. They stayed with Magoun during long excursions, more or less. For every mile she walked, they must have covered three, bounding, probing, wrestling, and tumbling, overflowing with life energy. They're not perfect hiking companions, but nobody could ask for ones with more enthusiasm for being afoot.

Not long afterward, Copeland accepted an invitation to hire on with a team of federal scientists at the Missoula, Montana, laboratory of the Rocky Mountain Research Station (RMRS). A branch of the U.S. Forest Service, RMRS has labs scattered in a number of western states, and it is a leading force in studies of midsize forest carnivores. As a rule, wildlife research is not high on the Forest Service's list of priorities. The usual staff at a district office includes truckloads of foresters and engineers, focused chiefly on timber harvest and road building, and a single biologist. Support from higher levels of the agency for protecting imperiled species and other wildlife resources sometimes all but evaporates when a new, anti-environmental administration assumes office in Washington, D.C.

"The beauty of the research station," Copeland told me, "is that it was designed to remain fairly independent of political pressures. It creates autonomous think tanks in the field of natural resources. RMRS had just completed a successful national survey of lynx by doing noninvasive hair sampling. Now conservationists were pressuring the federal agencies to find out what shape wolverines were in. My assignment was to come up with a scent lure and a hair-collecting device for surveying them.

"A lot of people still assumed musk was the territorial marker for wolverines. We established that the marker was urine, which could also be an attractant. Trouble was, the samples we set out weren't drawing in other wolverines the way we expected. What were we missing? I spent a ton of time collecting wolverine pee at Dale Pedersen's place and working with RMRS specialists to analyze the chemical makeup."

Along the way, Copeland became an expert in all kinds of details that might make some aspiring naturalists switch to careers selling deodorizers. "What gives urine its smell as a marker aren't just the organic compounds in it but the way certain ones ferment after they soak into bark or soil," he noted. "Wolverines don't raise their leg when they urinate; they raise their tail. At marking sites like the base of a tree, I'd often find a disgusting-looking, greenish, gelatinous goo left close to the urine. This blob was like, I don't know, the world's worst bowel movement – something excreted by a sick animal. It comes from the anus, but it's so common, the wolverines can't all be having digestive problems. I must have stuck my nose down by fifty samples in the field. Nothing – the stuff's almost completely odorless . . . What is it? No one has figured it out. Our search for a scent lure that would work for a large-scale survey was fascinating, frustrating, and a failure."

In the meantime, Copeland and Mike Schwartz of RMRS started a wolverine study in the Lolo/Lochsa area on the Montana/Idaho border at the northern end of the Selway-Bitterroot Range. After laying out a gauntlet of wolverine traps for almost 40 miles along the Lochsa River, they caught only a couple of wolverines but a number of rare Western fishers. The Lochsa wolverine project morphed into a fisher study.

Around the same time, the state game department relayed news of quite a few lynx tracks being seen in the Pioneer Mountains of southwest Montana. The Missoula RMRS lab commenced a study there and discovered that most of the reported lynx tracks were misidentified wolverine tracks. As with the Lolo/Lochsa project, research on one midsize carnivore turned into research on another.

A young field biologist named Todd Ulizio got a series of log box traps up and running to catch wolverines and radio-track them through the winter. Copeland was slated to carry out summer surveys. As he continued struggling to devise a reliable method using scent lures and hair traps, the Pioneer project developed more serious complications. Ulizio was finding his box traps ringed with steel-jawed traps intended to catch and kill the wolverines. While some of the local trappers were just extra-eager to score a pelt, Ulizio felt that others, fired up by rumors that the study would lead to restrictions on trapping or snowmobiling, or both, appeared bent on sabotaging the project. He found evidence of a couple of wolverines learning to avoid the trapper's sets on their way in to raid his log box traps. But that was one of the few things Ulizio was able to learn. With half the animals he radioed being killed, RMRS had to fold up the project early.

⬦⬦⬦⬦⬦⬦⬦⬦⬦⬦⬦⬦⬦⬦⬦⬦⬦⬦⬦⬦⬦⬦⬦⬦⬦⬦

Copeland enjoyed the idea-factory atmosphere of RMRS. He found himself pondering questions about carnivore ecology and genetics in ways that hadn't occurred to him before. New theories about the long-term survival of metapopulations across large, often fragmented landscapes drew his attention. A metapopulation of a species consists of groups that are separated from each other but, like a network of villages, stay interconnected by movements such as migration or dispersal. He'd made the decision to devote his career specifically to understanding wolverines and helping them thrive while back in the Sawtooths, and he remained intent on living up to that promise. But how was he supposed to study *gulos* and apply new scientific thinking to the results when it was so hard to find a single viable population to work with?

A little north in Glacier, Rick Yates was skiing through the mountains winter after winter carrying out his midsize carnivore track surveys for the park. He became friends with Jason Wilmot and his wife Kate Richardson, who were caretaking the grand old Many Glacier Hotel for the winter. Richardson worked summers as a ranger. Wilmot had been on the park's trail crews and was headed for wildlife graduate school. They both spent much of the winter following wolverine tracks in the Many Glacier Valley and were impressed by the number of them. The National Park Service happened to be seeking proposals for natural resource studies at the time. With Yates advising, Wilmot wrote up a study plan for wolverines that won funding.

By the time the money finally made its way through government channels, however, Wilmot was in school on the East Coast, and Yates was off in far western Montana catching bears for a U.S. Fish and Wildlife Service research project. Lacking the in-house expertise to capture and radio-tag wolverines, Glacier Park turned to RMRS. Copeland became the principal investigator. He hired Yates as his field coordinator. Yates and Kate Richardson went into Many Glacier to prepare for the first winter trapping season. And the Glacier Wolverine Project was officially underway in 2002.

⬦⬦⬦⬦⬦⬦⬦⬦⬦⬦⬦⬦⬦⬦⬦⬦⬦⬦⬦⬦⬦⬦⬦⬦⬦⬦

Ever since he'd found Socks traveling with his daughter, Number 203, Copeland felt he'd been given a glimpse of behavior that called for a do-over of the traditional view of wild wolverines. Despite the evidence he'd gathered of adults associating with juveniles after they left their mother's full-time care, he hadn't been able to make the case for wolverine social relationships more fully. Too much hinged on a small sample of animals and particularly on one: Socks. Sure, this father could have been unusual in his altruism. But what about the adult male wolverine Todd Ulizio recorded traveling with a yearling male in the Pioneers? If these males were both exceptions to the rule, so be it. If they weren't, wildlife biologists were going to have to admit that the 21st century had arrived without them knowing what kind of animal a wolverine actually is.

"My hunch," Copeland said, "was that a resident male, his mates, and their offspring form a kinship group. As this social unit becomes established, things like pair-bonding and 'responsibility' come into play, not because wolverines are kindly critters, but because extended relationships help the species contend with a tough environment. They have survival value."

You can call hunches by a finer name – scientific hypotheses – if you like. They're still only guesses until you've gathered proof. Where better to search for it than in a national park, the gold standard of natural laboratories? Since no fur trapping is allowed, wolverines couldn't be taken even accidentally in Glacier by someone going after the pelts of other targets. Nor would the balance of carnivores and the animals they prey on and scavenge be affected by trapping and hunting, which are permitted nearly everywhere outside national parks, even in wildlife refuges and wilderness areas. For that matter, a number of Alaska's national parks permit trapping and hunting as well. Finding a listening post where you can hear what nature has to say without human interruption is far harder than most people suspect.

"Glacier gave me an opportunity to do something I'd never been able to do before and never may again: study a fairly robust, intact population in an undisturbed setting," Copeland concluded. "If we could capture and keep in contact with a major segment of that population – always a big if with *gulos* – we were going to crack a few mysteries." And, he hoped, change a few minds.

Several-week-old captive littermates. DANIEL J. COX

CHAPTER TWELVE

Growing Up *Gulo*, Part I
The Brothers

You have to do your own growing
no matter how tall your grandfather was.

ABRAHAM LINCOLN

"AN INSATIABLE NEED TO KEEP MOVING IS THE HALLMARK OF THE WOLVERINE," is how Copeland once put it. When radio signals show one staying around an area day after day, it might mean that the animal made a kill or discovered a large carcass. Even then, some wolverines pause only long enough to stuff themselves and cache the surplus before continuing on the rounds of their territory. Lingering can also be a sign of sickness or injury. About the only other factor that will keep a *gulo* on hold is pregnancy. When Copeland and Yates saw a female beginning to confine her travels in late winter – "localizing," they called it – they took it as evidence that she was preparing to den and give birth.

In February of 2005, F2 localized on Mount Allen at the upper edge of tree line above Cataract Creek which flows into the Grinnell Valley. High on the valley's opposite side, F4 localized a mile or so from a notch that she used for crossing over the Divide. During the first week of May, Copeland, Yates, Savage, Jason Wilmot, on break from graduate studies in wildlife, and another volunteer gathered in Many Glacier. They were making ready to visit both dens and try to implant the kits with radio transmitters.

The route the men took to F4's suspected site was long and hard; it crossed avalanche-prone slopes and required crampons, ice axes, and ropes on the upper reaches. Where radio locations for the female had promised an active den, they dug for hours at two different sites where tracks led to small openings and found only mountain goat remains cached in the snow. They widened the search, mindful of the sheer cliffs waiting below, but ran out of daylight and had to descend.

The next morning, the men departed the ranger cabin to try for F2's kits instead. Rain was falling without let-up. After slogging miles up the valley, they started climbing again, kicking their snowshoes into the steep hill and hoping, as the trees thinned out, that the whole sodden slope wouldn't begin to slide. Two thousand vertical feet later, the crew fanned out looking for the den entrance that Yates had located from the air a week earlier. At noon, they found it. Empty. F2 had moved to another site.

While scouting the ridge and the alpine basins behind it, they finally picked up her signal. It seemed to be coming from cliff bands farther up, so they continued climbing. Then they made out F2's dark form against the snow. She was still a mile distant and much higher up toward the very top of Mount Allen than they had thought. All at once, she started bounding down in the intruders' direction, a strong hint that they were somewhere near her young. "That dark body was coming toward us so fast, it was like watching a boulder roll downhill," Savage recalled. "I began to understand how wolverines could travel from one drainage to another as fast as they do." But F2 disappeared into a rock cleft, and they didn't catch sight of her again. Nor could they find any sign of her current den.

Copeland said, "We were completely beat by the time we snowshoed back home and started stringing up wet clothes all over the cabin to dry out. The next morning, it's still raining. My leg muscles are talking to me. I'm going to need a day before I'll be ready to crank out another trip after F2's kits. That goddam Dan says, 'I'm going up there.' You're what? 'I just feel like going for a ski in the rain,' he says. And Jason says, 'If you're going, I'm going.' God, what are these guys made of? Count me out. Rick decides not to go, either. When Rick doesn't want to go, you *know* it's a tough trip."

Savage and Wilmot, both on skis, retraced the previous day's route uphill and this time found fresh wolverine tracks near the suspected den area. They followed them to four holes dug into the snow and started shoveling. The first three holes yielded empty tunnels; the fourth hole, said Copeland, growled as soon as they stuck the shovel in. "They caught the kits, and Dan did the surgery on them. When they skied back and we found out how the day had gone, Rick and I were devastated that we'd missed out. We're worse than useless. We're the biggest candy-asses in the world! But of course we couldn't have asked for better news. We had two new young males on the air."

I missed out on everything about the formative months of those kits, M18 and M19, having been away on magazine assignments. By the time I caught up with them, it was nearly fall in the high country again. Yates had been tracking the brothers over summer as they roamed with F2. She often led them across Mount Allen and into a lush little bowl. Plump marmots and ground squirrels abounded among the natural herb gardens. Boulder piles and rock walls with crevices offered the kits safe hiding spots when F2 went off hunting other slopes. Yates scrabbled up there one afternoon seeking more details about the kinds of habitat and physical structures wolverines select for rendezvous sites. The signals of all three animals were coming from the same crack in the rocks. He made his way over and peeked in. F2 let out a snarl, and Yates was suddenly all done peeking.

Later in the year, he sighted M18 in a larger basin sprawled at the base of an amphitheater on Going-to-the-Sun Mountain. He lost sight of the young male but tracked him by radio to a saddle on the skyline. M18's signal became stationary. Yates was able to pinpoint the location: a small crevice beneath one of the rocks along a projecting cliff band. When he peered in, M18 snarled the way his mother had, and the biologist once again agreed with a wolverine that nothing good was going to come from poking his nose in any farther.

Based on what we'd learned the year before from F4's pair of male kits, M9 and M10, Yates and Copeland expected M18 and M19 to become independent of F2 sometime after the start of September. The scientists hoped to have someone monitoring the family's movements as often as possible to try to discover more about the nature of the separation process and subsequent behavior of the young. That sounded like a mission to me. I was finished with my other work and more than ready to be back rambling Glacier's autumn landscapes in a wolverine frame of mind.

∞∞∞∞∞∞∞∞∞∞∞∞∞∞∞∞∞∞∞∞∞∞

The following are field notes from that period when I concentrated on following F2 and her sons. I kept two types of daily logs. While hiking or skiing, I recorded radio-tracking data and other basic information in a pocket-sized notebook that I could quickly flip through for reference. During rest breaks and back at camp, I set down longer descriptions and impressions in a bound journal. Below, you'll find material from both logs in *italics*. I won't pretend that I haven't gussied up the raw passages a little bit here – fleshed out shorthand notations and rearranged some sentences to make the subject more intelligible. The paragraphs in between are my later summaries and interpretations.

9/8/05: Up Siyeh Creek and around Matahpi to the head of Baring Creek with Dave Murray. Mostly clear skies, temperatures in the 50s.

Murray says, "We're in amazing country, we've got the whole day ahead of us, and wolverines . . . just the idea of wolverines. Man!" It's a fine attitude to have, especially since we don't pick up the slightest signal anywhere. We watch mountain goats, bighorns, eagles, and white-tailed ptarmigan. On the upper scree slopes, the wind hits like a bullet train. We drop down out of it into the alpine meadows called Preston Park and rest among the season's last wildflowers. Within minutes, we're horizontal, snoozing like fat marmots in the afternoon sun. The huckleberries and serviceberries we pass in the lower meadows on our return hike are globes of wild candy.

9/9/05: F15 on the north side of Many Glacier Valley, early morning. The day's route is up Grinnell toward the main glacier. Light cloud cover, light wind, 50 to 60 degrees F. Mountain goats scattered across the side of Mount Grinnell and the lower contours of Angel Wing. Bighorn rams not far below the glacier. M18 and M19 transmitting from the heights of Cataract Creek Valley. From the way the signal strength keeps varying, the kits are moving about. Later, get cheeps from the mother as well as from both kits near Piegan Pass but rarely from all three at once. The family could be together among boulders and dips that temporarily block individual transmissions or spread out across varying slopes. Too distant to tell.

Audrey Magoun found captive wolverines already caching food and scent-marking by the age of three months. M18 and M19 seem to be spending less time staying hidden and more time out exploring and hunting around rendezvous sites. The older kits get, the more they need to practice for life on their own while waiting for Mom to return. If she returns. Does she just not do that one autumn day?

In the afternoon, one of the last hikers descending the trail from Grinnell Glacier comes holding a rock in each hand and banging them sharply together. I figure this must be a hastily improvised bear warning system. His eyes are not merely wide; they're enormous and darting around as if the place were crawling with ninja assassins. He describes encountering a band of bighorn rams near the glacier the way someone might tell of running into a street gang late at night in a bad part of town. Those Grinnell rams do include some big boys with stupendous full-curl horns and – being park sheep – show no particular fear of humans. Instead of giving way as he neared, they strolled over to inspect him. Unnerved, he scrambled on a detour, jumped back up onto the trail, rushed on around a bend to complete his escape, looked uphill, and saw a mother grizzly with a cub looking back down at him from, he said, 30 feet away.

I don't believe the man has been enjoying his outdoor experience. I'm not smirking, though. Being in the great bears' homeland is an existential commitment. You'd have to be a wolverine to say you aren't scared of grizzlies and mean it. There are no points for pretending to be brave in the wild, no points for faking anything out here. You can learn to be braver, but it's just as important to learn to be honest about what you are and are not ready for.

9/15/05: One to two feet of new snow on the heights, starting to melt back toward the peaks a bit. Cloudy, 40 degrees, and sprinkling rain. 09:18 hrs: Get M18 weakly up Grinnell. 11:12: Both brothers intermittently, nothing from Mom. 13:38: Light rain squalls continue, clouds gathering around the peaks. Sporadic signal from M19 near the top of Allen, no M18, no F2. 14:39: F2 at last, variable signal, occasionally strong, from the mountain's northwest side, no kits. 15:46: F2 and M18. 15:52: M18 gone. From 17:34 until 17:56, I have all three family members on the air, but along different bearings. If they are moving as a group, they must be spread out on different routes. The wind picks up as the sky clears slightly. 18:37: M19 and no one else. 19:17: No wolverines.

I'd say that the three of them still qualify as a family unit, though a rapidly loosening one. What can I prove? Not a thing from today's readings except that the mom and kits were all on the same part of this immense mountain at the same time for a while.

9/16/05: *Drizzling rain out east over the plains. The moist air beginning to condense on the Divide and spill down in slow-motion cloud falls. Across Josephine – up in her favorite bowl – F2 and both kits sending steady signals, all on identical compass headings. (UTM – Universal Transverse Mercator – coordinates: 0303948 East/5407083 North. Bearing: 170 degrees. Signal strength: Level 1 – very strong – for F2 and M19, Level 3 – average – for M18.) They stay close together from 12:37 until 13:58, when M19 moves off to the south. F2 and M18 follow, but not until 20 minutes later. At 14:48, I have the three wolverines together again, traveling up the side valley of Cataract Creek.*

My guess is that F2's family will cross from Cataract Creek into the Siyeh Creek Valley after first pausing around Piegan Pass, another favorite site. When you sit to rest there in warmer weather, marmots make themselves at home on your outstretched legs while they chew on shoe tops, pack straps – anything with salt soaked into it. There may be a few that haven't yet gone into their dens for the winter. If not, the wolverines may stop anyway and try to dig some out. Wolverines will tunnel down through more than a dozen feet of snow in midwinter to excavate hibernating marmots.

9/17/05: *No radioed wolverines up Grinnell, Cataract, or Siyeh. Just gale-force winds and rain coming sideways.*

9/20/05: *Clear. Frosted last night. Driving over the Divide from the west side, I pick up F4's beeps near Logan Pass. On to Many Glacier in search of kits. A few faint cheeps from M19 somewhere on Mount Allen. An hour later, F2's signal strong from fairly low on Allen's slopes, down in the old-growth spruce forest perhaps. But no kits. I have her on the receiver a couple more times during the afternoon, then nobody for nearly two hours. 17:52: Signals from F2 and M19, close together now, moving up Grinnell Valley. No hint of M18 all day.*

9/22/05: *AM – With Yates. Track signals of M1 and F4 not far from one another on the west side of Logan Pass. M1 crosses east through the pass, slipping by traffic and strollers in this busy tourist area. We stay to watch a sow grizzly and yearling cub in a hanging valley. They mosey through fall foliage picking berries until they plonk down on their rumps in a shallow stream – the headwaters of Logan Creek, one of the starting points for the Columbia River. Something purely wonderful about bear butts flavoring the mightiest of Northwest rivers at its origins while wolverines roam nearby. Yesterday, Yates found M19 in Lunch*

Creek, the first drainage east of the pass. No sign of M18.

PM – *In St. Mary's Valley. Sweep antenna toward incoming Otokomi drainage, the southeastern portion of F2's range. Get her signal strongly, M19's weakly, same bearing, possibly together. Still nothing from M18. Savage hikes toward valley's head today but reports no wolverines. We search other portions of St. Mary's. Nope. Nada.*

9/23/05: Around 40 degrees, overcast, occasional spot of sun. F15 somewhere above Apikuni Falls, Many Glacier. F4 has crossed from the west side of the Divide to the portion of her territory in the Grinnell Valley. She's near where the team went to look for her den in May. Drive around to St. Mary's Valley and pick up F2's signal toward Otokomi again. No kits.

9/24/05: Hike length of Otokomi Valley. F2 near intersection with canyon leading to Goat Lake. Signal strong but highly variable – moving. Monitor for half-hour beginning 11:15. No kits. M16 somewhere on south side Curly Bear, distant signal.

I think we've got a breakup underway this past week. To gather more proof, Savage and I cover as much of F2's territory as possible by car in early morning to search for cheeps from her and the kits, without success. As we drive, he tells me that he hiked back this summer to F2's denning area on Mount Allen, where he had implanted M18 and M19. He and Yates wanted to inspect the site after the melt. F2 had chosen to burrow down through the snow to where a large, weather-bleached whitebark pine lay on its side. The trunk was suspended several feet off the ground by its stout branches, like a backbone above a downward-curving array of ribs. She dug her horizontal tunnel and side chambers through the ready-made crawl space beneath the trunk, chewing wood here and there to enlarge the corridor and using the chips to line the chambers.

Savage and I talk about how often we take a compass bearing toward the point where a wolverine's signal seems strongest and then, squinting along the antenna's axis, find it pointing directly at a mountain goat. For the most part, this is probably sheer coincidence. Goats going about their lives on open cliff faces are the park's most conspicuous hoofed animals much of the year, and the wolverines here also show a strong preference for steep subalpine and alpine habitats. However, we can't dismiss the possibility that the *gulos* are going out of their way to check out goat bands and weigh opportunities: a kid separated from its mother, a member lagging behind, limping on a newly injured leg, a loner asleep on a ledge easily reached from above. The most obvious remains in the feeding chambers and latrine areas of F2's den were mountain goat hair, bones, hoofs, and horns.

Since we have no leads on the wolverines' whereabouts from our road tour, we'll just have to arbitrarily pick hiking routes and hope somebody gets lucky. Doc Savage will do the hard miles, going up the Siyeh Creek Valley and climbing

Den sites in Glacier were often associated with whitebark pine snags fallen among weather-stunted subalpine fir. The mother would tunnel through the snow taking advantage of the space beneath the trunk and branches. Due to a fungal disease and insect infestation, possibly accelerated by warming climatic conditions, whitebarks are dying out across much of the northern Rockies. RICK YATES

different directions from there to shoot (point the antenna) down into Cataract Creek and upper Grinnell, Boulder Creek, and finally Baring Creek. He'll be knee-deep in snow while covering the upper reaches. I'll hike Otokomi, the lower-elevation drainage east of Baring Creek.

Within the first mile, I pick up a faint signal from F2. Then nothing until I'm directly across from the steep-walled side-basin whose bottom is Goat Lake. All at once, her frequency comes booming in from every direction, and I haven't even attached the antenna to the receiver yet. I'm getting her with the antenna cable alone, which means she's almost within a stone's throw – or else perched up on some cupola-shaped part of the cliffs that concentrates her signal and bounces it my way as powerfully as if she were a hundred times closer.

No, she's got to be close, because the signal is moving quickly past me. I'm in a meadow created by an avalanche that came off Goat Mountain and crossed Otokomi Creek, leaving only a few busted tree trunks where thick forest had stood. Racing here and there to get a fix on F2, I keep thinking I'll see her at any moment trotting through the thimbleberry and false huckleberry brush. I live in the unrealistic expectation of observing wolverines, always forgetting, because they stand so large in my mind, that they can disappear behind a shrub two feet high. The signal moves down along the course of the creek, which has cut through a fracture zone in the rock to create a deep gorge. Then the cheeps fade, and she's gone.

To check for signals from the kits, I continue up the valley another five miles under partial clouds as the day warms to 60 degrees. The only people I meet are a Blackfeet man, his wife, and their young child on horseback. Yet the forest has a busy feel to it because squirrels are dashing everywhere in hyperactive fall mode, harvesting seed-bearing cones. The trail is littered with green tips of Douglas fir branches nipped off in the process. Townsend's solitaires take the lead where I walk through lightly wooded meadows. These mountain thrushes have a habit of flying from a perch in front of you, landing a couple hundred feet ahead, and repeating this behavior over and over. I like the illusion of traveling through the mountains with them as guides – partners in the business of keeping an eye on things.

For all the high miles he covered, Savage found one wolverine track. No signals. I have nothing to report on F2's family except her signal. Useful negative data: The absence of kits anywhere we searched within miles of F2 only bolsters the case for a breakup. I'm calling it a productive day, made better by the fact that while I was still fairly high in the Otokomi Valley, I took an antenna shot over the St. Mary's Valley and picked up M16 miles to the south on Curly Bear Mountain. A welcome bunch of cheeps, as this adult male hadn't been heard from for months. We might have found his signal a lot sooner by searching from an airplane, but Copeland and Yates have cut back sharply on flying to conserve the project's rapidly dwindling funds.

9/25/05: AM – On a hunch, I hike with Savage from the Many Glacier Valley up Canyon Creek toward wind-whipped Cracker Lake below the north face of Mount Siyeh. We get M18! Only two readings in 15 minutes before he vanishes, but it's the first sign of him in nine days.

Brilliant, russet-and-gold-leafed morning with a crisp northern wind. Pikas busy making hay, peeping at us where the path crosses boulderfields. Mountain goats look like they just came back from a shopping spree at the outdoor clothing store. After shedding their long, matted-down winter coats through summer, the climbers are all outfitted with spotless, puffy-looking new ones. Light up like lamps on the ledges whenever the sun breaks from behind the clouds. Fresh diggings all along the Canyon Creek trail, plus large, fresh piles of scat – roots, bulbs, berries, and rodent remains. We're on a grizzly bear freeway. Where it winds through dense forest, we pump up the volume of our conversations. I give my canister of red pepper repellent spray a friendly pat from time to time to check exactly where it is holstered on my belt.

PM – Returning toward our homes in the Flathead, Savage and I stop at Siyeh Bend, take a shot up the Siyeh Valley. Get M19's signal – directly in line with a big mountain goat billy on Matahpi. The kit is six miles from where we located his brother in Canyon Creek earlier. Not far by wolverine standards, even if you count all the cliffs and broken ridgelines in between. But far enough for us to be almost certain that these juveniles are operating separately from each other as well as from F2. At dusk, record the signals of M1 and F4 below Haystack Butte west of the Divide. Same bearings: Big Daddy and this girlfriend are traveling together.

Yates has also recorded M1 and F4 either together or quite close to one another for several days this fall. So even as we're documenting young wolverines becoming independent at the age of about seven months, we're accumulating evidence that a resident adult male will continue to associate at times with his mates outside both the summer breeding season and the late-winter denning season. He and those adult females seem to maintain long-term bonds; not a constant closeness by any means, but relationships that endure nonetheless, season after season, year after year. They seek each other out. They get along. Would it be going too far to say they like each other, wolverine-style?

9/28/05: M13 on Mount Cannon, overlooking the McDonald Creek Valley. F2 on west side of Going-to-the-Sun Mountain. No kit signals. Mountain bluebirds migrating in large flocks through Logan Pass against a bullying wind.

Savage told me that when he spays dogs in his veterinary practice, he holds them overnight after the operation and urges the owners to then keep them confined for a week. After he began working on the project and releasing wolverines within hours of completing surgery on them, he kept half-expecting a telephone call telling him that a serious problem had developed. A couple days after he stuck a radio in M13 at the Two Medicine Valley trap site, this yearling male wolverine was located near Avalanche Lake, next to Mount Cannon, which meant he had covered 23 miles across steep terrain through deep winter snow. "Until that happened," he said, "I still didn't have an appreciation for what these animals were. There's tough, and then there's wolverine." Now 19 months of age, M13 is already roaming a tremendous area that doesn't seem to be claimed by any known adult male. If he's able to defend this territory, he's going to rule several hundred square miles south of M1.

10/5/05: *Many Glacier, high haze, sun on an inch or two of softening snow. Sow grizzly and two cubs of the year on Altyn's lower slopes. Black bear and cubs of the year surprisingly close by. Moose bedded with snow on its huge antlers at edge of Swiftcurrent Lake. Lone adult grizz just above trail to Grinnell Glacier in blind corner section. Cow and calf moose at Fishercap Lake in Swiftcurrent Valley. Two cow elk, 200 yards away from moose. Two sets of sparring bull elk, St. Mary's Valley. Scores of other elk grazing around them on Two Dog Flats. Mountain goats wherever I stop and scan the cliffs. Bighorn sheep rams still in Grinnell; more than a hundred ewes and subadults on side of Altyn. Several mule deer in Many Glacier Valley bottom. Did I miss anything? Wolverines, but it would be pigheaded to complain about not finding something today.*

10/6/05: AM – *M18 up lower Canyon Creek*

PM – *M18 moving east onto side of Wynn Mountain and on toward Boulder Ridge. Same sow grizzly and cubs on Altyn.*

10/13/05: AM – *Leave early from Flathead with Savage. Logan Pass closed, so we drive the long way, circling south around the park to reach the east side. No signals.*

PM – *Dave Murray and I wander up the highway toward Logan Pass from the east and get M13 on Heavy Runner Mountain. F2's signal is bouncing around in the Siyeh Creek Valley. We're not going to try to narrow down the direction. Snow squalls are ballooning outward from the high passes, while heavy rain down below threatens to soak the radio receiver's circuits. No kits.*

◇◇◇◇◇◇◇◇◇◇◇◇◇◇◇◇◇◇◇◇◇◇◇◇◇◇◇

A week ago, Savage and Yates hiked up Boulder Ridge watching large herds of elk in the Boulder Valley below. Their destination was the east face of Wynn, where they would more carefully measure and describe F2's natal den from 2003. There, too, they found she had chosen to tunnel through the framework of a fallen whitebark pine at tree line. The den would have been about 10 feet deep in the snow, and it ran horizontally beneath the trunk for about 45 feet. She chewed a great deal of wood to make a soft base for the corridor and chambers. To Savage, "It looked like the decorative bark you buy for your garden." F4's natal den from 2004 and two nearby maternal dens, which I examined with Yates and Savage earlier this year, were all within the structure of fallen snags as well.

Whitebark pines, *Pinus albicaulis*, take 50 to 60 years to mature. For the next 250 to 300 years, they produce an abundance of large, tasty seeds. Rich in fats and oils, the pine nuts are a critical autumn food source for Clark's nutcrackers, red squirrels, grizzlies, and black bears. A wide range of other mountain birds and mammals make occasional meals of these seeds. (This includes wolverines, though those seen rummaging through the squirrels' large caches of seeds, hulls, and cone remains may have been equally interested in the squirrels themselves, which sometimes burrow in the middens.) Adapted to endure the extreme cold and deep snows of the subalpine zone, whitebarks have tough, twisted trunks specifically designed to withstand the battering mountain winds. Cavities in the wood become prime nesting sites for mountain bluebirds, northern flickers, and squirrels. The wolverine's use of this high-altitude conifer for denning is intriguing, not only as a newly discovered behavior but also because this link reveals how modern influences can affect *gulos* in more ways than anyone suspected.

To begin with, pine blister rust, an Asian fungus accidentally introduced to North America around 1900, is killing off the whitebarks in the Lower 48 wolverine range. Glacier Park suffers one of the highest rates of infection yet recorded, approaching 90 percent. The pathogen has a complex life cycle that involves currant bushes as additional hosts. Rising temperatures and heat stress may make both the pines and currants more susceptible to the disease.

In his spare time, Yates earned some extra money climbing the whitebark pines still alive in the park and collecting cones so that nurseries could grow new stock from the seeds. Perhaps seedlings that show resistance to the fungus can be used to help reestablish wild populations through a planting program. But rust fungus or no rust fungus, global warming threatens to eliminate whitebark pine stands anyway.

One of the main reasons whitebarks are tied to high elevations is that their seedlings can compete successfully with the dwarf subalpine fir and Engelman spruce at the uppermost limit of tree line. As average temperatures rise, however, the spruce and fir start growing taller, and forests of them advance upslope. Whitebarks won't be able to keep pace because it takes them so much longer to mature. Once they finally begin reproducing, their new seedlings, which do poorly in the shade, can't establish themselves where other conifers have already grown up to form a canopy of branches.

Climate change also appears to be behind the dramatic recent rise in infestations of Western forests by the mountain pine beetle. Warmer temperatures accelerate this insect's life cycle, allowing the beetle to multiply more rapidly than it could before. Whitebark pine is currently under heavy attack by this enemy as well as by the exotic fungus.

Captive siblings form a growly three-part ball, wrestling being a favorite way to relate during the early months of wolverine life. DALE PEDERSEN

Populations of Clark's nutcracker are declining because they rely so heavily on whitebark pine nuts. Ordinarily, each bird makes hundreds of caches of these seeds by burying them or tucking them into crevices. Like the pika, the nutcracker relies on its stored food to get through winter and the spring nesting season. Since not all the caches are recovered, some of the leftovers sprout to establish new whitebark groves. But diminishing numbers of nutcrackers lead to ever-fewer such accidental plantings, and the whitebark-nutcracker loop becomes a downward spiral. Webs within webs –the whitebark pine/blister rust/currant/pine beetle/greenhouse gas/rising temperature/shifting tree line/grizzly/nesting bluebird/nutcracker/denning mother wolverine connection underscores the saying that every part of an ecosystem is ultimately hitched to every other.

10/14/05: *M18 in Grinnell toward the base of Angel Wing.*

10/16/05: *Up Canyon Creek in windy rainstorm. No wolverines.*

10/17/05: *Wind clocked at 106 mph at Logan Pass.*

10/18/05: *Headed south by car, with stops to radio-scan followed by short hikes. The elusive M16 again, now near Amphitheater Mountain in the Cut Bank drainage. F17 on Appistoki Mountain in the Two Medicine drainage farther south. Weather deteriorating, Logan Pass closed for the year. Going home for a while.*

11/8/05: *Up McDonald Creek Valley from head of lake almost to Logan Creek. No wolverine signals.*

A sunny morning turns sullen and cold. I'm hiking through several inches of fresh snow on the Going-to-the-Sun Road, gated off for the season. I pass a number of deer, among them a rutting buck following a doe so intently he pays no heed to the fresh cougar tracks he steps over. Two returning hikers tell me they crossed grizzly tracks by Logan Creek. Farther on, I meet park biologist John Waller, also on his way out of the valley. He asks what my plan is. I tell him it's to keep walking upstream searching for wolverine signals until I run into that grizzly, at which point I intend to leave. Waller is the last person I see for miles. The clouds keep lowering, draining color out of the world.

What I told Waller wasn't a joke, as it happens. Not far from Logan Creek, a large, dark grizz emerges onto the road. I assume it's a male; it's a big bear, and nearly all the females and young are in their dens now. He's 150 yards ahead. Given the way he popped up from the steep bank of McDonald Creek, Mr. I-Can-Break-a-Moose's-Neck-With-a-Swat and I might have met all at once at extremely close quarters if I'd been hiking a tad faster. Though he turns and begins coming my way, Mr. I-Can-Also-Run-35-Miles-Per-Hour keeps his nose close to the ground and his speed to an amble. He shows no sign of being aware of me. The wind stays in my favor. I'm actually outpacing him as I head home, sticking to the side of the road so my silhouette blends with the dark trees.

11/9/05: F17 on ridge south of Appistoki near Glacier's southeastern corner.

11/10/05: F2 in Boulder Creek. F15 to north by Swiftcurrent Ridge. Both kits! M18 and M19 near mouth of Canyon Creek. Problem interpreting signals . . .

From a hill out on the Blackfeet Reservation, I have a straight shot with the antenna deep into the park's Boulder Creek drainage, and I get F2's signal coming out of it. After opening the locked gate across the Many Glacier road, I drive a short distance, stop and wave the antenna around again, and pick up F15. I'm on a roll today. Four miles farther, near Windy Creek, I have cheeps from each of F2's kits toward Canyon Creek, and the signals seem to be coming from the same location. Booyah! This is blockbuster news in our wolverine world. Nobody has picked up M19's signal for the last 45 days. The brothers went their separate ways more than a week before that. Now they're possibly together, and . . .

Hold on. Aw, no. M18's signal is pulsing at twice the normal rate. Aw hell no. That's the mortality signal. The implanted radios are programmed to start transmitting this way – double-time – when the animal has been motionless for a long period. But something's screwy, because the bearing I'm getting for M18 seems to keep changing. He can't be moving if he's dead, right? What if he's not traveling and it's just the signal bouncing around, and I'm picking it up most clearly first from one direction and then from another depending on how I hold the antenna?

At this distance, about two miles, we don't get a very precise fix anyway – plus or minus 5 compass degrees at best. It doesn't help that I have to lean into the wind in order to even stay upright. Normally, you can refine the accuracy of a reading a little by gradually turning down the volume on the receiver. Weaker signals keep dropping out until you can only detect those coming from the narrowest possible slice of the countryside. But as soon as I lower the volume more than halfway, all I can hear is wind hissing in my ears.

I drive to a point directly across from Canyon Creek. From here I can tell that the brothers are in among the broken contours of the canyon mouth, always a rough place to get a decent reading from. M19 is definitely moving around. M18? I just can't be sure. I want so badly for him to be alive that I know I'm biasing my own readings, taking any variation that I perceive in signal strength or direction as evidence that, yes, he's up on his feet and busy at something. I'm also pinning a lot of hope on a vague memory of Yates telling me that the implants sometimes switch into mortality mode solely because of faulty circuitry. I drive to the ranger station and telephone him. He and volunteer Alex Hasson are about 25 miles south at the Two Medicine Ranger Station moving a freezer to store bait and provisioning the cabin with winter supplies. Interpreting radio signals in rumpled mountain settings can be as much an art as a technical skill, and Yates is really good at it. I'm desperate for his advice. He tells me they'll drive up to meet me in a few hours and try to solve the puzzle.

"You say M19 is right there with M18?"

"Yeah, and M19's signal is normal. Varying strength, so he's active."

"You think he met up with his brother again and then killed him?"

"Cain and Abel? I have no idea what's going on. I can't eliminate the possibility that M18's signal is shifting around, too."

"Well, maybe M19 is carrying his brother on his shoulder, trying to get him to a hospital."

"You're a big help."

"Or packing him off to eat."

"Thanks. See you on the road later."

I stay another hour and fail to resolve a thing. The very fact that two young male wolverines have remained in one area for hours since I first caught their signals is unusual. I go for a hike through half a foot of slushy snow up the adjoining Grinnell Valley on the off-chance that I'll discover something there related to this mystery. But the place holds no radioed wolverines today.

I remember now: It was Savage who was traversing the slopes above Helen Lake in the Belly River drainage when he picked up a mortality signal from M3. This male's implant had stopped working earlier, but he was wearing a GPS collar with a VHF radio built into it, and that radio was telling Savage that M3 was a goner. The mountain goats on the headwall above strongly disagreed. "It was obvious that they were bothered by something," Savage said. "They were telling me that M3 was up there moving across the ledges. I kept checking the radio locations, and they were telling me the same thing: M3's location kept changing." The transmitter was on the fritz; M3 was healthy. The team captured him again several times in the years to come.

When I meet Yates and Hasson, we angle our antennas this way and that, huddle with our backs blocking the wind, and compare findings. In the end, Yates goes with the possibility that M18's radio is malfunctioning, because he, too, thinks the signal is moving in the canyon's mouth. If so, we've got two live, reunited brothers, and the only downside is that M18's battery will give out in half the time because it's powering twice as many cheeps per minute. My company leaves. I stay on until dark, which comes at 17:40 hours these days.

After dinner at the closed ranger station, our headquarters for another Many Glacier winter, I drive back out on the road and listen to the brothers' signals. Same results. Troubling. At least one of the males ought to be headed somewhere else by now. On my way back to the station, I count 80 head of elk crossing the road in my headlights near Windy Creek. Perhaps the brothers are dining on number 81, and that's what's holding them up there in the canyon's mouth. I'll have to keep an eye on the weather tonight. If the temperature drops and a storm moves in, I've got to run my car out past the gate so it doesn't get snowed in for the winter.

11/11/05: AM – *40-mile-per-hour wind driving waves of rain and sleet past. Slopes above the canyon's west side buried in clouds. 08:39: M19, same locale as yesterday, but can't pick up M18 from my first three stops. Now what? Continue farther east. From 09:05 on, get both brothers in Canyon Creek mouth. M18's signal still in mortality mode. Repeat readings from various sites for the next couple hours. No change. Uh-oh.*

PM – *Confirm M18 dead. Cause unclear. Possible predation. Possible fratricide. Collect body for autopsy.*

All through the morning of a new day, I'm going up and down my side of the valley trying different shots with the antenna, not liking the results. In this windstorm, readings aren't superprecise, but they all seem to agree that M18 hasn't moved. M19 is with M18 or very close. I call Yates and suggest he come for another look. I'll hike the trail around the head of Lake Sherburne to the mouth of Canyon Creek and try to pinpoint each brother's location. Yates should be the one to examine the site if it turns out to hold a body. He says he and Hasson will meet me on the trail in a few hours.

The hike is less than two miles. It's a slow trip, though, in a foot-deep mix of damp new snow atop slush. Canyon Creek cuts sharply through a benchland of old rubble deposited by floods over the centuries. I continue high atop the bench on one side, taking a bundle of readings as I go. According to my triangulations, M18 is across the stream course in a forest of young spruce. M19's signal is no longer coming from near his brother. He's some distance downhill toward Cracker Flats and moving fairly quickly through a mix of conifers, cottonwood, and aspen.

My teammates reach the canyon in the afternoon. We scramble upstream until Hasson scouts a place to cross by jumping from boulder to boulder. Leading the way up the cutbank on the opposite shore, Yates sweeps his antenna back and forth like a Geiger counter or metal detector. Within minutes of entering the forest, we have M18 in view. He's lying as if asleep on a bed of moss, forepaws tucked beneath him, rear legs splayed out, his body cold as the day.

Snow has accumulated to a depth of more than two feet in parts of these woods. But here in the bower where M18 rests, the young spruce grow so thickly that very little snow has sifted through their interlaced branches. Only a sprinkling of flakes covers the young wolverine's fur. No signs of a struggle or other intense activity disturb the skiff of snow around him. A coyote attracted by traces of blood on the forest floor has visited but left the body alone. About 50 feet out, I find fresh wolverine paw prints in the deeper snow. Presumably from M19, the tracks circle among those of deer, spruce grouse, and dozens upon dozens of squirrels. This continues to be the busiest squirrel autumn I can remember.

"Looks like they ganged up and killed him."

"Who killed him?"

"Squirrels. There's a billion of 'em here."

"Whatever got him didn't really tear him up that I can see," Yates says, running his hands through M18's coat. "I'm looking at one small hole – probably a tooth mark – on the side of his head. A tuft of fur over there by some blood. Not many clues to go on."

"I've got M19's signal coming in strong, still running around down below us," I tell the others. "Nobody else on the air."

"Until we do an autopsy, all I'm going to say is that some carnivore got him. Could have been a cougar or bear or a wolf, but I doubt it. They would have done more damage."

Hasson and I spread out farther to look for evidence of a fight in the surrounding forest but find nothing out of the ordinary. After taking photos and making a final inspection of the scene, Yates looks over M18 once more. The kit appears to have been healthy. His fur is long and plush. He is nearly full size, and his body feels reasonably filled out, definitely not emaciated.

"Hoofh! No, he's not too skinny," Hasson says as he places the carcass in his pack and hoists it onto his back. Moose, elk, and deer tracks have perforated most of the trail since we were on it. In no time, Yates and Hasson are far out in front of me. These are long-stride men. Ground-eaters – summiteers. I hear them chatting away as they hustle up a hill, oblivious to the fact that they're postholing through heavy, slurpy snow. I feel a little like the weenie in the scout troop, the one forever falling behind and panting, "Hey guys, wait up." The difference is that I fall behind quietly. There's no whining allowed at wolverine camp.

The next day, I meet Yates and Savage at the vet's clinic for the autopsy of M18. The body weighs 10.6 kilos – 23.3 pounds – a bit on the light side for a male of eight-plus months. But Savage can feel a fair amount of mesentery fat stored on the membranes supporting the stomach. It's a sign that the kit's overall condition at the time of death was reasonably good. Probing the head, Savage discovers more puncture marks, and feels loose bones beneath them. He X-rays the carcass. The film reveals cracked and crushed portions of the skull. Yates skins the body. Everything else looks OK, but we can now see four holes penetrating the braincase. We measure the distance between M18's upper canines – the fangs: 3.3 centimeters (1.3 inches), exactly the distance between the two most obvious holes. In other words, a predator with teeth just like M18's bit down on the top of his head with jaws as strong as his. Then, judging from the second set of holes, the predator did it again.

In court, the prosecutor would be asking: And whose teeth more closely match M18's than those of his brother, found lingering around the scene of the crime for two days? Let me remind you, members of the jury, that no other wolverine was recorded in the vicinity during that time. Quickly, the defense attorney would rise to object that the evidence against M19 was purely circumstantial; that for all we can tell, an unknown, unmarked wolverine did this. Or that the killer was M1's older son, M3, who is, if you'll pardon the expression your honor, a notorious badass. His territory runs very close to where the victim was discovered.

How do we know M18 wasn't attacked by him while exploring a bit north, and despite suffering mortal wounds to the head – you have all heard how fiercely wolverines cling to life, ladies and gentlemen – somehow staggered back to that strangely peaceful little grove in his family's homeland to lay himself down and rest? In closing, I would also ask the jury to consider the possibility that the Scandinavians are right about adult male wolverines killing their offspring after all. Perhaps M18 was met in Canyon Creek and slain (dramatic pause) . . . by his own father, M1.

Where, I wondered, had M19 been during the month and a half we couldn't find him? Why, if he killed M18, did he stick around so close to the body? He wasn't feeding on it. Could the death have resulted from an excited reunion in which a tussle got out of hand? All through the fall while keeping tabs on the breakup of F2 and the kits, I felt that we were making progress in uncovering the secrets of wolverines' lives. M18's fate is a harsh reminder of how little we truly understand about the animals. I can only look at the flayed corpse on the table – the one whose thyroid gland and heart and lungs all struck Savage as remarkable in their size and like a turbocharged engine in combination – and imagine the remarkable vitality that once defined this creature.

I picture him racing at F2's heels to keep up across featureless snowfields through May and June, then loping beside her over the rolling tundra uplands during midsummer. His was not a large figure. Even when nearly full size, it all but disappeared within the grandeur of the landscape where he was born. Yet he was proving to be a match for this realm. By mid-September, M18 was covering this country the way the rest of us yearn to, tirelessly, alone, and unafraid. More than unafraid – burning to see what lay over the next ridge. He made multiple ascents during ordinary journeys that we would need days to do and talk about for years. He was embarking on a life of wild intensity.

Then, for a few moments, all that he had become was not enough. Not quite. Not yet. He needed to be a twitch faster. Or an ounce stronger. Or more experienced, better at reading another's intentions. He wasn't, and it is over. And we may never know whether his brother was the murderer or in mourning or simply waiting there, uncomprehending, for M18 to get up and go with him for a run.

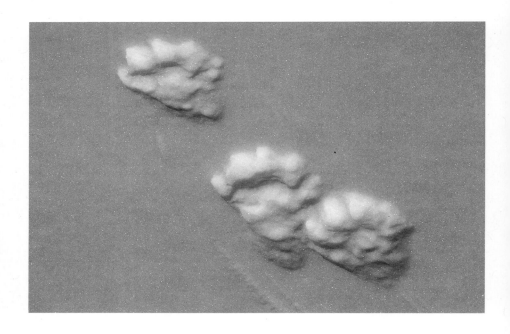

In powder conditions, winds can whisk away loose snow on the surface leaving crystals, compacted earlier by a wolverine's broad five-toed feet, higher than their surroundings. ALEX HASSON

CHAPTER THIRTEEN

Growing Up *Gulo*, Part II
The Sisters

When we reflect on this struggle [for existence], we may console
ourselves with the full belief that the war of nature is not incessant,
that no fear is felt, that death is generally prompt, and that the vigorous,
the healthy, and the happy survive and multiply.

CHARLES DARWIN
from *The Origin of Species*

IT WAS NOVEMBER OF 2005. I'D SEEN ANOTHER YEAR OF LIFE. Some of the wolverines hadn't. Both F2 and M19, her surviving son, divided much of their time between the adjoining Canyon Creek and Grinnell drainages. They moved separately but often used the same locale on the same day. Ordinarily, the territories of F2 and F4 split the Grinnell Valley more or less down the center. Both Yates and I had seen tracks of one female or the other go partway across and then turn back in the middle, as if she had detected the invisible boundary and beat a retreat. We knew F4 did trespass occasionally, because she was caught several times in the Josephine Lake trap, which stood on F2's side of the drainage. We discounted that as a result of an artificial temptation: the bait and hanging scent lure we placed there.

On the 17th of November, both M1 and F4, who had been traveling together in F4's territory, crossed the Grinnell Valley and went up onto the northwest flank of Mount Allen, well into F2's turf. M19 was also in that area at the time. On November 21st, I found M1 together with F2 instead. After moving around the base of Allen, the pair climbed to where I had located M1 and F4 four days earlier. M19 then joined his parents there. I hadn't recorded anything like this before.

Hiking up the forested slope to see what I could learn, I encountered tracks almost right away and felt sure they would lead to answers. They kept leading to more and more tracks. Soon, I was climbing among so many wolverine paw prints mixed with so many elk and bighorn sheep hoofprints that I may as well have been trying to decipher patterns in a crowded livestock pasture. I tromped through the deep, soft snow in every direction, ducking under spruce boughs and shoving through the alder brush growing from mountainside gullies. There had to be a carcass somewhere – a banquet to which all these *gulos* had invited themselves. But I never managed to sort out directions to the dining room.

Toward the end of November, the unusually mild, rainy autumn finally yielded to winter. Fresh snow fell and deepened. I moved from boot soles onto skis. That meant I had new sets of muscles to tune up and a brain that needed some retraining in the balancing-on-narrow-planks department before I could slide along concentrating fully on what was around me rather than on skiing. But once I got back into condition, the countryside opened up to me again.

The farther my daily travels extended, the more I began to realize how often the wolverines were doing what I was: following wolverine tracks. They weren't following other *gulos* indiscriminately. Predictably, they kept mostly to tracks of family members and mates. Sometimes M1 traipsed after his girlfriends, and if I read both the patterns in the snow and the radio signals correctly, sometimes they traipsed after him. M19, meanwhile, appeared to be tracking M1 and, especially, F2.

I don't know that any lingering desire for a parent's company motivated the kit to do this. As Copeland suspected in the case of the newly independent female in Idaho – Number 203, tracing the routes of her father, Socks – the chief virtue of following a parent is likely to be that it increases the chances of coming upon a good foraging area or a carcass – one the younger animal will be allowed to share rather than forced to fight for. I also came to appreciate how often coyotes shadowed wolverines, a relationship Yates had often mentioned to me before. Researchers in other parts of the Rockies have reported wolverines being tailed by foxes. Those canines, too, were improving their chances of finding a carcass.

The days grew colder, the snow drier and lighter. Under certain conditions, the crystals compressed by the weight of animals' feet remained in place while winds whisked away the loose uppermost layer of surrounding snow. I would set out after a blow to find all the tracks raised on pedestals, as if on special display. Even the delicate paw prints of voles and mice stood forth like meandering lines of tiny snow flowers.

I continued to regularly record M19 in the same part of F2's territory that she happened to be using at the time. In a few instances, their radio locations were so similar that I felt they were either together or else he was following within a few hundred feet of her. He seemed to favor the Canyon Creek drainage. More than once, I found his signal coming from the forest of small spruce where his brother had died.

On the 5th of January, I took a lengthy sequence of readings that showed M19 traveling in tandem with M1 across the head of the Grinnell Valley. Nine days after that, the son and both parents were all near one another on the side of Mount Allen. Because we had baited traps in the general vicinity, we could never be sure how much of what looked like sociability in that part of their range was a natural result of the wolverines seeking each other out as opposed to a consequence of them congregating near an artificial food source. Either way, these family members consistently tolerated each other in close proximity.

Copeland and others on the project team recorded M1 and M19 together for consecutive days later that January. No one was surprised, Copeland and Yates least of all, as they had previously tracked M1 traveling with his son, M3, when M3 was a yearling. Still, in light of the death of M18 in M1's territory, it seemed important to clarify through such sightings that M1 continued to accept the company of his juvenile male offspring rather than turn on them.

Savage skied in to join me at Many Glacier on January 14th. That night, we caught a lynx in the Swiftcurrent trap. We skied there and turned it loose and had no sooner returned to the ranger station than the signal for the Josephine trap went off. Along with the usual survival gear, we loaded the tarps, heater, medical supplies, and table Savage would require for surgery into the sled and took off.

It had been above freezing all day. The plunging nighttime temperature formed a strong crust atop the moist snow. Although Savage had already covered many miles on skis that day, he led the way for the last two-thirds of the trip to the trap site. I dragged our equipment in the path he broke, but the sled kept catching on the ragged edges of the crust. It made for a long, tiring haul in moonlight periodically blotted out by snow squalls. The hour was late when we arrived. Inside the trap waited . . . Ah! M19. This was our opportunity to remove his kit-size radio implant, which had limited battery life left, and replace it with an adult-size implant whose battery would keep the transmitter cheeping at us for the next two years or so.

For a trapped juvenile not quite a year old, M19 was exceptionally growly, promising to be a handful to immobilize. The weather was on the snarly side too, with blasts of snow swirling in off the lake. I had never seen Savage worn down before. He didn't quite look that way now, but he wasn't his usual vigorous self. "I don't feel on," he said, adding that he had reservations about operating on an animal when he wasn't energized and able to work quickly. Though he'd done implants in far worse conditions, he was inclined to leave M19 for the rest of the night. The likelihood of the yearling chewing his way out was small, since juveniles seldom attack the logs as determinedly as adults do.

To hear Savage speak forthrightly of his doubts only reassured me of his overall competence. Going against your instincts is almost always a poor choice in the backcountry. Far more than most people, Savage consciously practiced listening to what his body and his intuition had to tell him. They were saying to come back fully rested in the light of morning, and that is what the veterinarian did, performing the implant with his usual success.

On March 18th, 2006, when two locals skiing in for a visit stopped to watch a pair of coyotes on a talus slope toward the foot of Mount Altyn, a possible new element in the unsolved case of M18 came to light. Not far uphill from the coyotes, a wolverine was scavenging the bones of a small bighorn sheep carcass. If the coyotes' intention was to intimidate or distract the wolverine long enough to get a chance at the carcass themselves, they weren't even remotely successful. They were too busy picking escape routes when the wolverine walked down to confront them.

After hearing the visitors' account, I skied out to sweep the area with my antenna but couldn't pick up a signal from any of our study animals. Two days later, we had an unknown yearling male wolverine in the Boneyard trap, which wasn't far from the sheep carcass and little more than a mile from the mouth of Canyon Creek.

M19 happened to get caught again in the Josephine trap that same day. Since he had an adult radio implant now and it was working fine, the only action called for was to turn him loose. I volunteered to ski up and kiss him good-bye on the lips while Yates and Savage implanted the yearling wolverine at the Boneyard. As a result, I didn't get to spend much time directly observing the new animal. However, when I rejoined the others, they told me he was not unknown after all. This was M20, whom Yates and I had captured not long before at Fishercap and given a collar, which he had quickly lost.

I was able to follow the signal from his new implant the next day and found M20 looping south across the valley floor toward the mouth of Canyon Creek, where we had found M18's body. I couldn't help wondering if M20 had gone that way the second week of November and run into M18. After genetic analysis showed M20 to be M3's son by F15, I put M20 right next to M19 on the list of suspects in the killing.

◇◇◇◇◇◇◇◇◇◇◇◇◇◇◇◇◇◇◇◇◇◇◇◇◇◇◇◇◇◇◇◇◇◇◇◇◇◇

While most people seldom give a moment's thought to wolverines (apart from the indestructible hero of comic books and movies called Wolverine, who slashes villains with metal claws twice as long as steak knives), those of us on the project recognized that we probably thought about these animals a little too much. Our families and friends were very patient with us. Still, I had the feeling that they wished we would find something else to talk about more often, at least around home.

Hasson tried to give up the wolverine habit for a while. Implanting the animals with radios – or, as Copeland once described it, "this gruesome business of going into a national park, which is sacred ground, slicing wolverines open, and sticking gadgets in them" – got to Hasson. None of us felt that invading a creature that is the essence of wildness was justified strictly for the sake of science. On the other hand, implants had proved to be the most reliable means of obtaining information urgently needed for the sake of keeping this species from disappearing from the Lower 48 and elsewhere. Hasson understood this as well as anyone. Still, he said, he didn't have the heart for subjecting another wolverine to trapping, drugging, and surgery, and he left. Within a year, he was back with the team.

In pairs or small groups, we spoke of wolverines most of the day when afield, comparing notes, formulating new plans. In the stretched-out winter evenings at the cabins, we could finally relax and turn the conversation to any subject we wanted to talk about. And we would talk about wolverines. We puzzled over them night after night, no matter how long we'd been stationed somewhere. I could describe this as obsessive. It sounds nobler if I say we were enthralled. Everything we discovered about how high and steep and far and fast and relentlessly these creatures traveled was better than any outdoor adventure we had carried off in our lives, better than any we hoped to achieve. Better than most anything we had heard or read about.

To get from point A to point B, wolverines were as likely to go up the stone face of a peak and down an avalanche chute on the other side as they were to take a slightly longer but far gentler and safer route around the mountain's base. As we batted possible explanations back and forth one evening, Savage said he thought wolverines basically treated the spectacular topography as if it were flat. I remembered his comment because that was more or less how I would have described Savage's own approach to hiking these mountains.

Though we didn't know it at the time, Copeland was on the verge of proving Savage's theory essentially correct. In mapping out locations collected by the GPS collars that had briefly stayed on a few of our study animals, Copeland saw that the wolverines moved at about the same steady pace – 2 to 2.5 miles per hour – whether they were loping through a valley bottom or scaling the cliffy side of a massif. The key, Copeland found through further analysis, was that, with the exception of travels via a few spectacular drops routinely used as shortcuts and of the occasional jaunt to a summit, our *gulos* were expert at picking out the gentlest portions of steep areas for their actual paths. For them, route finding wasn't an issue of boldness and skill but a bottom-line business of energetics. The challenge lay in making it over the mountain – and then the next mountain, then the next – while getting the best mileage out of a tank of goat haunch or ground squirrel chunks.

We were chronicling the lives of some of the world's leading alpinists and adventurers. They happened to have four legs and fangs. Our team's attention hung on the latest tracks and cheeps from *gulos* the way other people devour gossip about celebrities. We wanted to know everything about these lives we admired. Yet we only had a few real facts in hand so far, and that was the other reason we talked endlessly about wolverines: Every aspect of their ecology and behavior begged for a more complete explanation. Careful analysis was clearly the best way to try putting the pieces together. But when you don't have many pieces to work with, it's fair to give wild speculation a try now and then. Contemplating wolverines was a journey through an open frontier.

In its fourth year that winter of 2005/2006, the Glacier Wolverine Project had been monitoring a greater number of known individuals more closely and continuously in an undisturbed natural setting than any wolverine study had before. We knew only too well how many hours and miles went into acquiring a single, solid piece of information. At the same time, we knew the project had reached a stage where each fresh bit of news about an animal generated more layers of information when put into the context of what we had previously learned, not only about that individual but also about its family, close neighbors, and other wolverines in the park. With this value-added factor building by the week, we felt that extraordinary opportunities for gaining insight into the nature of *Gulo gulo* lay within reach – if we could only make sense of a few more clues.

◇◇◇◇◇◇◇◇◇◇◇◇◇◇◇◇◇◇◇◇◇◇◇◇◇◇◇◇◇◇◇◇◇◇◇◇◇

I didn't become absorbed in M18's fate because I like the drama of murder mysteries. I was intrigued because one of the most obvious questions you need to answer if you're trying to secure a future for a species in decline is what the animals die from. Copeland could use the data we did have for M18 in calculations of birth rates and survival rates. These were valuable statistics for projecting whether a population was going up or down or staying even. But they didn't have much to say about the underlying causes. By contrast, an answer to the question of whether M18 had fallen victim to a member of his immediate family or to some other wolverine might help answer larger questions about the competitive pressures young animals face during their first year of life and the total number of wolverines that can coexist in a given landscape.

By one means or another – long hours of grunt work, the amassing of data, creative theorizing, and just lucking into a few of the right places at revealing times – the project was yielding results at a faster pace than ever. It was also going broke. As Yates and I were closing down the traps in Many Glacier so we could take a break for the Christmas holiday, he had told me, "Shut 'em tight. When we come back, it may be to take them down for good."

"It's that bad?"

"Right now, we've got about enough money left for us all to get together over dinner, shake hands, and say it was fun while it lasted."

The original grant from the Park Service was for three years of research. Of course the biologists were grateful to have had support for that long, but it wasn't nearly enough time to learn much about animals as elusive as wolverines. As the funding began to run out, Copeland kept the project alive with modest grants from various foundations. Inevitably, the coffers ran low again – too low to cover running expenses plus new radios, not to mention GPS collars at $3,000 each.

Unasked, several of us expanded our volunteer duties to include hitting up people for money. The job was beyond our pay grade, but it wasn't as hard as we expected. For instance, someone Savage had known for years – a sweet, gracious, elderly lady who was probably the least wolverine-like human alive – came forward on her own to donate $10,000. Her goodwill carried us through a critical period that winter.

I've been around biology projects most of my life. All but a few were chronically short of cash and searching for enough to carry on. I'm not complaining about the fact that we were in the same boat. I merely wanted to point out that for the next two years, no one could have accused us of constantly talking about wolverines. At least a third of our down time at field camps was now devoted to strategizing about dollars.

Through March and April of 2006, when I found F2 localizing on Mount Allen's north side in the hanging valley that held Snow Moon and Falling Leaf lakes, Yates and I had a difference of opinion. Having seen other females localize during late winter, apparently without having young, he thought that they might be motivated by seasonal hormones to practice this behavior whether they were pregnant or not. F2 had given birth to M18 and M19 just the winter before. Studies of captive wolverines showed that while some females were capable of having kits annually if fed extra rations, those on a regular diet produced young only every other year, and this looked to be the typical pattern in the wild according to other studies.

I drew on the same research results to argue that F2 was up there nursing a new set of kits because she *had* been given extra food: our trap bait. In addition to being an experienced hunter and scavenger, she was as clever as always at raiding the log box at Josephine. We knew of at least three recent visits during which she gnawed away the bait without tugging hard enough to trip the trigger. Aside from that, the reason I believed she had kits was that . . . well, I was really rooting for her to. The more wolverines the better.

Both M1 and his son M19 spent time in and around the hanging valley where F2 was staying. I'm fairly sure M1 visited the den, though I couldn't prove it since I didn't know the den's exact coordinates. I also picked up M19's signal from that site one day in April while F2 was away hunting. Fair or not, he was still a key suspect in his brother's death, and I have to confess that a vision of him devouring the helpless kits flickered through my mind. It wasn't a pleasant thought. On the other hand, if my goal was to ever see wolverines clearly, I needed to stay as wary of romanticizing them as of believing any of the sour assumptions made about them by earlier generations.

By late April, in view of F2's continued loyalty to the Snow Moon/Falling Leaf area, Yates was coming around to my point of view that she had given birth. At the start of May, he was downright eager to prove me right. With others on the team, he had just carried out a long, fruitless expedition across the high country on the Divide's western face to F4's natal den and excavated the snow tunnel system without ever finding her kits. F2 had become the project's best hope that year for gathering more information about the behavior and survival of young by putting some on the air.

She didn't disappoint. Members of the team found her den right away after climbing up into the hanging valley. A set of grizzly tracks led right past the entrance hole and on to a mountain goat head that F2 had cached nearby to snack on. Savage implanted two more of her kits. This time they were both females, F21 and F22.

In June, I heard signals from F2 and these daughters toward the head of Canyon Creek. Before I got close, she had left and stashed the kits at a rendezvous site within the uppermost copse of krummholz fir on a cliff face. The trunks and branches of the stunted trees were so dense and tangled, it was as though the youngsters were in the tunnels of a living cave. Some days, I wormed into the same kind of crannies for respite from the high-country wind. That day, I went only far enough to be able to tell Yates roughly where the kits were hidden so that he could come later to map and measure the characteristics of the spot.

Three days later, the mother and young were below Piegan Pass. There, she left the kits in a copse of krummholz with dead, weather-bleached whitebark pines towering overhead. July 11th, on my way back from Waterton Lakes National Park, Glacier's sister reserve in Canada, I caught faint, distant signals from her now 16-month-old son, M19, who hadn't been found on the air for some time. He was somewhere around East Flattop Mountain toward the easternmost edge of the territories of F2 and M1.

I left for work the rest of the summer and upon my return in early September learned that F21 was dead. An early snowstorm had swept through the high country, and she had apparently slipped while crossing a cliff face on Piegan Mountain. Perhaps over the summer of her brief youth, she had forgotten how slick a fresh rime of snow and ice on the rocks could be. She tumbled a long distance and smashed onto the ledges below.

Spidering along handhold by handhold, Yates could barely get to the body, which lay just above a deep *bergschrund* – the cleft where an icefield melts back from a rock wall. He found F2's tracks leading to a nearby section. She had etched scratch marks into the stone trying in vain to climb to her fallen daughter from one side. "I had all I could do to keep from falling myself," Yates said later. "But I'll tell you, seeing those claw marks, I just about broke down and cried."

Other commitments kept me from following F2 and her remaining kit as closely as I had monitored F2 and her sons the fall before. In fact, when I finally

The final resting place of the 6-month-old kit F21, who slipped crossing the cliffy side of Piegan Mountain and tumbled to her death at the edge of a snowfield. RICK YATES

freed myself to go look for the mother and daughter later in September, I thought the breakup might have already occurred. F2 was by herself in the Baring Creek drainage between Siyeh and Otokomi. Her signal was coming from the outer rim of the hanging valley carved by Sexton Glacier. Apart from two dozen mountain goats spread along the cliffs, this 25-pound carnivore was the only mammal I was aware of in all the miles and the thousands of vertical feet my eyes took in that day. I knew that was how it was for wolverines most of the time, how it worked out best for them: one per universe of stunted conifer forests and stone escarpments, blue glacial ice and waterfalls, turquoise tarns, and tan expanses of talus. Yet for some reason that day, I wondered if F2 felt lonely.

On the 9th of October, while Savage and I were radio-tracking on the park's east side, he related a story he'd heard from a man on the Glacier Park Trail crew. The guy saw a wolverine looking down from high on some cliffs near Jackson Glacier. Then he noticed a marmot sunning itself on a rock below. There was no tall vegetation between the two animals, no jumbled topography for concealment, either. The wolverine just bolted down the cliff face for 50 feet, sometimes diagonally, sometimes vertically, airborne much of the time, took a final leap of about 10 feet, and nailed the marmot. Though the trail crew guy was a rock jock – a serious climber himself – he was flabbergasted, unable to imagine moves like that.

Neither Savage nor I heard a cheep from F2 or F22 during that outing. Two weeks later, I found F22 in her birthplace, the Snow Moon/Falling Leaf hanging valley, together with her mom. Daughter in tow, F2 scaled the valley's headwall and crossed into the Grinnell drainage through a notch in the shoulder of Mount Allen. Extremely steep on both sides, the notch was the apex of one of those shortest-way-from-point-A-to-B/mountains-feel-like-flatlands-to-me wolverine itineraries. Like the rest of the countryside, it lay under a fresh, slippery blanket of white. I had to remember that this snowy route, which seemed so high and exposed and daunting to me, was a familiar neighborhood path to these animals. F2 had followed it winter and summer since I first got to know her. Where I pictured myself executing an exhausting series of braces and balancing moves over long distances, both up and down, the wolverines were walking a few blocks over to a grocery store.

On that particular afternoon, the trip led to F2's favorite bowl above Lake Josephine, the one well-stocked with plump rodents. Now in hibernation, they were tucked in underground dens, immobile, their body temperature only a few degrees above freezing – meat packets just waiting to be dug out of storage as far as the wolverines were concerned.

Hiking with three companions up the Grinnell Glacier trail, I took regular shots over the valley with my antenna. At a point above the head of Josephine, we stopped because F2 and F22 had dropped down from the bowl and were now moving in the forest below us. Mom was in the lead, daughter some distance back. From their signals, they seemed to be trotting directly our way, using the boardwalk built over the lake's marshy inlet. But, possibly because they smelled us, they abruptly began backtracking and headed up the trail into the Cataract Creek Valley.

We did the same. My companions were excited and kept breaking into a trot. They seemed to think that through the magic of radio telemetry, I would sooner or later be able to point out one of the wolverines up on a slope. How I wished. About a mile on, I noticed where mother and daughter, who'd been strolling the boardwalk earlier, had added a short side trip to a wooden viewing platform overlooking Hidden Falls. From what I could tell by the paw prints, the pair had stood at the outer edge facing the sight and sound of the plunging water, as if absorbing the scene. Toothy tourists. Then they returned to the main trail and resumed their travels up-valley.

I informed the others that the family's usual pattern was to carry on straight to Piegan Pass and over into the Siyeh Creek drainage, that there was two to three feet of snow at the higher elevations, and that if we went postholing through that, we would just keep falling farther behind and end up being cold, unhappy people floundering in the dark. My friends said, "OK, we'll go around to Siyeh tomorrow and watch them." I didn't play up the fact that the pair was likely to have loped into any of half a dozen other drainages by then or that even if I picked up the wolverines' signals in Siyeh, the odds of seeing the animals would be as slim as ever. Siyeh is an enormous place.

The next day was freezing, with a cloud fall spilling east over the Divide. From the road at Siyeh Bend, I got F2's signal; she was on the move. I was still trying to fix a location when one of my companions, whose expectations had seemed so unrealistic, hollered that he saw her. I swung my binoculars toward where he was pointing and caught sight of her bounding through snow higher than her shoulders. She was crossing the western face of Going-to-the-Sun Mountain where the highest-elevation copses of krummholz petered out and were replaced by talus and cliffs. I set up a telescope and saw that F2 was traveling in a path plowed by some other animal, whether another wolverine or a hoofed animal, I couldn't tell from that distance. She continued leaping through the powdery snow for almost half a mile, paused at a small clump of fir on the otherwise open slope, and vanished into it.

I retraced her route through my telescope and found F22 lunging along the path a third of a mile behind. She reunited with F2 at the fir clump. Ten minutes later, the mother bounded on to the southwest corner of the mountain. There, she paused, sniffed the air, and dove straight down some cliff bands. She dropped about 20 feet in three leaps that sprayed snow in every direction and disappeared into the old-growth forest. Whaugh! What it must be like to travel that way, going effortlessly vertical with four wide paws and powder snow for a cushion. Two minutes later, F22 flew down the same block of stone.

After some time spent imagining what wolverines could do on snowboards, I scribbled down my observations and moved to another spot to take radio readings. F2 and F22 remained in the forest. I made my way to that side of the drainage and started climbing in their direction among the giant, old trees. The understory was pocked with deer tracks and bigger hoofprints from a fairly large band of elk. The wolverines stayed together in the woods another hour, at which point I decided to descend rather than go closer and possibly disturb them. It was now five weeks later in the fall than it had been when M18 and M19 split off from F2 the year before. Possibly – in the case of female kits, anyway – there wasn't always a distinct breakup of mother and young. With these two, it looked more like a case of the mother simply going about her daily business, and if the daughter still wanted to come along and could keep up, fine.

Yates and I spent the morning of the second day of November chopping and stacking another winter's supply of firewood at an east-side cabin and then drove up the Going-to-the-Sun Road – gated for the season now – to listen for signals. A short distance beyond Siyeh Bend, we found two sets of full-size tracks on the snow-covered road. While they could have been the tracks of F2 and Big Daddy, they could also have been left by her and her daughter, since F22 was as large as an adult by now or very close to it. We didn't know of any other wolverines likely to have been using the area, much less any pair likely to be socializing within F2's territory.

Yates told me the details of a trip earlier that fall. He said he had climbed up the Two Dog Creek drainage between Otokomi and East Flattop, the mountain where M19 appeared to be located when I last heard from him back in July. Yates went because he'd picked up the male's signal once more after a long period of silence, but this time it was a mortality signal. Another young wolverine gone. Yates never found the body. Like that of the male kit M10, it must have been dragged off and strewn about. Or maybe carried off in pieces by a golden eagle; a pair had nested less than a mile away. Only the radio in its implant capsule was left, and even that had been gnawed on.

From there, Yates continued uphill to analyze a rendezvous site that Savage had pinned down during summer while tracking the signals of F21 and F22. The sisters were holed up together in a krummholz patch on a 60-degree slope with cliff bands above and below. Yates couldn't get to the spot without a rope. The last set of ledges between him and the stunted trees was too steep, the scree collected on them too slidey and covered in ice, and the view past his feet too dizzying – about a thousand feet straight down.

Backtracking, Yates was starting to notice elk tracks all over the slope when a mountain lion leaped out from the brush a hundred yards downhill and took off. This was – had been – the young wolverines' world: Big drop-offs. Big, meaty food on the hoof. Big, agile, rock-climbing predators contending for meals and territory. Applying every bit of skill you were born with plus every habit and technique you picked up from tagging along with your mother – and later your father at times – might just keep you in the game. No guarantees. Not ever, not here.

◇◇◇◇◇◇◇◇◇◇◇◇◇◇◇◇◇◇◇◇◇◇◇◇◇◇◇◇◇◇◇◇

Yates last located F22 the following summer at Piegan Pass – Marmot City – the general area where her sister had been lost. Whether F22's implant soon quit or she dispersed from the park out of radio range is anyone's guess. We know only that we never found her again. F7, F2's daughter born in 2003, is alive and producing young of her own in a territory that encompasses Logan Pass, Mount Cannon, Avalanche Lake, and Sperry Glacier – a collection of some of the prettiest settings Mother Earth has ever raised skyward. F7's implant battery gave out some time ago. But people have seen her and photographed her. She is readily identifiable by a gaping tear on her upper lip that left several teeth permanently exposed. Did she, too, tangle with another wolverine? A mountain lion? A grizzly bear over a carcass? Like the saying goes, if figuring out this stuff was easier, somebody would already have done it. And speculating about wolverine mysteries late into the night around a cabin stove wouldn't be nearly as much fun. We felt in no danger of that happening.

Man meets wolverine. The wolverines at Dale Pedersen's captive facility often follow him around the large compound and accept chin scratches and tummy rubs. DOUG CHADWICK

CHAPTER FOURTEEN

Wolverines From a Recliner

A man cried: O Heavenly Spirit, speak to me that I may know You exist and care for my fate. And a sparrow appeared on a nearby branch, singing its heart out.

The man didn't understand. O Creator, he cried again, let me hear your voice.

And in front of the man's face, a bee buzzed past bearing pollen from flower to flower. A butterfly followed, floating on rainbow wings to sip nectar.

Still the man did not understand. Instead, he called more loudly yet: O Maker of All That Is, if You won't speak to me, let me feel Your touch just once, I pray.

The Creator touched him. As the wolverine that had just bit the man on the ass loped away, the man shook his fist toward the sky, yelling: Now I am suffering because of a beast with a terrible nature. Why, oh why won't You ever give me a sign?

And the Creative Spirit sighed: I wish I had designed these hairless apes with more intelligence. But even I don't always get it right the first time.

- very loosely adapted from a homily I once read

WHEN I STARTED WITH THE GLACIER WOLVERINE PROJECT IN 2004, you could have taken everything I knew for sure about wolverines, wadded it into a ball, and tucked it inside your shoe right under the heel; you wouldn't have felt much difference hiking. I had thought that I knew some things about them – the usual: that they were skulking, antisocial, perpetually and dangerously pissed-off, et cetera – until a day in the early 1990s. I was in the Northwest visiting a compound where red wolves, a species native to the U.S. Southeast, were being bred to restore their critically endangered population. The biologist I was with asked, "Want to take a look at something really interesting?"

Well, seeing as how that's basically my profession, a defining trait of humankind, possibly the point of our existence, and that it didn't take us very long to look over the handfuls of red wolves left in the world, OK.

He led me to the edge of a different pen. The ground on the other side of the wire fence was mostly bare with a scattering of trees, logs, and rocks – and dozens of wolverines. They were ambling and loping about, clambering on the logs and branches like stocky monkeys or giant flesh-eating squirrels, rooting around in freshly dug dirt, mock wrestling, and tumbling together in multiwolverine heaps. Several took turns play chasing each other. One lazed on its back with its legs in the air, baby bear-style.

After a few minutes, the biologist asked if I wanted to go inside the enclosure. Still not quite able to believe what I was seeing – even in this artificial environment, a herd of lighthearted wolverines struck me as a complete oxymoron – I took a deep breath as another man let us through the gate and guided us in. Within seconds, a gang of the animals came hurrying toward us, bent on checking out this latest diversion in their confined world. More deep breaths. Our guide seemed relaxed. The biologist was trying to act that way. Standing out as the most nervous one in the group is never a good idea around carnivores of any kind, so I drew in the tentacles of my fear, stuffed them way down inside, and decided not to be scared.

I didn't register too much of what our guide was telling us at first, because I had wolverines investigating my ankles or standing on their hind legs to sniff higher – crotchward – like house dogs greeting a guest. No fear, no fear. I watched dumbfounded as the man squatted down and began to chuck some favorites under the chin and dole out tummy rubs. None of the animals acted aggressively toward any of us. The biologist and I wandered about for another 10 minutes before the other man and half a dozen wolverines escorted us to the exit.

That other man was Dale Pedersen. It would be a decade before I discovered his association with Jeff Copeland. During the brief time I'd spent with Pedersen, I learned only that he was fascinated by animals and kept several kinds on his large property. A private businessman who managed an assortment of enterprises, he enjoyed assisting scientists and zookeepers. He'd given the captive red wolf breeding program a boost by allowing the U.S. Fish & Wildlife Service to use his land and facilities for their work.

On separate acreage he owned somewhere over by the coast, you could find the bones of monsters sprawled like ancient ruins across a field. This was where researchers and museum workers sometimes brought carcasses of washed-up whales in order to render them and prepare the skeletons for exhibits, out of the public's sight and smell.

The wolverines, however, were Pedersen's. In addition to those roaming the pen we'd been in, he kept a couple dozen more in a second pen and segregated some breeding females in a third. Between the enclosures stood a long shed divided into cages, where he isolated a few females with newborns and also some individuals that proved unable to get along with others in the outdoor enclosures. Pedersen acquired his first wolverine from a zoo out of curiosity in 1983. Smitten, he placed advertisements for more in trappers' magazines. "Pretty soon, I have guys calling up and saying, 'If you don't buy this one I just caught, I'm going to kill it,'" he told me. "I never intended to get so many."

When I departed, I could say this about wolverines: The traditional lore that portrays them as not merely mean but amped-up demon nasty, like Beelzebub on crack, had to be either wrong or merely part of a larger and far more interesting picture. And that's about all I could say.

◇◇◇◇◇◇◇◇◇◇◇◇◇◇◇◇◇◇◇◇◇◇◇◇◇◇◇◇◇◇

By late spring of 2004, I'd had my first taste of checking on traps and skiing in search of radio signals with various members of the wolverine team. I'd listened to spellbinding descriptions of what certain tagged animals had done and listened carefully as the crew debated what the latest sets of data were telling them about the species' natural history. The information kept piling up in my head unsorted, though, leaving me more excited and confused than enlightened. It's always like this when I jump into an unfamiliar wildlife subject: The more I'm told, the dumber I feel until the turning point comes when things start to fall into place. But with *Gulo gulo*, the unknowns outnumbered the knowns so badly that a turning point was nowhere in sight, and this kept me wondering what my level of commitment as a volunteer ought to be.

I was drawn by the aura of discovery surrounding the project, by the fact that so many more secrets lay waiting to be uncovered. But for all I'd been hearing about the study animals, I still hadn't seen any. M3, F5, and their like were chirps on the radio receiver and paw prints in melting snow – mountain ghosts. After I found out about Copeland's long-standing connection to Pedersen, my first impulse was to rush over to those pens in the Northwest, get my hands on a wolverine and its paws on me, and see what that had to tell me about the future. I needed Copeland to vouch for me, though, because despite the spontaneous nature of my original meeting with Pedersen, he was very selective about whom he allowed in his private facility. Copeland made the telephone call, and I was invited to come.

"You know about the whale graveyard on one of his properties?" Copeland asked. "Giant bones sinking into the ground?"

"Yes."

"Well, at the place you're going to, he has a wolverine graveyard where he's buried his favorites. Some of those animals have bigger marble tombstones than any of us are ever going to get."

"Maybe they did more to deserve it."

"That could be," Copeland said. "Don't forget to ask Dale about his artistic wolverine."

Karen and I started driving west and arrived at Pedersen's home on a May afternoon that same year. His place lies among farmland rapidly being made extinct by new homes and strip development – the 'burbs. Our host had let most of his acreage grow up into tall fir and cedar forest around a lake with nesting ducks and geese. To enter through his gate was to pass from generic, metastasizing Mini-Mall World into a haven for the imagination hidden away behind dark green boughs.

Pedersen led us to his "office," a shed and workshop adjoining the animal compound. Big boulders of copper ore rested near the entryway, prospecting and mining being one of this man's many interests. In addition to minerals, antique guns, and a variety of large mammal skulls, he collected art. The walls inside his office were covered with prints and paintings. Every one featured wolverines. Above a stuffed *gulo* hung a portrait of a landscape that reminded me of Alaska or Glacier National Park. The *gulos* in its center were gorging on a wooly mammoth carcass while a saber-toothed cat looked on.

"Wolverines are real Ice-Age creatures," Pedersen said. "Their heyday was the Pleistocene, when so much of the northern hemisphere was boreal forest and tundra." But being superbly adapted to life amid ice and snow didn't make this species a leftover when the great continental ice masses retreated. Like wild yaks, musk ox, caribou, and mountain goats, wolverines adjusted their ranges apace, moving northward or higher on the mountainsides. They were at home where winter still came early and stayed late, and there was no shortage of such environments across either Eurasia or North America.

If an air of obsolescence seems to hover around these creatures today, it isn't due to shortcomings on their part. They got through the Ice Ages and the post-Pleistocene period alike in vigorous shape. Granted, their chances of making it through the Industrial Exhaust Age in good shape don't appear to be nearly as high. But then neither do ours.

Photography being another of his interests, Pedersen led us to a back room to see a series of images he'd made with the help of computer software. They showed broods of little wolverinelets hatching out of eggs while their proud mothers looked on. Sure enough, he told us, he got visitors who commented that they never knew this was how wolverines came into the world. Having only recently learned that baby *gulos* are pure white, I wasn't entitled to snicker too much. Besides, platypuses are mammals, and they do hatch from eggs. To many people's minds, wolverines are every bit as exotic.

"The newborns weigh one hundred to one hundred fifty grams [*3.5 to 5.25 ounces*]," Pedersen informed us. "They're cute as anything, but they stink so bad, I can hardly go near them. They have a waxy substance around their neck, and I think the smell comes from that. It may be a predator deterrent. Female weasels can breed at six weeks of age. Wolverines are capable of breeding at two years of age and giving birth when they're three, but they don't, not in captivity, anyway. Ours don't have young until four. Our first captive litter was born in 1994, and there have been litters every year since. This is the first year a female born here has produced a litter of her own. The mother was hand-reared, and she allows me to go in and play with her kits."

From the outset, Pedersen made it clear that he didn't consider himself an authority. "I just think wolverines are so interesting," he said. "When it comes to interpreting what they do, I'll leave that to the scientists." For someone who had by then been observing the animals close-up for more than two decades, this was a refreshingly modest attitude. No pretensions about being a *gulo* guru, no claim to be the wolverine whisperer. "But," Pedersen continued, "I know this much: Everything you read about wolverines is wrong, and everybody ends up with the wrong idea about them. The sociability I've been seeing for years? Now they're seeing it in the field.

"Once I got my first wolverine, I realized there's no animal that can compare. I think their sense of sight is fair, but everything goes through their noses first. They give me the sniff test every day to see what dogs and other animals I've been around. They hide stuff from me. I hide stuff from them, too. I put things for them to find on the bottom of the pool, and they'll dive down to get it. Some do that anyway – go completely underwater – at times. They like to swim, they like to climb, and they love to play. A male named Silas used to pick up sticks all over the yard and work them into the chain-link fence. He'd make these installations and spend time rearranging them. Then he'd take them down for a while before starting all over again. He was our resident *artiste*."

Ah yes, the one I might have remembered to ask about if I weren't so distracted by all the other facets of Pedersen's universe.

"Wolverines are busy, active animals," he went on, "kind of like an otter; they enjoy life. Ninety-nine percent of the time, males play with other males, and females play with other females. The males form bonds with other males, and they're very particular about which ones. There's a lot of individualism. It's very amazing how different they are from one another.

"Of course, this is a controlled set of conditions. Our wolverines get regular meals – a dependable food supply. They're fat and happy, not competing for their dinner, so they're not as likely to be antagonistic as in the wild. But you know, we've taken in wild, fresh-trapped wolverines, and you can feed them out of your hand. Now, here's what to do if for some reason the animals get you down and grab you by the throat . . . Just kidding. I've never owned an otter that won't bite you sooner or later. Our wolverines aren't like that. They don't just suddenly attack. They might give you a pinch with their teeth, but the only time I'm liable to get bit is if I try to force one into a closed area. And it will give me plenty of warning first."

On that note, Pedersen led the way out into the rain and on toward one of the pens, where a score of wolverines waited in coats that varied from silver striped over light gray to gold or foxy orange streaked over rich brown. His two big Labrador retrievers joined us. As soon as our host opened the pen door, about half the wolverines turned from what they were doing or rose from a resting spot and started our way. Yet they seemed most interested in the dogs out in front. Quickly surrounded, the retrievers didn't show the slightest alarm as they and the *gulo* pack exchanged sniffs. "They're friends," Pedersen commented. "They grew up together."

The distraction provided by the dogs gave me a few moments to take in details of my new surroundings. The pen was just under half an acre in size. To make the environment more stimulating, Pedersen had placed rock piles with small caves here and there and added a waterfall to go with the pool. An assortment of logs raised high off the ground formed ramps and trestles for more interesting climbing, and . . .

Here we go. The dogs had moved on toward some bones, and it was our turn to provide fresh stimulation. All at once, Karen and I had a passel of burly mustelids resembling martens crossed with bears sniffing warily at the edges of our feet. "Watch your shoelaces," Pedersen warned. "They'll shred 'em if you let them." Shoelaces were not our foremost concern. The hesitancy of these big-pawed beasts quickly evaporated, and they had begun standing on their hind legs to inspect crotches, buttocks, and waists, claws pressing into the fabric of our pants.

Though bold and insistently curious, the wolverines dropped onto all fours and backed away if I turned a little or made ready to take a step forward, so I didn't feel under assault. Not exactly. I sat down on a broad stone bench. That, it turned out, was an invitation. In no time, wolverines had jumped up beside me and were eagerly poking noses into my armpits and ears, across the back of my neck, and along the top of my head. One standing behind on the stone pressed its forelegs down on my shoulders as if giving me a massage.

I felt the dampness of noses sniffing me here, there, abruptly somewhere else. Where my skin felt wetter, I realized, I was being licked – tasted. Next came tugs on my hair and shortly after that, a nip – a pinch, as Pedersen would say – on my earlobe. "Ow! Knock it off!" The wolverine pushed away from my side. I wasn't alarmed so much as impressed by how finely this animal must have tempered the strength of those jaws, which had reduced massive cow femurs in the yard to splinters, in order to squeeze a soft earlobe between its teeth without drawing blood.

It wasn't as though these animals viewed us as chew toys. Sniffing, licking, tugging, and mouthing – these make up the wolverine way of asking questions and seeking answers. Same business I'm in, different techniques. *Homo sapiens* is the last species on Earth with any right to criticize another as overly curious, and to do that after strolling into a pen full of bored wolverines would just be absurd. Or so the part of my mind still working rationally was saying. The rest

Ember, one of the young, inquisitive wolverines that kept me company at Pedersen's place. DALE PEDERSEN

had been knocked off kilter by the bizarreness of what we were doing. "Want to take a look at something really interesting?" echoed in my mind.

Turning toward my wife, I saw her kneeling on one knee to interact with her share of the crowd. One wolverine had its arms wrapped around her other knee, and a second wolverine was exploring her neck on the opposite side. A third had climbed up her back leaving muddy paw prints and was poking its nose in among her tresses. Moving very slowly, Karen looked back at me and said, "This could all go horribly wrong in a hurry." But she said it with a smile and a look of amazement in her eyes. She was fine. Stepping a bit closer, knowing his familiar presence had a steadying effect on the animals, Pedersen, who is bald as the proverbial billiard ball, said, "They're just so glad to meet someone with hair."

As things progressed, Karen tried to pet a yearling named Smokey. Gray-coated Smokey was having none of it. Pedersen cautioned us that wolverines seriously disliked being touched in the place we naturally put our hand on tame animals: the top of the head. I appreciated our host's alert but casual style of keeping us under scrutiny. He knew that watching too intently would only cause us to think, "If he's that concerned, maybe we should be more worried."

Had either of us acted very rigid or jumpy – the two reactions tend to go together – or tried to force the animals into doing something, I'm fairly sure our time in the enclosure would have been brief. For that matter, if during our get-acquainted time in the office he had sensed that we came looking mainly for thrills, we likely would have been restricted to the other side of the chain link fence. Dale Pedersen has found ways to live his life doing what most interests him. Though generous and considerate, he follows his own course and sets his own standards. I don't think he could be persuaded for a minute to ignore them.

Following Pedersen's lead, Karen gradually worked her hand under Smokey's chin – at the cost of a few light pinches on her fingers – and ended up stroking the throat of a contented-looking wolverine. For his part, Pedersen had a wolverine in a near trance, hugging it with one arm and rubbing its nose with his other hand. "I don't know why they like their nose and cheeks rubbed so much, but they do," he said.

To show us how loose the skin over a wolverine's cheek is, he pulled the fur on one side until the width of his animal's head practically doubled. The creature could scarcely have shown less concern. None of this in itself made wolverines seem easygoing, cuddly, or affectionate. It meant only that they would tolerate certain kinds of contact in this unnatural setting and that they reacted positively to certain kinds of stimulation. Keep in mind that you can soothe crocodiles and sharks by stroking their underside. That said, it was fantastic to be able to have the wolverine's inquisitiveness and mine meet in circumstances that allowed me to explore active animals by touch.

Inspecting my companions' outsize paws, I ran my fingertips along the rough pads on the bottom. According to Pedersen, the feet develop more fur on the underside over winter. This may add traction as well as help spread the body's weight further on snow. Both the front and rear legs felt quite heavily muscled. Long, thick fur makes wolverines appear low-slung when on all fours, but when the limbs were stretched to reach higher on me, I couldn't get over how long they actually are. It was while sitting on that stone bench holding the paws and legs of wolverines that I was first able to imagine how this species might achieve the mastery of miles and mountains that its lifestyle in the Rockies seemed to demand.

We rose and walked slowly through the enclosure in light rain. One by one, our wolverine retinue drifted away. The novelty of our presence was wearing off. Subadults remained our most loyal company. Even they got sidetracked by other activities until only Smokey and another grayish yearling, Ember, were left. The biggest, fattest, grumpiest-looking, most bulldog-faced wolverine in the galaxy wandered past in a kind of rolling trudge. Pedersen introduced him as D. B. [so *named because he arrived on Dale's birthday, I found out later*], but D. B. was too busy being disgusted with everything and everybody to bother acknowledging us. "He weighs 48 pounds and is in his late teens," Pedersen said. "We've had several reach 20 or so [*close to twice the average life expectancy of wolverines in the wild.*] They get more grouchy as they grow older. The others just leave them alone."

A number of large, live Douglas fir grew from the packed soil of the pen, providing shade on bright days and partial shelter from the rain. Partway up each trunk, a band of slick sheet metal kept the wolverines from climbing up and working their way outward along branches until they escaped. The inmates had clawed out spaces between the roots and also chewed into the sides of several stumps, fashioning cubbyholes where they could avoid the weather or, when they tired of the hubbub around them, crawl in for a little wolverine alone time. Toward one end of the pen stood several small, hard-used maple trees that the *gulos* treated as jungle gyms, scampering along the slender branches with surprising agility.

At any given time, several animals would be loping round and round the pen's perimeter. This was classic behavior for a confined carnivore, a wolverine version of the pacing you might see big cats or wolves carry on at a zoo. In the large enclosure, this seemed more like working out on an exercise track – wolverines getting in their quotient of miles for the day. One wolverine jogger was often joined by another, and the jog might become a low-level chase. Sometimes, the chase would turn into a wrestling match. Rarely, this play fighting would escalate into a more serious spat. When an animal roaming the yard passed too close to certain individuals or tried to claim a bone from another, this could develop into a fight as well.

I'm sure there were a hundred other scenarios that might cause a battle to break out. However, *fight* and *battle* are such loaded terms for us warlike

One of the hand-reared, burly brothers named Rascal and Rowdy approaching a visitor. DALE PEDERSEN

primates that I can appreciate why behavioral scientists stick with unwieldy but neutral jargon such as *antagonistic encounter* or *aggressive interaction*.

The wolverine conflicts certainly looked horrible and sounded even worse. Deep, guttural warning growls, snarls, and metallic-sounding *gra-a-a-aks* rose to *chirrs*, roars, and screeches while the combatants were still squaring off. They didn't face each other preparing to rear up and swipe and slash or grapple with both front legs. The *gulos* stood parallel to one another with tails lifted out straight or upward, often making violent scraping displays with the rear legs. Then, resting their weight on the outside foreleg, they lifted the other front leg and began striking sideways at the opponent in a downward raking motion, lightning fast.

At that point, noises that could pass for a chain saw starting up or a Harley-Davidson going full throttle were issuing from the animals' throats. Twice, I saw wolverines balance their weight on both legs of one side and lash out with the other front and rear legs at once. It looked more like a smokin' kung-fu move than like any carnivore fighting techniques I'd seen.

And yet . . . and yet there were no clumps of fur flying, no gashes opening. Not a drop of blood spattered onto the dirt, because the flurries of strikes were carefully calibrated to just miss. This was all for show, a display of power and resolve. It was two wolverines negotiating. Call it arguing angrily if you'd rather, but to label it fighting is misleading. Were one to grab the other with its teeth and force the foe to the ground and hold it there, biting at the face and head while continuing to rake its body with the hind claws, *that* would be fighting – if carried out with enough intensity. Juveniles performed all those maneuvers, but they were measured, under control. Two could keep mock fighting hard for 10 minutes straight without either one showing signs of wear and tear.

I never saw any serious physical clashes between adults. For one thing, the rituals of roaring and swiping alone effectively settled disputes, sometimes within seconds. For another, Pedersen knew his animals well enough to recognize when a particular pair were becoming increasingly unable to tolerate each other. Before the ultimate smackdown took place, one of them would find itself moved to a different pen or possibly into a cage for a while. Those individuals were the exceptions. Getting along well enough to confound almost everyone who came to watch wolverines was the rule.

After we left, Karen refused to wash the wolverine paw prints off the back of her raincoat for weeks. Although I didn't feel that I'd come up with many answers to the questions I'd had about wolverines, I did figure out what my level of volunteer involvement with the project would be: High.

◇◇◇◇◇◇◇◇◇◇◇◇◇◇◇◇◇◇◇◇◇◇◇◇◇◇◇◇◇◇◇

Over the next three years, I returned to Pedersen's twice more, once with Copeland and Yates hauling a disassembled log box trap in the bed of a pickup truck, and again with Copeland and Savage. The office was much as I remembered it, except that Pedersen had added the gleaming angel-of-death wolverine skeleton mentioned in Chapter 6, and that evocative piece of animal architecture dominated the main room. He showed me a couple of new photos, including one that leading field researcher Audrey Magoun, who often visits to observe Pedersen's captive animals, had taken of a stuffed wolverine in Alaska. The specimen was more white than brown – a panda *gulo*.

Our host had done more landscaping with giant rock slabs since I was last there, and he planned to add the log box trap to the setting's décor. Over one side of the largest pen, Pedersen had constructed a new viewing stand, complete with a roof to keep out the rain, a coffee table, and three plush chairs, one of which was a recliner. There are hobbies, then there's volunteering to look for wolverines, and then, by God, there's wolverine-watching from a cushy lounge chair with snacks and a cold drink in your hand.

<hr/>

As we sat back during one visit and surveyed the score of *gulos* in the big pen from above, Pedersen said his captive population was holding fairly steady at 40 to 45 animals. "They're reproducing well enough here to replace those that die of old age or disease now." Forty-five wolverines in pens and cages covering less than two acres was almost exactly the number living in Glacier National Park's more than 1 million acres.

During a freewheeling discussion about sociability, Pedersen remarked that when it rained hard, all 20-plus wolverines in the pen below would head into a covered cage near the pen's entryway. There, he would find them in the morning in one huge, dry pile. It should have been an appealing image to contemplate, but I kept envisioning the scene in terms of half the Glacier population, which comprises the largest and densest single group in the contiguous states, huddled in a space the size of a large bathroom.

Drawing our attention to the larger bones strewn about the pen, Pedersen observed, "Throw these animals a fresh one in summer or fall, and they'll eat the meat off it. They might crack some bones to get at the marrow, but they're more likely to bury them. Come January, they start digging out the bones and chew them right up. They consume the entire thing in winter." To me, this suggested that the bone-eating documented in Glacier and elsewhere might be a standard part of the species' feeding habits and not necessarily a measure to fend off extreme hunger. Pedersen's animals were definitely not facing starvation. Compared to other wolverines, they were sitting in recliners with snacks set out on the coffee table.

Late in the morning, Susan Behrns arrived. Pedersen's longtime, trusted assistant at the wolverine compound, she was the main reason he so often said "we" and "ours" when speaking about the animals. We'd been waiting for her to arrive because Copeland wanted to experiment with a radio collar, and we were counting on Behrns to cajole an untranquilized wolverine into letting her put it on. She had a special relationship with two dark-faced, young, but full-size males that she had hand-reared from infancy: Rascal and Rowdy.

Without any preliminaries, she scooped the brothers up like house pets when they came to her in the pen. She could then dangle either male off the ground by his front paws or hug him all she wanted, and all the demon-devil-carcajou did was squirm. Behrns managed to buckle a dog collar on one to let the animal get used to the procedure. Yet neither she nor Pedersen could persuade Rascal, Rowdy, or any other *gulo* to hold still long enough for someone to fasten the ends of the more rigid radio collar around its neck. Enough was enough. That experiment wasn't going to happen, even with the tamest wolverines in the 'burbs.

When I entered the enclosure, I watched four wolverines tumbling together in a free-for-all mock battle, each one's jaws grabbing another one's hide. Among the most common targets of tugging were the cheek and side of the face. The advantage of having loose skin that could be pulled out so far, I saw, was that the animal under assault could still twist its head around to gets its jaws on the aggressor in turn.

Later, another element of behavior fell into place, or seemed to. If play fighting spiraled upward in intensity, it looked to me as though the targets of attack more often became the back of the neck and the top of the head. Not long after that, the animals would abruptly break off, and I assumed it was because some sound or posture – the equivalent of crying "Uncle!" or a wrestler slapping the mat – signaled submission.

For mustelids, the head and neck are the kill spots when attacking prey and territorial rivals. Recalling the wolverines whose facial scars or skull punctures we suspected of having come from clashes with other *gulos*, I could understand the penned animals' reaction to being petted on top of the head. That was a no-go zone.

⬦⬦⬦⬦⬦⬦⬦⬦⬦⬦⬦⬦⬦⬦⬦⬦⬦⬦⬦⬦⬦⬦⬦⬦⬦

During much of this time, a little white-faced juvenile was making it his life's mission to circle around behind me for a pinch of my heel. His presence was so distracting that I couldn't concentrate very well. I noticed Savage standing off by himself wearing the same baggy, flimsy, fast-drying black pants I've always seen him in outdoors when the temperature is above zero. What struck me as vaguely odd was that he also had the same expression he gets among the peaks, quiet and inward looking. I'd have thought the vet would be totally focused on nearby wolverine activities. He had been the last time I'd looked. I went over to speak with him.

He said, "Ah, I think one of the wolverines may have punctured the skin on my scrotum."

"Damn, man! You OK?"

"It was just a light nip. You know how they get up on their hind legs and poke around."

"I know you just became part of a very exclusive club." Odds are, he's the only living person in it.

I exited the pen, settled into the world's spiffiest wolverine-watching furniture, and started trying to figure out why *gulos* appeared to expend more energy walking than running. They have what's called a plantigrade style of locomotion, which simply means that they place the heel of the foot as well as the front in contact with the ground (as we do.) A greater surface area helps distribute the body's weight and balance.

The drawback to whole-foot striding is that it tends to be slower than skipping along on the front of the foot or just the toes as many mammals do. What I'd noticed was how ungainly wolverines were in low gear even for a plantigrade species. Their walk had a lumpy, lumbering, swaying quality that looked terribly inefficient. I'd seen more graceful porcupines. Not really, but the wolverines themselves seemed inclined to choose another gait even when they had only a short distance to go.

Their second gear covered the range between a fast walk and a trot. In this gait, the wolverine was no longer humping along. Its body stayed level, which generally improves speed, while the legs seemed to be doing the swaying somehow . . . I got it! From above, I could see that the long hind legs were taking turns swinging outward, tracing a wide crescent as they moved forward. So long as the back stayed level, the rear limbs combined with those prodigious feet were simply too long to be brought ahead directly under the body without dragging on the dirt or snow. They had to arc outward for the animal to maintain its faster pace.

The next gear up was the one that ate the miles in the wild – the lope, which looked to me like the most economical gait by far. Now the rear legs were back underneath the body, swinging directly forward and rearward like the front legs were. All the flexing joints from toes to ankle to knee were working in line now to provide better propulsion. Pushing off with both rear legs together, then both front legs together created an up-and-down rocking motion rather than a side-to-side sway that subtracted from the forward momentum. Though at least as complicated as it sounds, the result was smooth, and it translated into more speed with less apparent effort.

In winter, this lope creates the classic two-by-two mustelid track pattern across landscapes of otherwise unbroken white. The front feet land with one slightly ahead of the other, and as they lift off again, the rear feet come down onto those same two spots where the snow has already been packed down. Obviously, this can be an invaluable energy saver for long-distance travelers living where snow covers the ground more than half the year.

Play fighting in the Pedersen compound. DALE PEDERSEN

The highest gear I saw involved bounding with all four legs striking the ground in rapid succession – an all-out, leaping run. Such a gait is also called on when wolverines travel in deep powder snow, where the tracks they leave amount to craters roughly three feet apart, sometimes farther. Basically, the animals are making a series of powerful lunges that can go on for miles. I get tired just looking at this wolverine way of covering the countryside. It's another tribute to the snowshoe effect of huge paws for an animal weighing only two to three dozen pounds. The potholes that the *gulos* create are barely a foot deep in the kind of soft fluff that, were I to take off my skis, would have me floundering up to my thighs and moving at the speed of frozen yogurt.

Wolverines have one more slot in their gearbox – one more gait, if you can call it that. Judging from a couple of examples I saw in the pen, one near a box trap, and brief videos of varying quality that I'd viewed, it may be more an expression of high excitement, including both alarm and exhilaration.

Whatever the case, the wolverine hops high into the air, repeatedly, using the joints of all four feet and ankles at once to spring upward while keeping the legs and body more or less rigid. From a distance, you'd think the animal was on a pogo stick. By angling its feet, it can direct this movement to go bouncing forward or sideways across the terrain. Different members of the deer and antelope family employ this stiff-legged hopping gait as well. Behaviorists refer to it as *stotting* or *pronking*. But they're divided as to whether it's an altruistic social signal that warns fellow herd members of a threat or a selfish action intended to signal to an approaching predator that the pronker is healthy and uncatchable; go find somebody weak in the herd, and you'll have better luck.

Yet wolverines are predators and scavengers themselves. The purpose behind their pogo-ing around is . . . yet another wolverine secret.

The author carries M3 back to the trap, where he can recuperate until fully alert and ready for the mountainsides. M3 finally went limp after absorbing *three* times the normal amount of drugs required to sedate a wolverine; then researchers removed him from the trap and downloaded his GPS collar. RICK YATES

CHAPTER FIFTEEN

Mr. Badass Himself

In order to carry out great enterprises,
one must live as if one will never have to die.

MARQUIS DE VAUVENARGUES
from *Reflexions et Maximes*

Grub first, then ethics.

BERTOLT BRECHT
from *The Threepenny Opera*, translated by Marc Blitzstein

M3 IS A WOLVERINE'S WOLVERINE: curious, canny, fierce, tireless, and unconquerable, the King of Attitude in a trap, the Genghis Khan of local *gulos*. Clad in a cape of dark chocolate fur with bronze blazes on the sides, he rules an ever-expanding empire along the Great Divide, which the Blackfeet called *Mistakis*, Backbone of the World. When first captured and radio-tagged in 2003, M3 was only a yearling, but a big, heavy one and furious in a trap compared with others that age. Though it would be months before lab technicians got around to analyzing his DNA, the project researchers already had a good idea of who his father was, as the young animal's radio locations were clustered within the territory of M1. For that matter, the crew occasionally found Big Daddy and the yearling traveling side by side. M3's mother was durable, prolific F2. Well cared for and well taught, this was a juvenile being groomed for wild success.

As mentioned in an earlier chapter, the young wolverine soon began to extend his range northward into the territory of M6 and his son, M8. M3 reached sexual maturity during his second winter, which is when the team discovered him trying to chew his way into a box trap that held M6. The old male subsequently abandoned his former territory and vanished somewhere to the south. M8, found with fresh wounds on his face, left the park for lands far to the west.

Though the evidence for M3 being the rising power that drove both of them into exile wasn't airtight, the scenario surely looked like a takeover. For the remainder of 2004 and every year after that, the only radio signals from an adult male in the former territory of M6 were those of M3.

Among the females within M3's new domain was F15, who had previously mated with M6 and given birth to M8. In the summer of 2004, M3 bred with her. They had a son, M20, born in the winter of 2005, when M3 himself turned three. F15 localized again the next year. The team's efforts to find her den failed, so we couldn't be sure whether or not she had again produced young with M3. But we knew by the signals from M3's implanted radio that he not only maintained his claim to the lands usurped from M6 but also continued to enlarge his territory, especially on the northern end.

I'd never actually sighted M3 in the countryside or been around during the times he was captured. When I was tracking his signal and tried to envision his pace and moods on the mountainsides, all I had to go on was his reputation among those who'd handled him. Even by the explosive standards of cornered wolverines, the others told me, M3 was the incarnation of shock and awe. They said he went completely nuclear; that trying to stick him with the drug-filled syringe on the jab pole while he swatted and bit and roared wolverine curses would demolish your nerves; that if you finally got the sedative and muscle immobilizer into him, the drugs scarcely made him lose a step. You had to hit him with another dose, and another after that, for it took at least three times the amount prescribed for an animal his weight to keep M3 down.

Mostly for fun, we made him out to be a paragon of general unruliness and defiance. But there was a serious side to the "What would M3 do?" question – an awareness that you occasionally have to be as badass as the wilderness's worst moments to get through them. Suppose you're faced with fording a wide, icy stream in winter. You start across barefoot with your ski boots tied around your neck, and your legs go numb so quickly that you're at risk of losing your balance. Falling in and soaking your clothes could bring on a losing battle with hypothermia in the wrong kind of weather. Before that happens, you have to marshal a deep resolve to ignore the deep pain in the parts of your legs that still have sensations for as many steps as it takes to get across. Total commitment; right here, right now, you need to clench your whole being around a conviction that you will not fail to stay upright. And keep clenched, keep clenched. *Ungh!* Roaring and snarling are good. Mania is your helpmate. You're badass. Nothing's going to mess with you, because you utterly refuse to let it.

For us, the drawback to M3's unrelenting push to increase his holdings was that he was often far away from the core of Glacier, where we focused our efforts, and closer to the Canadian boundary. He might have begun spending part of his time on the other side, roaming Alberta's Waterton Lakes National Park or the upper North Fork of the Flathead River Valley in British Columbia (B.C.). We simply didn't know. Much of the topography was hard to reach from our usual routes, especially when the high country was loaded with snow and hiking across the international border had become a more complicated process in terrorist times.

Shea Wyatt, a friend from B.C. who had just graduated from high school and was planning to study biology at university, volunteered with me for several weeks in the summer of 2006. Tall, lean, and long-legged, he was built for covering ground. Nevertheless, he was slightly slower than I on hikes and considerably more sore at the end of the trails. Then again, he had just come from a home at sea level on the B.C. coast and was packing about 30 pounds of photography equipment along with ordinary field gear. He judiciously pared down his array of camera lenses and tripods. He ate like a wolverine that hadn't sniffed food for days. His forgiving, 18-year-old muscles and tendons quickly adapted to the miles and heights. Within two weeks, Wyatt was politely waiting at the passes for me to catch up. Punk.

After a series of day hikes to search for other wolverines, we set out in July to look for M3, his mate, F15, and their yearling son, M20, in the hub of his territory, the Belly River drainage. He wasn't in the part we rambled the first day before making camp, and he wasn't anywhere we checked the next day as we continued beyond Elizabeth Lake and then backtracked to swim in its waters and pitch our tent by its shore. Then Wyatt picked up a signal from F15 a couple thousand feet above, toward Seward Mountain on the east. The third day of the outing, we set off early to climb in that direction and cross the Ptarmigan Wall into the Many Glacier Valley. By midmorning, we had reached a high enough elevation to take a straight shot with the antenna toward Helen Lake, nestled beneath the Belly River Valley's headwall. We were still hoping to hear from M3. Instead, we got F15's frequency just upslope from the lake, about five miles from her previous location. We also heard cheeps from M20 emanating from the same spot. The yearling may have been traveling with his mother.

Later that summer, several different visitors reported seeing a grown wolverine with a smaller wolverine around Ptarmigan Wall and Ptarmigan Lake. This was within F15's territory. Since M20 was already adult size, the small wolverine that people described would have been a kit. Which suggested, first, that F15 did produce at least one new offspring while denning that winter and, second, that when Wyatt and I recorded F15 and M20 on identical compass bearings near Helen Lake, we were documenting three generations of wolverines – mom, yearling, and four-month-old kit – in a group or very close together. DNA from the youngster, who was captured during the winter of 2007 and known thereafter as M23, verified that he was indeed the second generation to come from a mating of F15 and brawler/lover/empire-builder M3.

Details of M3's whereabouts remained sketchy through the fall of 2006. However, son M23 was caught in January of 2007 and fitted with one of the GPS collars set to record his locations at five-minute intervals for about 10 days. Shortly afterward, M3 was trapped at the Boneyard site and given the same kind of collar. With father and son on the air simultaneously, the crew eagerly awaited a burst of information from these two hard-to-find males. To retrieve it, they had to capture the animals one more time. But as March arrived, the wolverines still hadn't shown. The snow was beginning to soften fast out on the flats of Many Glacier Valley. Ice was breaking up here and there in the streams. A few cliff bands on the south-facing slopes were almost bare of snow, and the mosses on them were turning a luminous green.

The signs were pointing to an early spring, which meant that adult male grizzlies would be leaving their winter dens somewhat sooner than usual. A few would probably emerge within a couple weeks to linger groggily around the entrance holes, rubbing five months' sleep out of their eyes and wishing bears knew how to make coffee. One or two might head directly for the valley bottoms to see what winter had left lying around in the way of carcasses to scavenge. If M3 and M23 didn't show up at one of our baited box traps fairly soon, someone was going to have to make the call to shut down capture efforts for the season – and maybe for good.

Originally proposed as a three-year effort, the project was now a highly successful operation in its fifth year, accumulating information at a faster clip than ever. We thought that having been able to prolong the study was a wonderful thing, but some park officials were showing signs of impatience, preferring to see our efforts wrapped up and off their list of activities to keep an eye on. I worried that they might get their wish. Although we'd acquired independent funding for the fieldwork from private groups and individuals, keeping those dollars coming in was a never-ending drama of last-minute reprieves. Then on top of that, Copeland was told that the Rocky Mountain Research Station might not be able to cover his salary any longer due to budget constraints.

I still hadn't laid eyes on M3. It was beginning to look as though I might never get the chance. When he was caught in Many Glacier earlier that winter, I was tending the trap near Avalanche Creek. I was scheduled to ski into the Two Medicine Valley in mid-March. I'd be there a while tending two traps with Lacy Robinson, recently out of wildlife graduate school and hired for the season, and helping her search for a collar F17 had lost. In between, while I was at home catching up on nonwolverine living, the Many Glacier team caught M23 again and downloaded his locations. That was something at least. But still no M3.

Then Yates telephoned.

"Want to keep me company on a trip to Many?"

"Sure. What's going on?"

"Buck [Hasson] just called. He's got M3 in Boney."

"My pack's by the door. Give me time to throw in some groceries."

"I'll swing by and pick you up in about fifteen minutes."

We'd got lucky.

I skied in behind Yates to help with M3 and finally had my first look at Mr. Badass himself. Rattling off warning growls, he was as big and fearsome as promised. Hasson made sure I was standing directly in front of the trap when he moved behind it and levered the lid up a crack so I could peek in. Instantly and massively, M3 flew at me roaring and snapping. I couldn't help jumping back with a shout. Hasson let the lid fall. "Just wanted to see your reaction," he said. "He's something, isn't he?" Yes. All kinds of things. And yet as he faced us down in his glossy, rich brown winter coat with russet streaks, he was, above all, beautifully, indomitably wild. He was perfect.

True to his reputation, M3 withstood two normal doses of drugs before a third finally made him still. The drugs we used lowered the body temperature of other wolverines. By contrast, the thermometer readings from M3 stayed near normal while we downloaded his collar, cleared it, and replaced the battery, hoping he'd give us one more round of data before the season's end. When I carried him back to the big box from the tarp on which he'd been lying, his body warmed mine through layers of clothing. He started coming around in my arms. Two minutes later, as Yates opened the trap lid to check on the patient, Mr. Badass tried to lunge at him, having regained most of his faculties in a quarter of the time most other wolverines required after being given an antidote to the immobilizer.

Once upon a time, field naturalists would gather around a warm, flickering fire in the evening. Now they huddle around the glow of a computer screen. We were in the Many Glacier Ranger station when some of the 1,900 locations just obtained from the GPS collar M3 had been wearing first popped up on the desktop monitor.

Picture scruffy guys in sweat-stained, bait-stained clothes at a cabin deep among the peaks, staring at pixels representing the whereabouts of a hard-to-find individual member of a long-mysterious race. Imagine the radio waves that fixed each of the positions being sent from at least three different satellites hurled into precise geosynchronous orbits by rocket ships, and the waves then being received and interpolated by miniaturized circuitry borne around the neck of this Ice Age-made beast as it loped and stalked and fought and fed among billion-year-old rocks until it was caught in an axe-hewn, fang-gouged log box set among lodgepole pines with a deer head hung from one of the branches to rot and waft more alluring odors into the big winds that swirl through the country-side and into scavengers' noses. Then visualize all the information, existing as electrical polarities on an intricately segmented chip of silicon and coded as 1s and 0s, being shunted from the collar into a laptop field computer, from there to a desktop computer at the ranger station, and on to Copeland's computer in Missoula, where software turned the subsets of data into dots superimposed on a topographic map and transmitted the result back to us.

I'd never really grasped the dimensions of the Glacier Wolverine Project before, I suddenly realized, never appreciated just how amazing the technological advances that underpin modern wildlife research have become. I'd never seen the computerized choreographies of electrons dancing from Earth to space and back again for the nigh-miraculous extensions of human senses and physical abilities that they are, never given much thought to how quickly we have come to take such inventions for granted, and never, ever, for all my admiration of wolverines, truly understood what a breathtaking invention each one of these life forms is.

"Holy shit! He summitted Cleveland!" [*the park's highest peak at 10,466 feet.*]"

"And he did the last forty-nine-hundred feet straight up in ninety minutes."

"Yuh. In frickin' January."

"All riiiight! We've got him traveling with M23 for a while first. [*Copeland had also sent the movements of the yearling son, adding them to the map.*] Identical times and locations."

"After climbing Cleveland he goes way up into Waterton Lakes. First, he crosses into British Columbia, then into Alberta. No wonder we couldn't find him. His territory's several hundred square miles."

Mr. Badass had gone international.

Yates climbed Cleveland once. Hasson had, too. Mountain goats went up to the crest as well in the warm months; in fact, Yates had taken a goat trail part of the way. He was one of the first to report an abundance of grizzly dung on Cleveland's upper reaches. Hasson had seen a sow with two cubs near the summit. Other climbers ran into a veritable crowd of grizz there on the very tip-top of Glacier.

We now know that bears are drawn to these heights by astronomical numbers of adult army cutworm moths, which congregate on the uppermost talus slopes of Cleveland and certain other peaks in the region. While the presence of bulky bears on or near Cleveland's summit tells you there are ways up the mountain that don't involve scaling sheer cliffs, even some of the safest paths include a section or two where a slip could be fatal.

M3 didn't choose any of the routes that humans, goats, or bears have followed. Passing near Whitecrow Glacier, he blasted right up the mountain's soaring south face, a cliffy exposure with the shape of a logarithmic curve, becoming ever closer to pure vertical near the top. The walls would make for a dangerous technical climb in the best of summer conditions. M3 bagged the summit by this route in midwinter when the face was a solid, icy white barricade – a solo first ascent so impressive that it won M3 a bit of fame as word of his accomplishment got out.

M3 summitted the 10,466-foot Mount Cleveland – Glacier's tallest peak – in January. Based on data from his GPS collar, M3 climbed the central wall of the cirque basin to the summit, ascending 4,900 vertical feet in 90 minutes. RICK YATES

Inspired, a group of experienced human mountaineers set out to duplicate his route in June but discovered the face still largely cloaked in compacted snow. The challenge it presented seemed less like rock climbing than like working your way up an Olympic ski jump thousands of feet tall with few obvious break points and some of the snow undercut by running meltwater. Wisely, the climbers abandoned the effort before going very far, leaving the M3 route up Cleveland unrepeated.

But why would a wolverine summit a foodless winter peak buried in corniced snow high above the passes? And why by such a formidable route? We'd asked ourselves the same thing when F5 powered up Bearhat Mountain to the highest point of that lonely fang in late winter. Like all living things, these animals need to test their limits, but wolverines have more than enough opportunities to do this without taking on extra trials. I seriously doubt they view mountain walls as stages for dramas of self-discovery and personal growth. They're not up there hoping for glory, fulfilling promises to themselves, seeking visions, or any of that.

After scaling Cleveland's south face to a point on a ridge just east of the summit, M3 crossed the mountain's apex and then followed its western extension some distance before dropping down toward the Waterton Valley. Harking back to the Dan Savage theory of the world being more or less flat as far as wolverines are concerned, it's possible that if we knew how to analyze the topography from the standpoint of *gulo* energetics, putting ourselves in their oversize, clawed paws and four muscular legs, adding an extra-big heart, lungs, and thyroid gland, and subtracting a great deal of fear, we might find M3's tracks over Mount Cleveland marking out the shortest, most sensible route between the portion of his range in the center of the Belly River drainage and the Waterton drainage.

But from Waterton's gentler slopes, M3 soon climbed to high altitude again, roaming around the Stoney Indian Peaks. Which either proves Savage's notion – that when wolverines are deciding where they want to go next, they don't give much weight to the ups and downs in the way – or it doesn't. The only conclusion I can think of is the phrase heard time and again in wolverine camp: We don't know why they do that yet, but it's very cool.

◇◇◇◇◇◇◇◇◇◇◇◇◇◇◇◇◇◇◇◇◇◇◇◇◇◇◇◇

For most of January 2007, I helped tend the trap near Avalanche Creek in Glacier's McDonald Valley. I don't remember the temperature often rising much above zero (F). For part of the time, I was with volunteer Jack Noll, a computer software developer lending our crew a hand with fieldwork while on break from the East Coast. After noticing fresh wolverine tracks coming down from the valley's upper reaches, Noll and I decided to lay a fresh scent trail to the trap roughly a mile away. We went behind our quarters at the ranger cabin to a metal-sided shed, chopped off a haunch of the deer carcass hanging there, and started dragging the meat upstream.

A quarter mile later, Noll called out for me to take a look over my shoulder. Close behind, one of the wolverine's closest relatives, a pine marten, was bounding along scarfing up clots of deer meat and blood left on the snow's hard crust. Light brown with a blaze of orange on its chest and no more than a foot and a half long counting its tail, the marten stopped when I did and fixed its bright, bold gaze on the food in my hand as if weighing the chances of grabbing it.

Earlier in the study, when volunteer Alex Hasson stayed through the winter at the Avalanche Creek station, a marten got in through an unused heating vent and decided to stay. By storing food in the cupboards and inevitably spilling crumbs, he added to the number of mice to hunt. When Hasson tried to run off his new roomie, the marten refused to budge. Hasson went to plan B, blocking the vent and dangling a dead mouse by the tail next to the door to lure the hunter outside.

"The marten's by the back wall about 15 feet away," he had told me. "I'm standing there shaking the mouse around, saying, 'Here you go. Yum! All yours.' I look to the side for – I swear – a fraction of a second, and when I look back, the marten is right where it was, except it's got a mouse in its mouth. I stare down at my fingers. They're empty. That's my mouse! I never even saw the marten move."

Later in the week, Noll and I went to the bait shack to cut off another chunk of deer. We found a fair amount of the carcass eaten, though there was no way into the building larger than a hole for a missing drain pipe. As we were puzzling over the damage, we heard a chittering growl. It came from a marten poised on one of the rafters that crossed the open ceiling. The animal dashed along the board from one side of the building to the other so quickly that I realized Hasson hadn't been exaggerating; it was as though the marten was teleporting. Then it ran directly overhead and stopped to chirr more loudly, baring its teeth.

After a couple more of these rushes, Noll shook his head in wonder and said, "It's bluff charging us." Both Noll and I weigh upward of 175 pounds. Pine martens weigh one or two. This creature kept up its threats for a good three minutes, alternately zapping around the rafters at warp speed and then suddenly stopping to stretch down and flourish its teeth at us.

It didn't seem possible that an animal smaller than a house cat had been able to remove so much deer meat. Or that it could feel so strongly that we were the raiders destined to be driven off. We left to search the compound for something to protect what was left of the meat and found some old pieces of wire mesh. When we returned to wrap them around the carcass, the marten took after us again, bluff charging with maniacal intensity.

"I dunno, man. We might have to call for backup."

"If these things were just a couple of pounds bigger, it wouldn't be safe to go in the woods. We'd all die screaming."

Maybe, maybe not. In return for more bribes, the marten that grabbed Hasson's mouse agreed to live mostly outdoors. Still, the animal took to sleeping atop the woodpile right next to the front window, the better to keep an eye on the situation inside, it seemed. Neola, as he called her, and Hasson became one another's closest company for weeks on end. They renewed their relationship the following winter, though he couldn't prove that it wasn't a marten with identical markings, perhaps one of Neola's offspring. In any case, Hasson once again found himself passing many an evening hour, elbows propped on the sill, exchanging glances with a gremlin through the glass. We say of other creatures, "Ah, they're just animals," and they are. But we have to expand our definition of animal every time we get to know one better.

◇◇◇◇◇◇◇◇◇◇◇◇◇◇◇◇◇◇◇◇◇◇◇◇◇◇◇◇◇◇◇◇

During the first part of my stay at Avalanche, Dave Murray and I were on duty. There were fresh moose tracks in the understory of the forest near the waterway and small bands of goats overhead on the cliffs of Mount Cannon, but no sign of a mustelid larger than a marten. Finally, we crossed a lone set of smallish wolverine prints and backtracked them for miles upstream. Neither of us had the slightest clue as to which *gulo* might have left the tracks. We hadn't picked up any radio signals in the area. Murray started referring to the mysterious visitor as Elvis. We laid a fresh scent trail, which Murray literally beefed up by rubbing pieces of leftover steak from his dinner onto the hard crust of the snow at intervals.

The trap signal went off during the night. Though we felt the odds were high that it had been tripped by one of the valley's insatiable martens, we rushed the mile to the log box and stood over it listening, both with our ears and the radio receiver. Nothing. I ran through the entire sequence of frequencies for our study animals without hearing anything but the hiss of static. No grumble or growl nor any sound of movement issued from within the trap, not even when we tapped a branch against the side. If our captive wasn't a marten, it almost had to be a lynx, coyote, or fox. Otherwise, whatever animal set off the trap had somehow shot out of it before the lid fell shut. The only problem with these explanations was the fresh wolverine tracks that had led much of the way here, going from one spot where Murray had scuffed steak on the snow to the next.

Readjusting our headlamps, we lifted the lid and peered inside and found an unknown, unmarked *gulo* peering back.

"Elvis," Murray declared. "I knew it. I knew my steak would bring in a wolverine. Gawd, we're good."

Our prisoner was the antithesis of M3: a small, slender specimen that huddled at the rear of the trap just watching us, passive and quiet as a lynx. I guessed it to be a yearling female and an undersized one at that, trying to get through her first winter after leaving her mom's side. No matter what kind of commotion we made moving around the box or how far we stuck in our heads for a better look, Elvis wouldn't growl or even bare her teeth, a nonreaction I hadn't experienced with these animals before. I never thought I'd call any wolverine a sweetheart, but I found myself telling Murray that's what she was.

Savage wasn't available to surgically implant a radio, and the researchers were reluctant to put a collar on a little girl who was either a very small individual by nature or still had more than the normal amount of growing to do before she attained adult size. So when Yates came in the following morning, we just sedated the female, took measurements, and made a general inspection of her condition. Despite her petite stature, she seemed in good health and wore a long, lustrous, unmarked coat. After snatching a few hairs for DNA analysis and putting on ear tags, we let Elvis go free as F24.

Two weeks later, I returned to Avalanche, where Jack Noll had been stationed for a few days alone. While he hadn't detected any activity at the trap site, he'd recently seen wolverine tracks right around the ranger station and our bait shed – small tracks, possibly left by F24. We made a fresh scent trail to the trap and caught a wolverine that night. But it wasn't the yearling. It was F7, F2's daughter born in 2003. Her radio implant had been off the air for more than a year. Yates arrived and sedated her.

F7 had been full of fight inside the box. It wasn't until we inspected her out in the daylight that we realized how haggard this four-year-old adult female appeared. Her body was very lean, her fur dull and matted. She weighed barely 18 pounds, less than yearlings we'd handled. Some of her incisor teeth were missing. One canine tooth was chipped off on the end and discolored. Part of her upper lip was missing, and the tissue around it was scarred and shrinking, further exposing her gums. Her teats, still enlarged and elongated from nursing, told us that in addition to coping with this physical trauma, she'd been dealing with the demands of rearing kits through the past summer. No surgery for her, but since she was already sedated, Yates decided it would be all right to put on one of the newer, lighter GPS collars to gain at least a brief look at her current life.

"She hasn't been having an easy time of it, that's for sure," he said. "I'll bet she's the wolverine with two kits that people were seeing around Sperry Glacier last summer."

"Think F24 is one of them?"

"We'll know before long."

We learned very few details about F7 from the GPS collar. She worked the hi-tech necklace loose and dropped it shortly after we let her go. Nevertheless, she was sighted in her territory during the summer of 2007 with her telltale missing chunk of lip and exposed fang, and also during 2008, accompanied by a pair of new kits. She may have looked beat-up, but she was by no means beaten. One way or another, she was able to keep moving, keep breeding, and keep leading babies into the world.

American, or pine, martens gnawed many times their weight in trap bait intended for wolverines, their larger relatives in the mustelid family. Worldwide, mustelids form the largest and most diverse group of carnivores, with members ranging from tropical tayras and zorillas to sea otters. MARCI JOHNSON

It was the 26th of January the day we let F7 go from the Avalanche trap. That night, the trap's radio was chirping double-time, alerting Noll and me that something had tripped the lid closed again. We found wolverine tracks around the log box but heard no growling from within. Elvis! I mean shy, silent F24. When we looked in, she did finally grumble, but not loudly and not for long. Yates and Savage arrived early the next day. Noll and I had packed a card table from the ranger station for Savage to operate on. As we set it up on the snow among spruce and cedar and alder brush in the middle of nowhere, I wished somebody would come skiing by and ask what we were doing. I had my lines all ready:

"Why howdy there, friend! Care to try your luck in a little game of chance?"

Or: "What? You people eat your trail food on the snow?"

As usual, the implant surgery went quickly, and Yates and Savage were on their way back home by midmorning. Yates's final instructions to us were to let F24 rest another two hours to be sure the last of the drugs wore off, then position ourselves to discourage her from running toward McDonald Creek once released. Although she could probably swim across the broad stream with no ill effects, it didn't seem like a good idea for her to soak the bare, shaved skin on her belly around the freshly sewn and superglued incision.

We followed our instructions, but F24 shot past us and swam McDonald Creek anyway. Later in the day, she swam back. I think. It was tough to pin down her signal, which kept bouncing off the steep, goat-tracked face of Mount Cannon. Then all at once, her frequency started coming in at twice the usual pulse rate – the mortality alert. The location kept moving down the valley, so F24 wasn't dead.

We always had to keep the implants from getting cold when packing them around to cabins or traps because they would go into mortality mode if they dropped below a certain temperature. I could envision that happening to F24's implant when she swam the freezing river. Unfortunately, I could also picture her incision tearing open after being softened in the water or caught on a sharp branch and the cooled-down implant cheeping at us double-time while F24 struggled through the woods with parts of her guts poking out.

Calm down, Yates told me when I telephoned from the ranger station. He reminded me of other new transmitters that had started acting up after being implanted. She's probably not in trouble, he said, and he was right. Not only was F24 OK, her radio self-corrected after a few hours and switched back to the normal pulse rate. The reason I knew she was fine was that we caught her again at 3:30 the following afternoon. Fine, that is, but famished, and we had the best, most readily accessible food the yearling knew how to find in her wanderings.

This time, she growled quite a lot when we opened the lid to look her over. More than that, she rushed at us and tried to stick her head through the small opening. She had also been chewing away at the lid before we arrived. Noll and

I congratulated ourselves, saying we had successfully trained F24 to be a real wolverine, though we knew that she had merely grown more used to us and was no longer intimidated by two tall creatures. When we levered up the lid, she ran for about 50 feet, stopped, looked back, and ran another short distance. Then she circled around and went slightly uphill from us and stayed there watching.

F24 was waiting for us to go away. She clearly planned to dive back in the trap for another bite of deer forequarter as soon as we left, if not sooner. We'd need to close the trap to keep her out. She'd already eaten most of the bait. I'd end up tossing away the old deer leg and putting in a fresh one when the time came to open the box again. Suddenly, I couldn't help myself; I grabbed what was left and threw it her direction. She walked right toward us and started gnawing on the remains.

After a minute, she paused to take a long look around. With the scraps of meat and gristle attached to it, the leg weighed perhaps ten pounds. F24 weighed only about twice that. Nevertheless, she picked the entire thing up in her mouth, lifted her head high and then higher yet until the lower joints of the leg no longer dragged on the ground, and took off at a fast trot as if her prize were light as a twig. A couple more sessions like this, I thought, and we could probably get her to follow us home.

That would have been a counterproductive move scientifically, at odds with the project's goals of understanding natural processes, not to mention contrary to park policy. Still, I secretly loved the idea of staying at the ranger station with Elvis out demolishing carcasses in the snowy yard, growing big and fat.

At the station, I telephoned Yates again and told him we ought to keep the trap closed or we'd just keep catching our new best friend. He understood the problem but said that although the DNA results wouldn't be in for a while, he strongly suspected that F24 was one of the two kits reported from F7's territory during the summer and that her sibling might be close by at the moment. He didn't want to forego the opportunity to catch that animal. Data on the production and survival of young were central to the project.

Right. Noll and I were due to ski out of the park the next day in any event. Volunteer Guy Zoellner, a young mule skinner who led pack strings to supply Forest Service outposts in the Bob Marshall Wilderness and carried out snow depth surveys there on skis, came in to replace us at Avalanche. He duly rebaited the trap. Within hours, he had F24 inside. Hearing that, Yates gave up and told Zoellner to pop her loose and wire the lid closed until she left the area.

When the lab results came in, we learned that F24's father was M13, the young male who, like M3, seemed to be steadily expanding his territory and now claimed a huge swath of the park from its center to its southeastern edge. The mother was indeed F7, which made F24 the granddaughter of F2. Considering F7's injury and rundown condition, I wondered whether F24 was naturally small or undersized because her mother had experienced trouble hunting and keeping her offspring fed.

◇◇◇◇◇◇◇◇◇◇◇◇◇◇◇◇◇◇◇◇◇◇◇◇◇◇◇◇◇◇◇◇◇

In April, Yates climbed 2,000 feet up the side of Mount Brown, the next massif downstream from Mount Cannon in the McDonald drainage, and recovered the body of F24 from a small slide area below some cliffs. She hadn't fallen to her death, and she hadn't been caught in an avalanche. There was a hole in her belly not far from the incision site. The wound had nothing to do with the implant. F24 had apparently gone after one of the bearded white climbers living on the rocky ledges, for the hole was exactly the circumference of a mountain goat horn. Our hungry little girl had been given a lesson about how rapier-sharp the tip of those weapons are and how aggressively goats wield them with their muscular necks. She learned it at the cost of her life.

In late summer of 2007, M16, who occupied drainages between the territories of M1 and M13, was found dead on a high ridge when a park employee tracked down the mortality signal from this adult wolverine's implant. The cause of his demise remains listed as an unknown predator. Some of the holes in his skull resembled those that another wolverine's canines could have made. Other punctures might have been caused by a more massive tooth or teeth. M16's corpse was lying not far from the body of a bighorn sheep that appeared to have been fed on by a grizzly. Such evidence adds up to at least a hint that the most notoriously badass behavior *gulos* practice – competing with great bears for carcasses – is every bit as dangerous as it sounds.

While various naturalists have witnessed wolverines driving bears away, researchers have also reported instances of bears killing wolverines. *Gulo gulo* can't afford to be one iota bolder or more reckless than it already is, or the species would lose too many members. To thrive in the niche it has claimed for itself, this modest-size carnivore just has to be a little bolder and a little more reckless than everybody else. Which is why I think it's accurate to say: There's wild and then there's wolverine.

◇◇◇◇◇◇◇◇◇◇◇◇◇◇◇◇◇◇◇◇◇◇◇◇◇◇◇◇◇◇◇◇◇

We ended up marking down "fate unknown" for a lot of study animals including our oldest acquaintances – M1, F2, M3, and F4 – because Glacier Park officials rather abruptly announced in mid-2007 that the wolverine project had continued for long enough and was over. Finished. Exact cause of death undetermined.

We knew that some on the park's staff preferred wildlife research projects to be tidier than ours; that is to say, shorter, or at least bound to a definite end date. And we were keenly aware that others in the park were uncomfortable with all the manhandling of wolverines involved in attaching radios, particularly the surgery required to implant transmitters.

Copeland had chosen this technique because he knew very well how often wolverines slipped out of radio collars and how commonly the equipment (especially the expensive GPS units) failed even when the *gulos* kept it on for a while. Implanting VHF radios as capsules was the most reliable and effective means of getting key information year-round. Equally important, the technique allowed us to track juveniles too small and growing too rapidly to bear collars tightly fitted around their neck. Discovering more about young wolverines' lives and deaths – the high rate of early mortality we were picking up was striking – would prove critical to understanding population dynamics. Even so, Copeland was prepared to skip the implants and go solely with collars. The park officials were having none of it. They were done with this study. Period.

While we weren't totally surprised by the news, we were of course hugely disappointed. Yet this wasn't about us, nor should it have been about people on the park staff with no enthusiasm for continuing the project. It was about wolverines, perhaps pound-for-pound the most powerful animals in the entire warm-blooded wildlife community and yet one of the most vulnerable species in the lower 48 states.

Gulo gulo was the subject of formal petitions to list the last 250 to 500 south of Canada as endangered. The kind of information needed to stem its decline was in very short supply. Even some of the most rudimentary facts about the animals' natural history and habitat requirements were still unavailable, both to land managers weighing developments proposed for the backcountry and to game managers setting trapping seasons for midsize carnivores. For decades, when asked for details about wolverines, the decision makers mostly just mumbled about how mysterious and elusive the critters are.

Well, they *are* mysterious and elusive, especially where only dozens remain. Yet because of the Glacier Wolverine Project and the similar study led by Bob Inman in the Yellowstone/Grand Teton area since 2001, there is more to be said about wolverines – a good deal more. Cutting off further investigation of the most significant concentration left in the contiguous states – the Glacier Park group – at this stage made no sense.

For our part, I think we could have done a better job of explaining to the park service folks why there is no substitute for long-term study when the subject is a slow-reproducing, thinly distributed, hard-to-find, very-hard-to-follow, often nocturnal, peak-bagging, blizzard-beating, bone-crunching, badass mustelid. It's unreasonable to expect to figure out *Gulo gulo* at anyone's convenience. In an ideal world, the researchers and park officials would have drawn up a mutually acceptable plan to keep building on the data that had come out of the Glacier wolverine work so far. That didn't happen.

When others ask me what's going on with the project and I say there is no more project and they ask why, I still find myself at a loss for answers. In the end, I simply tell them they'd have to put their questions to the staff at Glacier. Asking a volunteer wolverine tracker to explain park politics and bureaucratic priorities is like asking M3 for a rundown on the fine points of Chinese calligraphy.

We were pleading with the park not for money but simply for continued approval and a minimum of logistical support. How Glacier's officials weighed that against all the other obligations they were asked to fulfill, from keeping more than 2 million tourists per year happy and safe to fending off external threats like an open-pit coal mine and monster coal-bed methane development proposed next door in British Columbia, is as complicated a puzzle as wolverines are.

From my vantage point, though, this wasn't a matter of either-or choices. The contentment of tourists, the integrity of Glacier Park, the expansion of knowledge about wolverines, the effectiveness of a bureaucracy created to protect natural resources, the dethronement of the hydrocarbon industry, the restraint of global warming, the education of the public about environmental values, and the salvation of wildlife in an era of widespread extinctions are issues that ultimately have to be addressed together. All are part of the challenge of learning as a modern society how to live the good life on Earth without abusing the generosity of our hostess.

I know of a sure way to shore up the connections that keep ecosystems healthy and wildness flowing, a way to knit the fragments of the modern world back into a whole for our own sake as well as for countless other species. The idea can be summed up as freedom to roam. It's not the same as the wolverine way; nothing is. But the closer we come to understanding the wolverine way, the more it helps illuminate the concept of freedom to roam. I want to explain this as best I can before the book comes to a close.

Freedom to roam for two-leggeds and four-leggeds alike. DAVE MURRAY

CHAPTER SIXTEEN

A Natural Selection
of Ideas

The whole is more than the sum of its parts.

attributed to ARISTOTLE

DOWN IN THE VALLEY BETWEEN THE SWAN RANGE AND THE MISSION MOUNTAINS lives a gentleman named Bud Moore, who built his cabin in the forest on a sweet rise between two cattail-edged lakes. He wasn't the one who picked out that site. A fishing and woods-rambling pal, the late Norman Maclean, did it for him. Maclean, the author of *A River Runs Through It*, is a Montana legend. Moore, a longtime forest ranger, hunter, trapper, conservationist, and dispenser of outdoor lore and wisdom, is an icon in his own right.

When I stopped in to visit one December day, he reminisced about a wolverine that used to make a huge circuit of the area. About once every week, this animal would swing down out of the Missions into the valley, cross through a stretch of woodland, and angle back up toward the heights again. Moore's description reminded me of the kind of movements our GPS radio collars recorded for M1 as he loped the perimeter of his territory in Glacier during the course of a week.

"If you catch a wolverine by a front leg, it can sometimes use its rear legs to push against the trap and pull free," Moore told me. "But if you catch it by a hind leg, the wolverine can't get loose from the jaws." He went on to tell me with delight that there were fresh tracks in the snow from four wolves on the corner of his property, and he urged me to go have a look.

In his 90s now, Moore hasn't trapped in quite some time. He's far more interested in doing what he can to save wildlife for generations to come. To that end, he's placed a conservation easement on his acreage, which he calls Coyote Forest, with the land trust Vital Ground to limit future development. His place

247

lies within a critical wildlife corridor between the public lands rising on either side of the valley. He took the wolf tracks for confirmation that his property was doing its part to keep the wild community whole.

I wanted to introduce Bud Moore here not only because he's helping reconnect ecosystems by adding private land to the habitat mix but also as an example of a hunter and trapper I admire. I've hunted. Most of my friends and acquaintances in Montana shoot wild meat, and that includes the Glacier wolverine crew. I discovered that many of the people on the project had done some fur trapping at an earlier stage in life and felt that it deepened his or her fascination with the natural realm.

I'm emphasizing this because I want to talk about game management in relation to wolverines and other midsize carnivores, and anything construed as a criticism of hunting or trapping has a way of quickly spiraling into a shouting match about rights and righteousness, lifestyles, cultural identities – everything but what was originally brought up for discussion. My purpose isn't to argue for or against either activity in general. I'm only trying to look more clearly into how we interpret nature and go about conserving it.

◇◇◇◇◇◇◇◇◇◇◇◇◇◇◇◇◇◇◇◇◇◇◇◇◇◇◇◇◇◇

When Jeff Copeland and Rick Yates analyzed the survival data collected by the Glacier Wolverine Project from 2002 through 2007, they determined that the population was stable to just very slightly increasing. Using the same figures, however, they were able to predict that the additional death of one more adult, particularly a breeding-age female, would have put the population on a downward trend. Two such deaths would have made for a much sharper rate of decline.

The loss of a single mature animal in 1,500 square miles causes a notable difference? A pair of losses marks a path toward scarcity? How can that be?

"Wolverine females don't produce offspring until at least age three and then have two kits per litter every other year, on average," Copeland explained. "So in a female's breeding life, which would end after around age ten, she'll have three litters and a total of six kits. The sex ratio is 50:50, so we've got three new males and three new females in the population. Half those kits will die before reaching maturity. Now we're down to 1.5 males and 1.5 females as the offspring. One of each has to survive and stick around to replace their parents in the population. That leaves half a male and half a female to disperse and carry the genes somewhere else. You can see how a small change in the number of breeding females would make a big difference."

Suppose the population isn't within a fully protected park. How many of those half-a-males and half-a-females – the vehicles for dispersing the gene pool – might get shot or trapped before they could leave? How many of the adult females might have been trapped while out foraging in winter to find food and bring some back to their kits? We recorded mothers in Glacier regularly traveling several miles from den sites to hunt. During his Sawtooth study, Copeland caught a female nearly 10 miles from her den.

If a nursing mother is taken in a trap anywhere within her wide hunting range, you'd have to subtract both that breeding-age female and her young starving back in the den from the population. Should the resident adult male be trapped instead during the course of his still wider and more frequent travels, a transient male could come in and kill the kits. If the newcomer doesn't kill them, the kits will still grow up with less protection from other wolverines and less experience gained from traveling with a father after they separate from the mother. Both factors lower the offspring's chances of successfully reaching adulthood and either replacing numbers in the population or transporting genes to other homelands.

How often would just one wolverine have to survive and reach another area in order for scattered populations to stay connected? "I don't know," Copeland replied. "That's one of the things I'm looking at: What does it take to keep a metapopulation going? I know that if a very occasional connection was enough, you'd still find wolverine groups in Oregon, California, Utah, Colorado, and maybe a few other parts of the West. This isn't a species crashing toward extinction; I'm not saying that. It's an animal with incredibly low densities and many of its populations in isolated mountain areas, and that makes it extremely vulnerable."

The mortality data from dispersing wolverines show that they run a fairly high risk of being killed by people outside strictly protected lands such as national parks (remember: wilderness areas, wildlife refuges, state and provincial parks, and other types of reserves permit trapping and hunting.) In British Columbia, studies by biologist John Krebs revealed that wherever wolverines were declining, the primary cause was mortality from trapping.

Here in the Lower 48, the number of traps specifically set for wolverines is no longer much of an issue. Only Montana allows *gulos* to be trapped, and the state finally reduced the legal quota to a token handful in 2008. What needs to be considered is the number of traps put out for other midsize carnivores but capable of catching a wolverine – or a protected lynx or rare fisher.

There are several thousand registered trappers in Montana alone and many thousands more in neighboring Western states. That translates into hundreds of thousands of traps lacing the backcountry and front country alike with jaws set for bobcats, coyotes, otters, and other furbearers considered legal game. Wolves were just recently taken off the endangered species list in the West. Game managers promptly opened hunting seasons on the packs and may go on to allow wolf trapping before long, as Canadian provinces and Alaska already do. This could create more problems for wolverines in the southern end of their continental range – the Lower 48, where populations are the smallest and most widely separated.

Officials hesitate to confront the side effects of trapping for fear of stirring up bitter controversy. Living in rural Montana, I understand that, and I understand that no one has much hard information about "nontarget" captures to begin with, because many are never reported. Just the same, I think the value of a ban on trapping midsize and large animals both in and around reserves with wolverine populations deserves more thought, as does the possibility of restricting trapping in some of the linkage zones between them.

Human disturbances, from snowmobiling and heli-skiing to cross-country ski touring, in high-country denning habitat should be examined as well. That's bound to make life more complicated for some people at first, but the objective should be to make life possible for wolverines. Maybe the creation of buffer zones with some restrictions on human activities during the denning period around core parks and wilderness areas already off-limits to mechanized back-country travel would suffice. I'm for trying and seeing.

◇◇◇◇◇◇◇◇◇◇◇◇◇◇◇◇◇◇◇◇◇◇◇◇◇◇◇◇◇◇◇◇

Exhaustingly large to those of us attempting to keep up with the owners, the territories of Glacier's wolverines are considerably smaller than those of other groups studied in other places, which means Glacier supports a higher density of the animals. Part of this is a trick of topography. If you were to magically flatten out all the vertical contours here, you'd find each wolverine's range covering a much broader area. The rest of the explanation for smaller home ranges has mainly to do with the quality of the habitat. Though high and steep and subject to brutal winter weather, Glacier supports a remarkable abundance of life adapted to its extremes.

Mountain goats are one of the most common big animals. The park may have close to a thousand. Occupying the same upper elevations as the wolverines, the bearded white climbers are a major item in the *gulos'* winter diet. Most are probably scavenged rather than taken as prey. Nevertheless, wolverines are perfectly capable of killing a kid or subadult when an opportunity arises, and the *gulos'* climbing abilities give them more opportunities than other predators have. Together with winter, they surely claim some of the badly injured, the weak, and the very old among adults as well.

Add perhaps 500 bighorn sheep to Glacier's high elevations, plus hundreds of mule deer, white-tailed deer, elk, and moose farther downslope, and you have tons of what ecologists term *ungulate biomass* – meat on the hoof – crowded among these formidable-looking peaks. Of the original fauna, the only midsize to large species currently missing are bison, mountain caribou, and possibly, fishers. Some 350 grizzlies, the densest population south of Canada, hundreds of black bears, active wolf packs, healthy populations of mountain lions, coyotes, otters, and a fair number of lynx also call Glacier home.

Don't presume that wolverines end up with a smaller share of food because they compete with so many other predators here. We're looking at another case of a whole being greater than the sum of its parts. What wolverines can't take away in a contest with another carnivore, they can later come back and munch down to bones, then munch up the bones. The better the hunting for other carnivores, the more *gulo* food gets left lying around. This could be one of the reasons most of the wolverines left in the contiguous states are found in the same mountain refuges as grizzlies, cougars, and other major predators.

We don't often think of how the activities of one carnivore might encourage the survival of another – wolves commandeering prey killed by cougars, for instance – because we're not used to viewing ferocious predators as a complex, finely balanced community. I've come upon late-winter carcasses of elk with wolf, cougar, grizzly, wolverine, coyote, and marten tracks together around them. If the forest were stripped away, the place might at times rival an African park with lions, cheetahs, hyenas, wild dogs, and jackals all out there in plain view maneuvering for access to kills.

Thriving predators require thriving prey. Our game management system is nicely geared to produce hoofed animals in good numbers – but primarily for human consumers. Devised during the first half of the 20th century, it's a semi-agricultural approach that openly defines wild herbivores in terms of crops, harvests, and surpluses. A primary goal is to provide what managers call the maximum sustained yield. To gauge the condition of a wildlife range, they measure how lightly or heavily the vegetation has been eaten. If it looks hard used, they take this as a signal to increase the harvest – reduce the number of eaters.

The underlying belief is that game animals naturally produce a harvestable surplus, and if we don't take that excess, wild herds will starve and suffer, having exceeded the carrying capacity of their range. It all works out in amazingly convenient and morally satisfying fashion so that we're actually helping animals by killing them – kindly neatening up the messy side of the wild world while having a good outing and getting some great-tasting meat.

This is a pleasant rationale, and I'm not out to poke holes in it. I just don't believe we should conflate it with the workings of nature. She has her own game managers. They're called predators and scavengers. Prey species don't produce a surplus; that's a human value judgment.

Prey species have high rates of reproduction; they produce relatively large numbers of young. Each generation makes its way into the world and is sorted out by the carnivores and the physical demands of the environment, leaving the fittest to join the reproductive population and give rise to the next generation. This is natural selection. Human hunting will not yield the same results until sportsmen go out to bag the least impressive specimens they can find instead of gunning for the grandest expressions of the gene pool. Humans have become the primary predators of many hoofed species and, thus, a dominant agent of natural selection. Over time, the trophy syndrome can only reduce the overall size and fitness of the species we prey on.

Game management is not a science. It is a utilitarian scheme to provide food and sport, dressed up as science. I wish it worked better for the predators, which often get blamed – and purged – when hoofed herds decline in part due to heavy pressure from human hunters. And I especially wish the system worked better for wolverines, which have been ignored compared with other wildlife. Just as we can expect *gulos* to fare well as part of a boisterous predator community, they would fare better yet if we weren't so intent on squeezing the maximum sustained yield from hoofed herds. Managers may prefer nature neat and orderly – cropped and mown. But *gulos* depend on the flux and swirl in wild communities – the bulging out to the sides, the slop and the spillover. As far as wolverines are concerned, there is no such thing as too many prey animals. The natural balance of predators and prey has always fluctuated around a level ultimately determined by qualities of the habitats that the landscape and prevailing weather will support. If ungulates periodically become overcrowded and more begin to grow ill or weak from hunger and the range has dozens of bodies strewn across it after a hard winter, why, then it's time for wolverines to shine. Selecting some of the less well-adapted prey animals for dinner and cleaning up the carcasses of others, ultimately reinforcing the stability of the community as a whole, is their job description – their niche, their very reason to be.

Drawn to wolverine bait, a captured lynx is freed within minutes of its discovery. ALEX HASSON

CHAPTER SEVENTEEN

Freedom to Roam

A thing is right when it tends to increase the integrity, stability, and beauty of the biotic community. It is wrong when it tends otherwise.

ALDO LEOPOLD
from *A Sand County Almanac*

Man is not totally compounded of the nature we profess to understand. Man is always partly of the future, and the future he possesses a power to shape.

LOREN EISELEY
from *The Firmament of Time*

AMERICANS HAVE COME UP WITH LOADS OF TREMENDOUS IDEAS. Many would agree with the Pulitzer Prize-winning writer Wallace Stegner that establishing a national park system was the best one this country ever had. Our national wildlife refuge system was another splendid idea, our national wilderness system yet another. The arrays of protected areas grew out of a more fundamental, profoundly democratic notion: public lands. Counting national forests and national rangelands, one-third of the acreage constituting these United States of America is deemed the property not of select individuals and giant corporations but of every citizen, rich or poor, in equal measure.

In addition to the various types of federal domain, there are state parks, forests, game ranges, designated natural areas, and ecological reserves also managed on the behalf of ordinary citizens. Canada has a similar spectrum of protected public lands, ranging from national parks and wilderness areas to provincial parks that allow limited industrial activities such as logging.

During a hiking trip in Glacier National Park, I would be considered a visitor. But I am also the owner. I can't build a house or do business in the park. I can't haul any materials out of it. I can, however, pass as many days as I want here, hike to my heart's content, and make Glacier my spiritual home for as long as I breathe. Though I'm nobody special, all its square miles and hundreds of thousands more from the Everglades to the Arctic National Wildlife Range and all the summits, canyons, wild rivers, desert sunsets, and seashore fogs within them are part of my holdings. I take the privileges and responsibilities that come with such an inheritance seriously. If I want to keep the likes of tree frogs, trout, bison, grizz, old-growth cypress woodlands, swans, prairie dogs, orchids, manatees, warblers, and wolverines on my place, I'm obliged to make sure they have what they need to flourish. What do they require most today?

A fresh idea.

On both sides of the international border, many of the best-known reserves are clustered along mountain chains whose craggy heights escaped development, namely the various ranges of the Pacific region and the spine of the continent – the Rockies. Here are the bulwarks, the strongholds, for the most powerful North American mammals left outside the Arctic and Subarctic, especially the carnivores. Each of these reserves is a star in its own right as well as part of the constellation that ornaments the modern landscape. And yet not one of them – not Glacier National Park, Montana, or the Glacier National Park 220 miles north in British Columbia; not even 3,470-square-mile Yellowstone National Park or the nearest national park of that size in North America, 4,200-square-mile Jasper, 500 miles north in Alberta – is truly large enough to sustain its great beasts over time by itself.

That's why a fresh way of thinking about conservation is so important.

Are visitors to one of our grand mountain parks going to stand there amid ranks of cloud-scraper peaks looming above valleys wider than an entire county back home and imagine that the resident wildlife need more protection? Nope. They're more likely to be thinking, "This is the biggest, strongest-looking setting I've ever been in with the biggest, strongest-looking critters I've ever seen. Maybe they're in fragile shape somewhere outside the entrance gate, but surely not here, not where the view toward every horizon promises room for large numbers to thrive indefinitely. What a hopeful scene."

And I'm the spoilsport who walks over and says, "You know, you could put the DNA that built all the magnificent creatures here into a bowl no larger than a contact lens. Imagine it resting gently on your forefinger. There's the park's gene pool. Hold it up against the mountain background for perspective. If some of the mixtures in this tiny container don't flow out well beyond those towering rock walls and new mixtures flow back in, the pool is in danger of turning stagnant and starting to evaporate. Now can you begin to see why even a place that feels so overwhelmingly vast and immune to the passage of time might require a little extra help to stay strong?"

Population genetics can be a daunting subject, so I'll bring in some wolverines to help open up the innards. In their high, harsh niche, a full belly isn't easy for *gulos* to come by, and it's sometimes filled only with old bones. As we've seen, these animals compensate by keeping on the move through immense territories the way no other beast quite can to uncover anything and everything worth biting into. Because each of the well-defended territories sprawls across so much tilted terrain, not many more than 40 to 50 adults and young are going to fit inside Glacier at any one time. Fewer yet will fit inside the park if global warming makes cool habitats and deep, lingering snow for den sites scarce.

The figure of 40 to 50 is the total, or *absolute*, population size. Biologists draw a careful distinction between that and the *effective* size of a population, which is the number of individuals that actually contribute offspring to the next generation. To determine this, take the overall count, subtract nonbreeding animals (immature, infertile, or prevented from mating by dominant individuals), then subtract the adult females that skipped breeding that year because they were nursing young or replenishing their energy reserves. Then subtract the mothers whose offspring of that year failed to survive to breeding age.

We know of five or so resident adult male wolverines that claim most of Glacier between them at the moment. Each breeds with two or three females, but not all of them produce young every year. We also know that quite a few of their offspring never reach adulthood to pass on the genes they carry, and that others disperse. Thus, the effective population within the park is somewhere around a dozen.

For a group of relatively slow-reproducing mammals to stay viable over time without serious problems from inbreeding, experts reckon that the effective population needs to be at least 50. To maintain their full spectrum of natural genetic variation, the effective population should be in the many hundreds, which would require a total population in the thousands. Glacier's wolverines are hanging in there. They'll continue to get by as long as occasional movement into the area by wolverines from somewhere else occurs. Should that end, however, so would Glacier's *gulos*. Maybe not right away, but inevitably. On their own, they're toast. Indeed, the effective population size of all the wolverines left in the lower 48 states appears to be less than 50.

To find another case in point, have a look 150 miles north at Banff National Park, the oldest and perhaps best-loved reserve in the Canadian Rockies. Though Banff is more than half again as big as Glacier, its total number of grizzlies has faded to just 50 or 60, because the bears get whacked by cars and trains along the major transportation corridor running through the heart of the park, killed in campgrounds where people leave out food and garbage, or leave and are terminated around settlements nearby. The effective size of the population is probably fewer than 15, a pitifully small number for a great silver-tipped carnivore. Banff's grizz may still appear big and burly and frighteningly active to a tourist on a trail. To a population biologist, they look more like the walking dead unless they get an infusion of breeding adults from elsewhere.

Wolverines returned to the Lower 48 principally through Glacier after coming from Canada during the 1960s and 1970s. They may well have arrived from Banff. The first wolves to inhabit the U.S. West in half a century came from the Banff area, trotting south to den in Glacier during the 1980s and spreading outward from there. Researchers have since radio-tracked wolves from Banff to Glacier and from Glacier back to Banff. They've done the same with a few grizzlies. Based on the distances some young wolverines venture when leaving home, I'd be surprised if *gulos* haven't also gone from Glacier to Banff over the years. As things stand, this pair of parks has the ability to back up each other's carnivore populations, so to speak, by naturally providing new seed stock once in a while. This is how the system of reserves is supposed to work.

But southern Alberta and British Columbia have grown awfully busy lately. An animal traveling between Glacier and Banff has to get past massive coal-mining projects and still more extensive logging operations, cross a major east-west highway with heavier volumes of traffic every year, negotiate a spaghetti-spill of backcountry roads associated with recently installed oil and gas fields, contend with rapid subdivision for new homes and resorts in the scenic valleys, more homesites and recreational facilities spreading upslope, heavier hunting pressure, et cetera, et cetera.

I wonder how much longer any park-to-park exchange of lives and genes and potential will remain possible. I wonder what will happen over the long run to the southernmost of grizzly populations, Yellowstone's famed bears, which no longer have any contact with other groups of grizzlies. What about remnant subpopulations of the rare mountain race of woodland caribou in wildland outposts of southern British Columbia and northernmost Idaho, cut off from the rest of their kind? And what about the impact of humans in the form of rapid climate change?

<hr>

The joys of trekking through the summer high country are too many to either list or give adequate thanks for. However, this part of the West has been stuck for the past decade in a moderate to severe drought that baked much of the pleasure out of being atop the continent some days and turned strenuous hikes into heat stress tests. The dry times continue as I write. How much of this trend is due to some cyclical weather pattern and how much is a consequence of global warming is open to debate. All I know for sure is that 2006 brought one of the fieriest summers in memory.

All my life, I've counted on the routes toward the peaks offering lower temperatures, stronger breezes, and snowbanks with meltwater rivulets where I could drink my fill and bathe my face in the coolness of the bygone winter. In 2006, the snowbanks were gone early. Streams ran dry. Even along the highest ridges, the air was often dead still and shimmering with heat waves. My favorite part of the world was no longer a refuge from the overcooked realm I thought I had left below. With temperatures hitting the 90s on the Divide itself, the alpine zone became the zone too near the sun – the treeless zone with no midday shade and scant atmosphere to filter out ultraviolet rays, a province of bare rock expanses that absorbed the heat and radiated it back like a giant solar-powered kiln.

Apart from mountain goats bedded beneath stone overhangs, the only large animals Shea Wyatt and I saw that summer while searching for M3 in the Belly River area and during other radio-tracking expeditions were in the water: mule deer wading chest deep in some lakes; a moose partially submerged in a higher tarn surrounded by open slopes, standing motionless as if asleep or stunned while we worked our way down the trail above, eyes filled with sweat, brains too hot to register much besides thirst and the placing of one foot in front of the other.

I apologize for whining; I know I've said there's none allowed in wolverine camp. But we didn't sign on for desert-type trekking complete with hyperthermia and dehydration. This issue of global warming was getting personal at a level beyond the sorrow of watching the last shining glaciers collapse into dirty pools of meltwater.

News articles about climate concerns often point out that Earth's polar regions are heating up at a faster rate than the lower latitudes. But I've seen little mention of the fact that many mountain realms around the globe – the high altitudes, from the Andes to the Himalayas – turn out to be the most rapidly warming places of all. Within the lower 48 states, the greatest increase in average temperature has taken place right here in northwest Montana: 3 degrees (F) over the last 30 years. Why? Because the region is mostly made of mountain ranges, crowned by the Divide in Glacier National Park, where the temperature increase has been two to three times the global average. The fact that the foremost wolverine concentration known south of Canada today lives where the environment is growing toastier at the highest rate is sour with irony.

In light of Copeland's map-based analysis showing wolverines absent from regions where the average maximum August temperature exceeds 70 degrees, the species' future seems questionable even in protected reserves like Glacier. I was thinking in terms of decades. But given just a few more summers like 2006, we naturalists might be able to find all the *gulos*, goats, and pikas left in the park merely by searching around the last icefields on the tallest peaks. And not long after that, locating a U.S. wolverine may require that we first plan a trip to Alaska.

Ah, for the good old days when people thought that if you drew a protective line around a wild place, you'd have its flora and fauna permanently preserved like specimens in a living museum. Compared with specialists in the present era of molecular biology and computer modeling, early reserve planners were practically working in the dark. Wildlife wasn't always the priority anyway. The folks marking out boundaries were often thinking harder about how to include geologic marvels and other scenic highlights. Or they were just trying to outline a nice, spirit-recharging stretch of the outdoors that wasn't coveted by industry and could therefore be set aside for public enjoyment without too much political fuss.

When Yellowstone was declared a park in 1872, Wyoming was a territory 18 years away from statehood. Glacier was established in 1910, 38 years after Yellowstone. Yet most folks in Montana still traveled by horse between small lantern-lit towns, and almost everybody, rangers included, was more interested in eradicating carnivores than in figuring out how to keep some around. Terms like *ecology* and *ecosystem* wouldn't come into common use for at least another half-century. No one was talking about wildlife population genetics, much less climate change. And not even the most foresighted of conservationists back then could have guessed how thoroughly skyrocketing human population growth coupled with technological advances would reshape the land in between reserves.

Back then, it would have taken a science fiction fan to envision snowmobiles capable of hitting freeway speeds allowing a fur trapper to run traplines covering a hundred miles or more while helicopters roar up the high ridges and deposit powder hounds among the peaks to ski back down. Hunters covering the same slopes while sitting in all-terrain vehicles. A feller-buncher machine that would let one person log a forest single-handedly without ever leaving his or her seat. Exclusive condominium/golf course communities with names like Wolf Hollow and Grizzly Glen displacing real wolves and bears on the mountainsides. I hardly need to add that the list keeps going and growing.

The faster surrounding habitats get chopped up, paved over, and turned into humanscapes, the more existing reserves begin to resemble islands. Much as I like real islands, this is not a complimentary comparison. Islands have had the highest extinction rates in the world. Compared with large islands, smaller ones invariably support not just smaller populations, but far fewer kinds of life forms. Big animals are generally among the first to disappear; either that or they shrink in size as natural selection favors punier versions adapted to more restricted space and resources.

As a reserve is more solidly barricaded by development, it becomes the equivalent of an island set farther away from any mainland and from other isles. The more isolated the island, the lower the chances of its fauna being replenished from another source. Once again, the result is a marked decrease in species.

Many animals that would be counted as residents of a reserve swing beyond the borders in the course of their daily or weekly travels. Some exit for part of each year to take advantage of better seasonal habitat elsewhere. Offspring are bound to try journeying farther still when they disperse as juveniles or young adults. And every so often, mature individuals blast off for parts unknown for reasons we can't fathom. The question is how likely that voyager is to drown in a sea of human activity when it passes beyond a reserve's protected shores.

As a rule, large to midsize carnivores will be among the first to drop out of confined wildlife communities. This is no surprise, in light of their huge ranges, high energy requirements, slow rates of reproduction, small effective populations, and the fear, intolerance, and human hunger for furs and trophies awaiting them outside should they make a break for it. The smaller and more isolated the reserve, the sooner some of the big, toothy hunters will vanish; studies show that they already have from a number of U.S. parks.

The disappearance of a top, or apex, carnivore ripples all the way down the steps of the food pyramid. Each loss skews the balance between other meat eaters, causing the community to become less stable. This reshuffles the numbers and movement patterns of the animals being preyed upon, which changes grazing pressures on vegetation, which alters habitats, creating more instability for smaller species.

I'm not pointing at the sky and shrieking, "Run! Th-th-that sucker's coming down on our heads!" None of these reserves is going to collapse overnight. Many facets of the island effect will be too slow and subtle for anyone but scientists to detect for a while. On the other hand, every influence that adds to the isolation of a reserve leaves both the wildlife and their habitats increasingly at the mercy of events that can sweep through a last stand quite suddenly: drought, wildfires, massive flooding, disease epidemics, insect outbreaks, invasions of nonnative species, and a host of other forces that we perceive as rare and unlucky catastrophes. Mind you, on nature's timescale, most of these are normal tremors in the system, and they are 100 percent certain to happen sooner or later.

The story of our age is nature going to pieces. Nature won't work in pieces, not even those we've made special efforts to safeguard. The future of wildlife is tied to its freedom to roam.

<><><><><><><><><><><><><><><><><><><><><>

I can't help pounding on this point that the model of setting aside samples of the wild world in scattered reserves is outmoded, because I can't think of a more crucial subject in conservation. Moreover, I can't shake my impression that the majority of citizens assume North America's premier natural areas and the wildlife within them have already been saved and are good to go for the future. Time to relax. Oh sure, there are environmental problems and endangered species issues to deal with. But we'll always have the best of the outdoor realm banked in our national parks and wildernesses and refuges, right?

Nature is an all-embracing web of processes and interactions that we arose from and remain very much part of and depend on for our survival. However, Western societies were conditioned to conceive of nature as a separate order of existence. To them, the untamed world was not so much a dynamic whole as an assemblage of curiosities and wonders – of different and strange, startlingly beautiful, and sometimes dangerous nonhuman things. However well-intended, tucking nature away in special enclaves here and there reinforced this sense of division between the human sphere and rest of the living world, and the consequences are catching up with us.

Once estranged from one another by development, preserves of nature become mere fragments of nature. And fragmentation, being the opposite of wholeness, is the enemy of everything that keeps ecosystems healthy and strong. I'm not suggesting that the old model of protecting the wild world wasn't a glorious idea. With the benefit of hindsight, perhaps we can say that a great deal of its glory lies in the fact that it was a start. Today, the challenge is to make more people aware that it was only a start and that the great work of conservation on this continent and the most enduring rewards lie just ahead.

If the problem is that our remaining patches of wildness are becoming smaller and more isolated, it seems pretty obvious that the solution is to make them larger and better connected. This doesn't necessarily mean expanding them all. Simply having a bridge in place between two islands makes each of them effectively larger, adds some slack to the system, gives the inhabitants a place to turn when something goes wrong on one of the isles. Bridging as many reserves together as possible re-creates a whole greater than the sum of its parts, which is a fair description of nature. If there's a better solution, a fresher idea, no one has yet heard of it. It's time to shuck the philosophy of separateness. Time to go big – big and bound together, rejoined, renatured.

Conservation biologists speak of shoring up what was accomplished by the old model and at the same time building on it through a strategy of cores and connections. Existing wildland reserves and *de facto* (unprotected but still unmessed-with) wilderness are the cores. Some do need to be expanded to take in vital seasonal ranges or other critical habitats left out by the original design. If the borders can't be redrawn for one reason or another, much the same result can be achieved by establishing buffer zones next door in which certain kinds of development and other human disturbances are limited.

As for the connections, they go by any number of names: habitat bridges, landscape linkages, corridors, and migratory or movement routes, to mention a few. Creating one might be a matter of controlling activities in the terrain that runs along the upper elevations of a mountain range. Or designating the brushy banks along a river's course a wildway. Or making sure that a few stringers of mature forest leading from one side of a mountain valley to the other are always left intact. Elsewhere, keeping an area permeable to wildlife can be as simple as

F4 studies a visitor along the Highline Trail. BILL GARWOOD

constructing underpasses or overpasses across a lethally busy highway at points where the topography naturally funnels animals on the move.

Ecologists, environmentalists, owners of backcountry recreation businesses, and ordinary citizens who don't ever want to know what life is like without a truly great outdoors have been promoting this goal of conservation at the landscape level for the past couple of decades. Associations such as the Wildlands Network (formerly the Wildlands Project), Alliance for the Wild Rockies, the Greater Yellowstone Coalition, and the Yellowstone to Yukon Conservation Initiative (Y2Y) led the effort. In 2007, Patagonia set out to begin enlisting not only conservation biologists and mountain adventurers but also politicians and major corporations to support its Freedom to Roam campaign, putting special emphasis on the need for north-south wildland corridors to give native plant and animal communities a means of adjusting to climate change.

Predictably, objections have arisen from different groups, who portray a plan of this scope as the biggest land grab ever by bear-smooching greenies and wilder-nuts. I've even met people who say too much public land has been safeguarded already. We should mine/log/drill/graze/bulldoze/commercialize some of our current reserves, they insist, as though if we could just get into those last corners of the frontier, especially along the rugged spine of the continent, we would finally have all the jobs/energy/economic growth/folding money we ever wanted.

Some guys relish a fight. I'd rather try something we haven't been doing for the last thousand generations. These days, it's about all I can do to haul my aging ass up to the tip-top of a mountain. If I have any leftover energy, I don't want to squander it on some outdated feud like jobs versus the environment. What hasn't gotten through to the opposition is that proposals like those advanced by Y2Y and Freedom to Roam could just as easily be interpreted as mainstream business plans, among the most solid ones going for mountain regions in the 21st century.

Throughout the heart of the Rockies, tourism and recreation have either replaced resource extraction industries as the major sources of revenue and employment or are on the verge of doing so. In particular, national parks and other reserves that dot the region are proving to be among its most reliable economic engines both for local communities and for the states and provinces that host the protected areas. The aim of connecting those dots for ecological reasons goes hand in hand with ensuring long-term financial stability and prosperity.

What's not to like? Opponents fear the possibility of more land being "locked up" in order to build linkage into the system. To them, the core-and-connection design somehow translates into a superpark or superwilderness running wild up and down the Rockies and coastal ranges, forcing rural people out of their homes. In reality, most of the countryside in between the reserves has long been federal domain such as national forest or its counterpart in Canada, known as crown land, or else state or provincial domain. It is not private property with homes. It's public property. In other words, a huge part of guaranteeing species the freedom to roam involves providing better protection for animals and habitats on government-administered domain that is supposed to be managed to maintain wildlife, diverse woodlands, fisheries, clean water, and recreational opportunities in the first place. If this is a landgrab, it's of land we citizens already possess. We just want to hold it a little closer.

Linkage zones don't necessarily require regulations as stringent as those in official reserves. As long as the corridors provide passing wildlife with food, shelter, real security, and the chance to find a way forward, they're doing their job. Some pretty smart people are poring over some very detailed maps right now to pinpoint acreage that leads through the most suitable terrain and habitats. These are pathways – survival lanes – that conservationists are calling for, not enormous swaths of countryside. Animals are pretty smart, too. They learn where they are safe and where they are not. It won't take millions and millions of acres with new layers of protection to keep the entire network humming with life. It will just take acreage in exactly the right places. What needs to spread far and wide is a deeper understanding of the power of connections.

◇◇◇◇◇◇◇◇◇◇◇◇◇◇◇◇◇◇◇◇◇◇◇◇◇◇◇◇◇◇◇◇

A badly disintegrating beaver drew a wolverine into the Josephine trap fairly late in the season when I was alone in Many Glacier one winter. As usual, the *gulo* went in after dark, and as usual, snow squalls were scouring the two frozen lakes en route as I made the ski trek up the valley and lifted the box's lid to see what I'd need to do next. Also as usual, the captive immediately made a dive for my face. It was good mother wolverine F4. She appeared to be in decent shape. No obvious signs of illness or injury, and her radio implant was working fine. I called Copeland on the satellite phone for instructions.

"We're not going to try putting a satellite collar on her. She might be nursing young back in the den this time of year, so we wouldn't want to hold her overnight in the trap or give her any drugs. You checked her condition?"

"Best I could without losing parts of my head. No problems I could see."

"Just pop her loose then."

"My pleasure."

"Before you do, though, see if you can get a look at her teats. If she does have kits, they'll be swollen, and the hair around them will be worn off. It should be obvious. That would be valuable information for us to have."

"Right. So all I have to do is persuade F4 to roll over and show me her belly."

"Just keep looking. You might be able to tell something. Good luck."

Forty-five minutes later, F4 and I had both worn down. The snow around the trap was high enough that I had to lie on my side to be able to peer in while lifting the lid slightly, ready to drop it at an instant's notice when she charged. After my arm grew tired from holding the heavy logs up, I tried propping the lid open with one leg. After my leg gave out, I wedged a branch in the crack to use as a lever. By then, F4 had started keeping more to the back of the trap, perhaps realizing that I wasn't doing anything more threatening than peeping at her.

But she had kits waiting somewhere high up on the slopes, growing a little cooler and hungrier as the night wore on. Why in the world would I expect a cornered wolverine to expose her underside? The only time she raised up off all fours was when she came at me and stood at the front of the box trying to push her head and front paws through the crack. To see her chest and belly, I would have had to look straight down past her jaws. Even then, the part I was supposed to examine would have been in the shadow unless I stuck in my arm with the flashlight.

My only plan was to give this trying-to-peek-at-wolverine-teats business about fifteen more minutes before turning the female loose. I was telling her out loud once again to just let me know whether she was nursing and she'd be free, when F4 abruptly sat on her haunches facing me. As if she'd made a conscious decision to meet my request, she raised her front legs in the air and gave me a square-on look at her underside. It was more than enough to reveal the swollen dugs of a nursing mother. The scene was so strangely calm and utterly unexpected, I could barely find my voice.

"Thank you."

A minute later, she was loping off into the mountain night.

"Say hi to the kits for me."

I gibber at marmots and ptarmigan. I wish passing mountain goats a lovely day and compliment nannies on their kids. When they hold my gaze for an extra moment or proceed to do something out of the ordinary, I can't help feeling that we're building a kind of rapport. Projecting feelings and motives onto animals is a normal human inclination. Assuming that wild creatures take an interest in us as individuals is mostly another of the many, many ways in which we flatter ourselves. Still, it's our nature to want an animal that we like to like us, or at least reciprocate our interest, and it's easy to convince ourselves that this is what's happening.

If the animal is one we don't like, our belief that we are the recipient of special attention doesn't waver much. It just twists. We think the creature is making a particular effort to bother us. This is partly why you hear people say bears are out to get us, wolves and coyotes want to destroy our flocks and "our" herds of wild game, and wolverines relish stinking up cabins and raiding traplines when in fact predators are simply impelled to get protein-rich food. Sometimes we happen to own it, sometimes we compete directly for it, and once in a great while we are that food. But it's not personal.

I'd never seen a *gulo* sit fully upright as F4 did, and I've no idea what caused her to perform such a move. Despite that, despite the fact that I talk to wolverines and care deeply for them and was especially fond of F4, I never had the slightest feeling that I was more to her or to any of the others than a threat or a potential competitor. At best, I was a tall, rather slow, odd-smelling annoyance. The only thing they would ever want or need from me personally was to be left the hell alone. I admired them all the more for that.

They're wolverines. They're indomitably wild. They want nothing to do with either our romantic tableaux of charming wild beasts that want to be our friends or our screwy fantasies where *gulos* play the role of diabolical enemies. They have no truck with illusions. It's part of what I think of as the wolverine pledge to never equivocate or deal in half-truths, which of course is really not their pledge but mine. I'm from the species that struggles daily to distinguish the truth from its own half-truths and lies. When you load nature up with human opinions, dreams, and nightmares, the results might make for more dramatic stories, but nature is always diminished in the end. Taken straight, the wolverine way, nature offers more real excitement, adventure, meaning, freedom, and hope than any version we've ever cooked up. That is what I learned from being on these animals' trail.

Gulos don't need a few secure areas to survive. They need lots of secure areas – big ones – and healthy corridors of protected land in between to link populations and the genes they carry. They need to be part of a robust community of predators, and they need an overflow of varied prey. As the wolverine becomes better known at last, it adds a fierce emphasis to the message that every bear, wolf, lynx, and other major carnivore keeps giving: If the living systems we choose to protect aren't large and strong and interconnected, then we aren't really conserving them. Not for the long term. Not with some real teeth in the scenery. We're just talking about saving nature while we settle for something less wild.

Park biologist John Waller hefts the frozen carcass of M29, a very large male yearling accidentally hit and killed on the Going-to-the-Sun Road. RICK YATES

Epilogue

The Journey of Life Is Long and the Path Unknown
Rest a While, Enjoy the Nature
Always Expect Unexpected
Keep Your Cool

BRO (India's Border Roads Organization),
Four of the many official advisories that I noticed displayed on road-edge
markers between 10,000 and 13,500 feet in the Himalayan province of
Ladakh while reporting on snow leopards

THE LAST FIVE ANIMALS CAUGHT BY THE GLACIER WOLVERINE PROJECT crew in 2007 were the following:

F25, a yearling female that had eluded capture as a kit when the team made two arduous but futile trips to find and implant radios in the young at F4's dens in 2006. Now the team put F25 on the air, and a couple of us continued to record her locations until early winter of 2008. She seemed to be establishing a territory next to F4's, squeezing in between the lands claimed by her mother and F15's turf. Her fate since then is unknown.

F26, also a yearling. She may have been F15's granddaughter, born to a female who had dispersed from the northeastern part of the park to its southeastern quadrant. Captured and implanted in February of 2007, F26 dispersed in turn during April. She left the reserve, crossing the river, railroad line, and major highway that outline Glacier's southern boundary, and made her way into adjoining national forest lands. In August, Yates located her in the Swan Mountain Range near an alpine lake about 50 miles south of Glacier. Savage tracked her in the same general area during October and November. The high country where she seemed to have settled was the very same part of the Swans where I'd studied mountain goats as a graduate student while wolverines occasionally tore up my tent and sleeping bag. This was also where Maurice Hornocker and Howard Hash subsequently carried out the first wolverine study in the Lower 48. The team lost track of F26 after late fall of 2007. Her fate gets marked down as unknown.

F27, an adult female. It had been a busy trapping season for teams at three different locations, and the only radio left when F27 was caught started malfunctioning. Yates just snatched a fur sample and let the female, who was a lactating mother, go. The DNA showed her to be most closely related to M1, Big Daddy, and she was probably denning somewhere in the Livingston Range to the west of the McDonald Creek Valley. Fate unknown.

F28, a kit. She was dug from F4's den in May of 2007 high on the steep, western side of the Grinnell Valley, where the team had searched unsuccessfully for another of F4's dens two years earlier. Father? Big Daddy, M1. I was away on assignments in Mongolia, northern India, and the sub-Antarctic seas south of New Zealand from May through July but helped monitor F28 as she traveled with F4 during August and September. Fate also unknown.

M29, a yearling male no one knew about until October of 2007, when the Going-to-the-Sun Highway was closed to the public to speed up work reconstructing sections of the road. One of the big dump trucks struck and killed a wolverine just east of the Divide. The body was recovered and designated as M29. From samples of the hair, the team learned that Elvis – F24 – did have a sibling. She and M29 were both the offspring of F7 and M13 from 2006.

<hr/>

After the Glacier Wolverine Project ended, park biologist John Waller, consulting with Copeland, designed the plan to sample wolverine DNA that several of us from the former project team volunteered to help carry out, setting up fur-grabbing bait posts on frozen lakes in winter. The data from that effort is still being analyzed. If it proves promising, the study may be expanded to every corner of the park and possibly beyond to neighboring national forest and other lands. We'll see. We did learn that Big Daddy M1 and Good Mother Wolverine F4 were still alive and roaming their territories through the winter of 2008/2009. Longtime wolverine friends and lovers, both had to be close to ten years of age, if not older.

As of the summer of 2009, Jeff Copeland is busy producing scientific papers. Still with the Rocky Mountain Research Station, he's involved in a wolverine study in the northern part of the Greater Yellowstone Ecosystem and another study in Idaho. From time to time, he also pitches in on an effort to trap and monitor the few wolverines found in the North Cascades Ecosystem of Washington. Rick Yates is working on a maintenance crew in Glacier Park, keeping an eye out for job opportunities as a field biologist, and occasionally leading a field seminar on wolverine ecology.

Manning the fire lookout tower perched on the Continental Divide atop Swiftcurrent Peak in the heart of Glacier, Buck Hasson is one of the first people to see the sun rise each morning over this part of the world and one of the last to see it set in a tide of alpenglow. He's doing this work as a volunteer and considers himself lucky beyond words. Dan Savage is busy with his veterinary practice in between hikes and climbs all over northwestern Montana. Dave Murray just returned from a trip with his mules through the Bob Marshall Wilderness and is back running his construction business. He loves those mules, his hot rods – he owns some classic Super Bees and a Shelby Super Snake – and wolverines, and is standing by, like all of us, to help them any way he can. Guy Zoellner is a full-time mule skinner, leading pack strings to resupply backcountry stations in Glacier and the Bob Marshall Wilderness.

Somewhere up above the Arctic Circle, Marci Johnson is studying musk oxen. Lacy Robinson worked for a while on a wolf research project and is currently on a bighorn sheep study run by the Nez Perce Tribe in Idaho. Karen Reeves is managing one of the two remaining stone chalets where visitors can stay high in the backcountry of Glacier. She's often awakened at night by mountain goats clomping along the wood planks of the porch. After earning certification as a master naturalist back in the Appalachian Mountains, Virginia-based Jack Noll returned to working as a software designer and volunteering his time with various conservation enterprises. He spent his vacation this summer hiking solo along the crown of the continent in Glacier. Shea Wyatt is once again at sea level in British Columbia, taking summer field courses in oceanography while preparing for his senior year as a biology major at the University of Victoria.

◇◇◇◇◇◇◇◇◇◇◇◇◇◇◇◇◇◇◇◇◇◇◇◇◇◇◇◇◇◇◇◇

In 2009, a new administration set up shop in Washington, and a new petition to protect wolverines was sitting before the FWS. This one incorporated some of the latest findings from the Glacier Wolverine Project and Bob Inman's research in the Greater Yellowstone Ecosystem. On June 10, 2009, FWS agreed to review the wolverine as a candidate for listing as a threatened or endangered species and deliver a decision by December of 2010.

DOUGLAS H. CHADWICK, WHITEFISH, MONTANA
July 25, 2009
Maximum daily temperature: 95 degrees

Acknowledgments

First and foremost, I'd like to thank Jeff Copeland and Rick Yates for the privilege of joining in the work, pain, pleasure, and boundless freedom of following wolverines around the mountainsides. Special thanks also to the volunteers with whom I shared so many full backcountry days and spirited talks: Alex Hasson, Dan Savage, Dave Murray, Guy Zoellner, Keegan Kenney (now Zoellner), Jack Noll, Shea Wyatt, and the best partner in the world, my wife Karen Reeves. Other volunteers who made the Glacier Wolverine Project go include Becky Petrashek, Jason Wilmot, Tabitha Graves, Jamie Belt, Michael Stevenson, Pete Lundberg, Brenna Forester, Jeff Stetz, and Mark O'Keefe. A succession of field assistants helped see that good science got done. More properly called research technicians, they were Kate Wilmot, Marci Johnson, Rebecca Hadwen, Allen Hoffs, Laura (Lacy) Robinson, Ryan Williams, Brady Dunn, and Todd Ulizio.

John Squires, Leonard Ruggiero, Michael Schwartz, Kevin McKelvey, and Kristy Pilgrim, all of the USDA Forest Service Rocky Mountain Research Station, advised and contributed to the science underway, as did Dan Pletscher of the University of Montana College of Forestry and Conservation, and Glacier National Park biologist John Waller.

In the beginning, the Glacier Wolverine Project was funded through Glacier National Park by a Natural Resources Protection Program grant. Other institutional support came from the Wilburforce Foundation Yellowstone to Yukon Science Grant Program, the Glacier National Park Fund, Earth Friends Wildlife Foundation, the Wolverine Foundation, USDA Forest Service Northern Region, Montana Department of Fish, Wildlife and Parks (special thanks to Region 1 program manager Jim Williams), University of Montana, Defenders of Wildlife, Northern Rockies Conservation Cooperative, Chase Wildlife Foundation, and the Wildlife Land Trust (thank you, executive director Robert Koons), an arm of the Humane Society of the United States.

Private donations to help continue the project came from dozens of open-hearted people. In particular, I'd like to acknowledge the generosity of Grace Kirshner, Richard and Carol Atkinson, Sean and Anne Coffey, and the Glacier

Park Trail Crew alumni, which couldn't have been expressed at a more critical time. The former and current executive directors of the Glacier Park Fund, Jan Metzmaker and Jane Ratzlaff, respectively, were also instrumental in keeping the project alive. Metzmaker put in many a trail mile keeping an eye out for wolverines as well.

It goes without saying that the study wouldn't have been possible without the support of Glacier National Park staff, which provided the wolverine crew with access and the use of cabins and other facilities. A number of rangers and other personnel helped out both officially and informally. I'd especially like to acknowledge the interest and efforts of Paul Downey and Kevin (The Law Above Treeline) Forrest. Steve Lautenbach, the Many Glacier winterkeeper for Glacier Park Incorporated, offered cold weather hospitality, as did his successors, Jessie Scipkovsky and Ron Hoppner.

For deciding to publish this book, Rick Ridgeway, Nora Gallagher, and Vincent Stanley of Patagonia have my deepest appreciation. Then, for guiding the book into finished form and for their combination of enthusiasm, patience, encouragement, and focus, I owe all kinds of thanks to Patagonia text editor John Dutton, photo editor Jane Sievert, and project coordinator Jennifer Sullivan. Thank you Judy Long of the Wolverine Foundation for help in hunting down illustrations. Thank you Copeland, Yates, Hasson, Savage, Murray, Noll, Wyatt, and Reeves for reading over drafts of the book and offering corrections and solid suggestions. You, too, my friends Amy Shapira, Christine Paige, and Carolyn Dobbs. And to anybody I forgot to mention: You know I'm not ungrateful, just a bit disorganized sometimes.

– Doug Chadwick

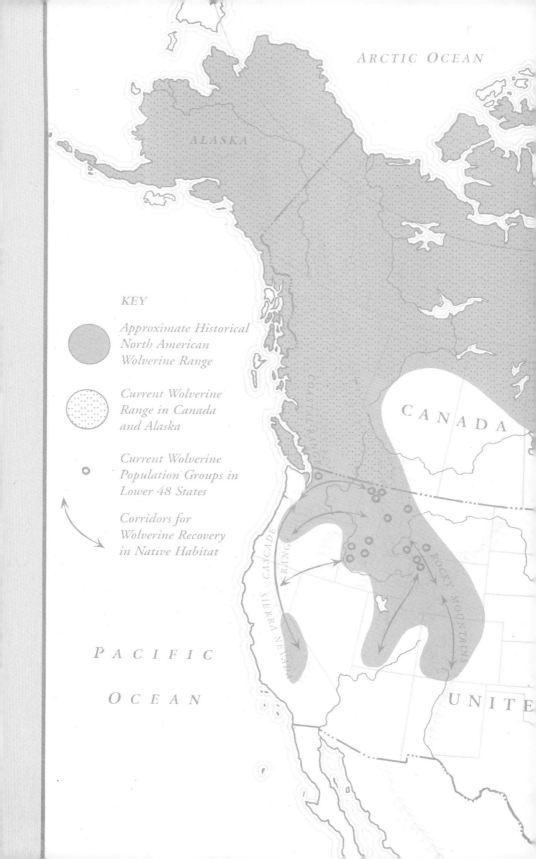

ARCTIC OCEAN

ALASKA

CANADA

KEY

Approximate Historical
North American
Wolverine Range

Current Wolverine
Range in Canada
and Alaska

Current Wolverine
Population Groups in
Lower 48 States

Corridors for
Wolverine Recovery
in Native Habitat

COASTAL RANGE

CASCADE RANGE

SIERRA NEVADA

ROCKY MOUNTAIN

PACIFIC

OCEAN

UNITE

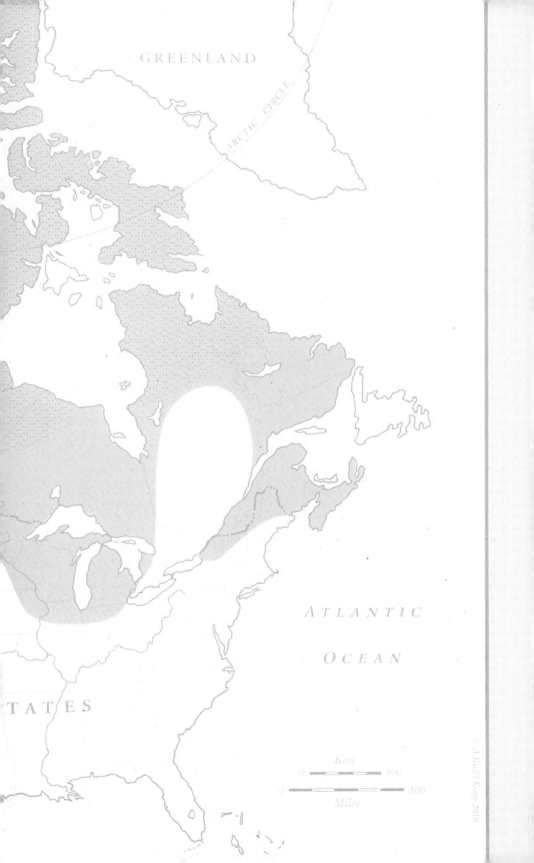

GREENLAND

ARCTIC CIRCLE

ATLANTIC

OCEAN

TATES

Kms.

0   500

0   500

Miles

© A. Karl/J. Kemp 2010